SOJOURNERS

SOJOURNERS

by John Borneman and Jeffrey M. Peck

The Return of German Jews
and the Question of Identity

University of Nebraska Press

Lincoln and London : 1995

Publication of this volume was
assisted by The Emily Schossberger
Fund, established in memory of
Emily Schossberger, first director
of the University of Nebraska Press

⊖ The paper in this book meets
the minimum requirements of
American National Standard for
Information Sciences Perma-
nence of Paper for Printed Library Materials, ANSI z39.48–1984.

Library of Congress
Cataloging-in-Publication-Data
Borneman, John.
Sojourners : the return of Ger-
man Jews and the question of
identity / by John Borneman and
Jeffrey M. Peck. p. cm. In-
cludes bibliographical references
and index. ISBN 0-8032-1255-0
I. Jews – Germany – Berlin –
Interviews. 2. Jews, Germany –
Berlin – Identity. 3. Jews, Ger-
man – Identity. 4. Holocaust,
Jewish (1939–1945) – Germa-
ny – Influence. 5. Berlin (Ger-
many) – Biography. 6. Berlin
(Germany) – Ethnic relations.
I. Peck, Jeffrey M. 1950–.
II. Title. III. Title: Return of
German Jews and the question
of identity. DS135.G5A1263 1995
943'.004924–dc 20 95-3125 CIP

CONTENTS

Intrigued by the possibilities of a German Jewish identity in a divided Berlin, we began research for this study in June 1989. The results are a video documentary and this book, *Sojourners: The Return of German Jews and the Question of Identity*, comprising eleven life histories and two essays. After over fifty interviews, hundreds of hours of discussion, and four years of work, we have changed as much as the countries that were the sites of our fieldwork and the identities that were the objects of our interest. Our project was begun when there were two Germanies; at its end there was one. Our prejudices about the differences between East and West Berlin German Jews—in terms of their own understanding of Germanness and Jewishness, in relation to life in exile in the United States, England, France, or the Soviet Union, and in political and religious affiliations—also changed. Instead of moving toward a unified point of view, we have tried to maintain some sense of the shifting nature of our project as we completed it over time, of the disagreements we have had, and of the partiality and incompleteness of the ethnographic rendering of experience.

No study exists, to our knowledge, of German Jews who fled, returned, and are now living in Germany. Much of what has been written about the uniqueness of German Jews in history has been written by German Jews living outside of Germany. Peter Gay calls them a 'metaphor for Modernity' (1978, vii). George Mosse says that what marks them is 'the search for a personal identity beyond religion and nationality' (1985a, 2). Sander Gilman writes that more generally 'the negative image of difference of the Jew found in the Gospel [is] the central referent for all definitions of difference in the West' (1991, 19). Despite differences, scholars are agreed that the German Jew has served—before and after the Holocaust—as a screen onto which others, Europeans in particular, have projected their wishes and anxieties. For us, what makes German Jews special is that they are a group of people who have tried to displace, if not transcend, traditional linguistic, religious, tribal, and political forms of identity. Today, given the post–Cold

War rediscovery within Europe of these older forms of distinction, the attempts by German Jews throughout the last two centuries to find other measures of belonging seem particularly relevant. Against all odds, German Jews tried to forge a cosmopolitan identity. And although the Holocaust seems to make a strong case for the failure of cosmopolitanism, or as Gershom Scholem argues, 'Love, insofar as it existed, has been drowned in blood' (1976, 73), the history of the German Jews is not over. Although few in number, some did return and are still living and working through this particular identity in Germany.

This book is foremost a chronicling, not merely of eleven lives (seven from East Berlin and four from West Berlin) and two generations (parents and children) but of a piece of German history experienced and created by men and women who fled Germany in the 1930s, became refugees and often citizens in foreign countries, and then returned to live in a divided Berlin. Their lives differ from those of most German Jews in two respects: first, they got away and did not perish in the gas chambers; second, they did not remain in exile, but repatriated. Because of their return, fellow Jews often view them skeptically, even, especially in North America, hostilely. The returned Jews stand in a number of uneasy tensions: between non-Jewish Germans and world Jewry; between the Germany they left and the one they returned to; between the Germany that forced them to leave and the one that took them back; between the Germanies they returned to and the countries of exile they left; and, most recently, between the Germany they wanted to change upon their return and a new, reunited, increasingly xenophobic Germany. Indeed, their last memories of a unified Germany were of a country that united against them, claiming that they no longer belonged.

Why, then, should they return to the country that rejected them so brutally? Who are these people who actually returned? What were our criteria for choosing them? These are questions often asked of us. We interviewed twenty-three people for this project, most of them two and three times, and then narrowed our selection to the eleven presented in this book. Seven were chosen for our documentary and were interviewed separately. Some are in both the book and the documentary; some appear in neither

but are frequently referred to by others and by us. Those autobiographies not chosen became an invaluable reservoir of material
that broadened our views and enabled us to generalize about the
experiences presented here. Initially we were interested in the
mutual influences of ethnicity, religion, and political ideology on
personal identity construction (Jewishness and Germanness) and
the relationship of Cold War politics (Soviet and American influences) and country of exile to the construction of everyday lives in
East and West Berlin. In focusing on people who were in exile in
one of the Allied countries, we limited our scope to those who
were willing to forsake life in a country that was a moral victor in
World War II. This choice also allowed us to draw significant
comparisons between the country of exile and the part of Berlin,
East or West, chosen as the place of return. Indeed, a variety of
trajectories from exile in the United States, England, and France
or the Soviet Union to East or West Berlin are represented.

We do not present statistically typical or 'representative' life
histories here. Rather, our interviewees represent prototypes of
possible responses to the problems of exile and repatriation experienced by these two generations of German Jews in Berlin. Our
interviews reveal a range of possible responses to the historically
specific situation of two generations. We were particularly interested in the narrative processes by which reconstructions, that is,
remembering and recounting a past, became history. We were less
interested in constructing 'objective history' than in the way a
particular subjectivity, German Jewish identity, was constructed
over time. With reunification, each version of a life history was
being reconstructed quite literally before our eyes. We took this
rethinking to be a demonstration of how the present constantly
intervenes to shape what history should look like and how it
might be understood.

As political events and history overtook us, our project became
more than a documentation of German Jewish lives and the vicissitudes of identity in East and West. Our video documentary,
especially, became a testimony to lives being transformed by
events that often undermined basic premises of cherished political and personal beliefs. Limited to repatriation in the GDR, the
video documentary's attention to voice, gesture, setting, perspec-

tive, and image provided another medium for documenting exile, return, life in the GDR, and reunification. Together our book and video introduce the reader/viewer to two generations of German Jews, whose common experiences of exile and return are also inflected by differences in personality and political ideology.

We dedicate this study to its subjects, the German Jews who tried to come to terms with the difficult and often traumatic experiences that have marked this century's European, German, and Jewish history. They have survived this sojourn, but not without wounds. The stories they tell are marked by scars, which now seem more apparent to their children, who now are also adults, than to the parents, who initially experienced the trauma of exile. For many members of this postwar generation, the xenophobia, anti-Semitism, and violent attacks on foreigners that have followed the unification of Germany are forcing them, much as their parents were forced sixty years ago, to rethink their relation to Germans and Germany as a culture, a country, and a home.

Aside from those who appear or are named in this book and in the video, there are, of course, many others to thank for their support—financial, emotional, and intellectual—of both projects. Specifically, we would like to thank the German Department and the Jewish Studies Program at the University of Washington, the Jewish Studies Program and the Institute for European Studies at Cornell University, the Center for German and European Studies and the School of Foreign Service at Georgetown University, the International Research Exchange Commission, the Fulbright Commission, and the many old friends who were with us from the start and the new friends we made along the way. For criticism and help in preparation of the manuscript, we wish to thank Leslie Adelson, Stefan Senders, and Elise Brayton. We especially want to thank Martin Patek for taking over production of the video in our absence and essentially making the video documentary possible.

This book begins and ends with essays written by the authors. These two essays frame autobiographies of German Jews edited and annotated by us. We did the interviewing together and therefore have transcribed our voices as a single one (J) unless it became apparent to us that one of us was solely determining the course of the interaction. We each translated and edited half of the interview transcripts. Those of the interviews with Benario, Klein, Cramer, Rödel, Thimm, and Münz were completed by Jeffrey Peck. Those of the interviews with Eisler, Kuczynski, Herzberg, Leiterer, and Jacoby were completed by John Borneman. Part 1, by John Borneman, is a description of the project as it developed and an analysis of the subject. Part 7, by Jeffrey Peck, is an analysis of specific recurrent themes in the interviews. Part 2 contains two life histories of German Jews who returned from the Soviet Union to East and West Berlin, respectively. Part 3 also contains two life histories of German Jews who returned to East and West Berlin, respectively, but from the United States. Part 4 documents three life histories of returnees from England to East Berlin. Parts 5 and 6 focus solely on the children of returnees, part 5 including two life histories that focus on carrying on traditions in East and West Berlin, and part 6, two life histories that center on the rediscovery of Jewishness in East and West Berlin.

PART I. IDENTIFYING GERMAN JEWS

John Borneman

How does one identify a German Jew? Why did some German Jews voluntarily return after 1945 from exile in one of the Allied occupation countries to East and West Germany, more specifically to East and West Berlin? Did postwar experiences change people's perceptions of themselves as German Jews? In June 1989 Jeffrey Peck and I began ethnographic interviews—some of which we later filmed —with formerly exiled German Jews in order to address these questions. History intervened: the Wall opened on 9 November 1989, the East German state dissolved, and its territories and people formally united with the Federal Republic on 3 October 1990. The extreme flux of this period, now called *die Wendezeit*, during which both of us regularly visited or intermittently lived in Berlin, continually dissolved many of the divisions and tensions that we were studying, only to replace them with ones that were not immediately identifiable. It forced us to continue our research for several more years, so that we did not complete work on this book until July 1993. We still cannot offer any succinct definition of a German Jew. But we can identify the motives for returning to Germany, and we can account for some of the changes in how, and in the positions from which, German Jews who repatriated and others have imagined German Jewish identities.

The number of Jews still alive in Germany after World War II is extremely difficult to estimate, as is the number of those who remained in the East and West, or returned there from exile, during the Cold War. Not only are such numbers hard to obtain but the very category 'Jew' or 'German Jew,' which the numbers are said to index, has been a politically contested one—by the Germans in the East and West, by the various members and organizations of the international Jewish community, and by the different Allied occupation forces. Moreover, for obvious reasons, many Jews did not want to identify themselves as Jews, least of all for the purposes of citizenship or statistical quantification. Subject positions are always political stances, placing an actor in a historical tradition and a present-oriented field of power and interest (Adelson 1993, 87–129; Martin and Mohanty 1986). Therefore the number of 'Jews' one cites will always be partially determined by polemical, political, and factual considerations. With these caveats in mind, how did we—how might one—identify a German Jew?

A census published in June 1933 registered 500,000 Jews living in the German Reich (around 1 percent of the residential population), of whom approximately one-quarter were foreign (non-German) Jews. Approximately another 100,000 people who were not registered had at least one Jewish grandparent. Around 72,000 of those registered by the government lived in Berlin. Between 1933 and 1945 approximately 270,000 were able to leave Germany; more than 165,000 were murdered; about 15,000 survived the camps; and another 2,000 survived underground (Benz 1991b, 10). In the spring of 1945 'as many as 100,000 Jewish survivors [the majority not being German Jews] found themselves among the eleven million uprooted and homeless people wandering throughout Germany and Central Europe' (Peck 1988, 5). Between 1945 and 1950 the number of Jewish 'displaced persons,' the official category used by the Allies, rose to nearly 200,000 (Jacobmeyer 1983, 421–52). International Jewish agencies then engaged in a massive, relatively successful effort to remove the Jewish population from Germany, so that by 1950 the number of Jews in Germany had dwindled to less than 15,000. Of this small group, 6,000 were displaced Jews from Eastern Europe who had settled in Germany, another 2,000 were from other countries, and only the remaining 6,000 were German Jewish returnees (Yahil 1971, 496–500). At most, then, only 6,000 German Jews repatriated. Those who remained in Germany or moved there after the war were seen as a pariah people by such groups as the World Zionist Organization, the World Jewish Congress, and the Jewish Agency, all of which issued 'ultimatums' to the effect that all Jews must leave Germany (Peck 1988, 9).

Jews' relations with the Allied occupiers and German authorities were entirely different from those they had with Jewish authorities. Within weeks of the defeat of the Third Reich exiled Jewish Germans began returning to Berlin to serve—initially with the Soviet Union, shortly thereafter with the other three occupation forces—in rebuilding Germany. The great majority of these returnees were highly skilled, politically motivated Jewish antifascists who had worked in the opposition during the war. Some had begun this oppositional activity on the side of the Republicans during the Spanish Civil War; they saw the fight against Nazi Germany as a continuation of these earlier battles, and the return to Germany as part of an international antifascist struggle. Many identified themselves more strongly as communists and members of the German Left than as Jews, and some were prominent personalities whose return to Germany was hoped for by a small group of non-Jewish German friends and antifascists who had also survived the war. Jewish returnees whom we talked to concluded, however, that most people who lived in or occupied Germany at that time treated all repatriation within the decade after the war with total indifference.

Initially, Jews who had returned to Berlin were not radically affected by the Allies' division of Germany. In fact many wanted this division, which they viewed as just punishment of Germany for the war, as a necessary lien on European security, and, especially for those in the East, as providing an opportunity to construct socialism. The Jüdische Gemeinde [Jewish Community] in Berlin remained united until 1953.[1] A majority of the early returnees to the Soviet Zone/GDR settled in the Pankow area of East Berlin. Officially acknowledged as Victims of Fascism and treated the same as other categories of victims, they received priority in allocation of apartments, and many were immediately incorporated into high-status political, cultural, and administrative work. For most of these people, political identity was more important than religious and ethnic aspects of Jewishness. In any case, political authorities in the East encouraged the development of identities not based on religion or ethnicity, and most residents, Jews and non-Jews alike, accommodated themselves to this norm. At the same time, the state recognized the principle of freedom of religion. The Jewish Community accordingly organized itself along religious lines, and some people did practice a Jewish identity—much as others practiced Catholic or Protestant identities—within the state-approved and -controlled confines of the confessional community. Given no alternative but a Jewishness reduced to religious practice, many East German Jews suppressed parts of their own histories, in the extreme case even hiding aspects of a Jewish heritage and history. Hence their children were often left on their own to rediscover or nurture relations to Jewishness or the Jewish Community. In 1986 the group Wir für Uns [For Ourselves], with approximately two hundred 'members,' began meeting regularly in East Berlin to cultivate a broad range of primarily non-religious-based Jewish traditions (Kirchner 1991, 35; Ostow 1989, 51–52, 149–54).

As the Cold War heated up in the early 1950s, people in both East and West, including Jews, were increasingly asked to take a position against the other side. In 1952–53 a wave of persecution of 'cosmopolitans' and 'Western immigrants' in Prague and Moscow had repercussions in East Germany: Jewish Gemeinden were searched, and the parliamentary representative and chairman of the Jewish Communities in East Germany, Julius Meyer, was arrested. Five of the eight leaders of the East Berlin Jewish Community fled to West Berlin one night in January 1953. The result of this exodus was a call by the rabbi for Greater Berlin, Nathan Levinson, for all Jews in the GDR to move to the West. Many responded to this call, and on 19 January 1953, the Jewish Communities were officially divided (Beigel 1953; Ostow 1989, 1–9).

Despite this turbulent political history, approximately 1,500 Jews were still registered as living in Greater Berlin in 1956. Yet the number of Jews in the GDR (the vast majority of them in East Berlin) continued to decline dramatically, even after the building of the Berlin Wall in 1961, when East German emigration was almost nonexistent.[2] The community in the West grew incrementally, however, throughout this period. By 1986 the number of Jews registered by the Community in the East had declined to 350, with 200 registered in the Berlin Community (Richarz 1988, 20). Approximately half of those with whom we became acquainted, either personally or only through hearsay, were not registered by the Community and therefore were not part of the official statistics. Most came from professional classes and worked in the occupations from which they had been banned during the Nazi period or in related ones. By the 1980s the East German regime, in search of the international recognition already accorded the Federal Republic, had begun to curry the favor of international Jewish organizations, granting most Jews in the GDR a relatively privileged status, with more travel and business opportunities and better access to political authorities.

For West Berlin Jews also, 1952 was also a decisive year, for at that time the Federal Republic began actively encouraging some prominent Jews to return. In its striving for international recognition and its desire to isolate the GDR, it formulated a reparations policy that did not focus primarily on the Jews who had suffered under the Nazis or on relatives of those who had been killed, but on the state of Israel and the Jewish people as a group. Policies earmarked as antifascist in the East and *Wiedergutmachung* (restitution) in the West helped to add prestige to and legitimate both German states, but especially the Federal Republic, in the international community. In this light, Y. Michal Bodemann (1994) has argued that the major 'function' of Jews in postwar Germany was to do 'ideological labor' for the two new states. Certainly this holds for the Federal Republic. Because it was more successful at this game of international politics—until 1973 only thirteen states risked going against West Germany's Hallstein Doctrine and recognized the GDR[3]—it experienced a net gain in Jews during the Cold War. From 1955 to 1959 alone, six thousand Jews migrated to West Berlin or West Germany, more than 60 percent coming from Israel and most of the rest from Latin America. It should be stressed that most of these immigrants were either of Sephardic ancestry or *Ostjuden* [Jews from the East], not German Jews; they were not returnees but new to Germany and to German culture. The Jews in the GDR, on the other hand, though fewer in number than in West Germany, were primarily German Jews, either the products of so-called mixed marriages, concentration camp survivors, or returnees from exile (Kirchner 1991, 30). Following the logic of the Cold War, the GDR developed a different, often contradictory, policy regarding Jews. Initially it supported Jewish claims for indemnity, but after the summer of 1952, following anti-Semitic show trials in several other Eastern European countries, it suspended all outstanding restitution claims. Its policy toward Israel, initially extremely supportive, also became increasingly hostile over the years (see Ostow 1989). One consequence of the official anti-Semitism in the East bloc, especially but not exclusively under Stalin, was a steady flight of Jews to the West. The West German Jewish Community, under the leadership of Heinz Galinski from 1949 to 1990, worked closely with the FRG in welcoming those from the East.

By the time of our study, an estimated seventy thousand Jews (defined as those with at least two Jewish grandparents) were living in the two Germanies, although only about half of them were registered as members of the Jewish Community. If one includes converts to Judaism and others closely identified with Judaism, this number might approach one hundred thousand. Of those registered by the Communities, there were approximately five thousand living in the East and twenty-five thousand in the West. Of this total, about two thousand lived in East Berlin, and six thousand in West Berlin. Included among those in West Germany were approximately ten thousand to twelve thousand Soviet Jews who had immigrated since the 1970s (see Bodemann 1983, 28, and 1994; Ostow 1989; and Richarz 1988, 25). Today more than 50 percent of all Jews registered with the Jewish Community in West Berlin come from the former Soviet Union (Hammer and Schoeps 1988). Of these numbers, only a small fraction are 'German Jews.' Of these German Jews, we were concerned with only those who repatriated, those who had lived in exile in one of the Allied countries and returned to Berlin.

With the help of many others, through hearsay and by referral, we identified approximately forty-five people who we thought fit our categories; we interviewed twenty-three of these between June and October 1989. Only one person declined to be interviewed. We selected people based on categories that revealed a particular range of experiences and differences in age, gender, nationality, and country of exile; we did not select them randomly. We also maintained a nearly equal balance between those living in the East and in the West, between women and men, and between two generations (those born between 1904 and 1926, the first generation, and those born between 1936 and 1955, the second). All members of the first generation were raised in Germany, left between 1932 and 1939, and were in exile during the war in one of the four Allied occupation countries (the Soviet Union, the United States, Great Britain, or France). They returned between 1945 and 1956 to either East or West Germany and eventually to one of the Berlins.

For the purposes of our study, we identified as German Jews those people who either 'subjectively' identified themselves as such or were so identified by ancestry, from the 'outside' through shared blood on the male side (a category employed by the Nürnberg race laws) or through shared blood on the female side (according to Jewish religion). Thus several of the participants in this study who had been labeled as Jews at various times in their lives insisted that they were not Jews. Obviously, we are aware of the danger in hypostasizing an identity for someone who insists that he or she does not belong to the group in question. We recognize and respect the right of people to represent themselves as they wish. On the other hand, our goal is not to prove people's belonging against their wishes but merely to probe the relation of subjective identifications to the two external definitions of belonging listed above. In this, we are following Leo Spitzer's (1989) study of the 'predicament of marginality' in the last two centuries, in which he examines the nexus between individual action, self-perception, and the institutional frameworks of the historical moment in which people find themselves.

Our open-ended, autobiographical discussions lasted anywhere from one to six hours at a time. In eighteen cases we returned for a second interview, and in eight cases we returned for a third. The discussions were taped and carried on in the language chosen by our partners, either German or English. About one month into the interviews we decided to make a film about these people in addition to working on our book, and we selected nine people for filmed interviews. Since August 1989 we have met again either singly or together with all of the people whose accounts are included in this book. After transcribing, translating, and editing the initial interviews, we made the resulting protocols available to the interviewees for further corrections and comments. After such intensive contact, people who were initially 'research subjects' have become friends. This study is also more narrowly conceived than most anthropological monographs in that it makes very limited reference to our participant observation, instead focusing on our formal interviews.

Our initial assumption that we would have access to these individuals, especially those in the East, only during a single period of their lives and ours has given way to an understanding that their subject positions have changed throughout the course of this project, as have ours, and that it was impossible and pointless to limit our interactions and their identities to a single ethnographic moment. Not only have my co-author and I changed universities but we have moved in and out of personal relationships, in both Europe and the United States, which in turn has influenced our relation to initially a divided and now a united Berlin. For example, in the summer of 1989 the Wall still divided our relationships into East and West, with very few people from the East being able to visit us in West Berlin, though sometimes we met our West Berlin friends in the East. This asymmetry in power in the relationships between East Berliners and us created a certain kind of erotics, as our relationships unfolded in a constant dynamic of violation of Cold War ideological barriers and the uncovering of public secrets. It also highlighted a tragic dimension, to which we were drawn, in the lives of people in the East—imprisoned by the circumstances and choices of a bygone ideological fight, partially hidden and sequestered from the West, accessible only to us as 'non–West Germans.' By contrast, West Berliners' lives appeared to us familiar and transparent, their concerns often even trivial.

Opening the Wall removed the shroud of secrecy surrounding the East, but only slowly. Accumulated intrigues—governmental, State Security [*Stasi*], and private—flooded the newspapers and electronic media daily. Each month resulted in a new East German ordinance changing the relations between East and West, but their impact varied greatly depending on whether one was a West Berliner, a West German, or an American. As U.S. citizens, we still had to wait in long lines to go to East Berlin, lines that grew in length for us as they decreased in length for West Germans over the course of 1990. The new status division during 'the transition' was between Germans and non-Germans. And as the so-called free world's media descended on East Berlin to witness the collapse of communism and the Cold War, we suddenly found ourselves classified as part of the non-German Western media competing to capture this moment in history. With formal unification on 3 October 1990, all restrictions on travel within Berlin fell away, only to be replaced with new emotional and material tensions between East and West friends. Unveiled and open for all to see, the city's underside of anger, frustration at thwarted expectations, fear of the unknown, and anxiety about the future increasingly came to light. Although we had come prepared to study the changing nature of German and Jewish identities in the two Germanies, we were nonetheless unprepared for the variety and kinds of differences generated by the collapse of Cold War division (see Borneman 1992, 1993).

This book belongs to a growing field of study that has become known as identity politics. It questions how its subject, the German Jew, is represented and tries to be explicit about how our representations were shaped in an interview process. It makes a historical constructivist (i.e., antiracial, antiessentialist) argument, maintaining that Jewish identity is syncretic and entails multiple subject positions. Also, we take a particular position on the relation of identity to politics. Instead of assuming that identity can be derived from political position or the authority of religion, state, or ethnicity generally, we explored how political authority is generated out of conflicts about identity that unfold over time. Therefore, we began not with the necessarily reductionist categories of the state, the census-taker, the doctor, the rabbi, or the psychologist, but with German Jews and their personal histories. People's histories reveal emergent and changing subject positions, variously willed by individuals, determined by outside authorities, or negotiated between the two, with regard to states, nations, religions, ethnicities, and, most strikingly, the Cold War. These positions should not be confused with 'opinions' or 'values,' idealist artifacts with which the cultural is often confused; rather, subject positions are indexical signs of the material conditions in which people actually live.[4]

Rather than examining the relationship between personal identities and politics as formally separate domains, we have focused on single interactions in which the two domains are inseparable yet represented as distinct. (We should not be misled by the fact that political instances, of which government is but one, represent themselves as separate from and somehow 'above' the people. Politics, like culture or identity, cannot be understood in terms of 'bottom-up' or 'top-down' models of imposition and resistance.) Following Foucault ([1975] 1979), we have assumed that meaningful objects—people, places, things—are constituted as discursive practices and that their historical significance is generated, and therefore to be found, in individual experience of and with instances of political authority. For this experience to be historical, it must somehow be inscribed as significant. One moment of inscription takes place in autobiographies, or remembered and reinterpreted experiences. Since autobiographical accounts tend to remain part of 'oral tradition,' they rarely achieve the historical credibility of written texts such as laws, demographic tables, or historiography. We are inverting these valuations here. In sum, identity politics is about the representation of experience with political authority, which obtains historical significance only from interested perspectives that reconstitute memories.

❦ THE GERMAN JEW

Formerly exiled German Jews offer privileged insights into identity politics, because they are an exceptional case. As Carl Schmitt has argued, because the political is defined by the exception, whoever decides on the exception necessarily determines politics. The Jews have often served as the exception in German, if not European, history; as such, they have been integral to debates about the limits in the extension of political rights and freedoms as well as to definitions of citizenship and human rights.[5] This 'decision' has not been just a German or Jewish one, but one of world historical dimensions, part of a 'global ecumene' (Hannerz 1992) in which a transnational flow of bodies, images, and interactions has contested the meaning of the term *German Jew*. Nowadays, for most Germans the German Jews' symbolic significance seems to be in inverse proportion to their number. Much like Native Americans in the United States, the fewer Jews in Germany the more significant they have become. This argument follows in part Sander Gilman's very suggestive analysis of 'blackness without blacks' in Germany. Gilman maintains that because Germans have so seldom been confronted with blacks, the image of blackness has become 'a mirage which evolved an independent existence in providing a structure for certain projections of anxiety' (1982, xii). The parallel between blackness and Jewishness holds except for the fact that Jews and blacks, though few in number, actually live in Germany; they are no mere mirage. The German Jew is signified not only by absence but also by the presence of the few who are living in a place where they were consigned to death and memory. Non-Jewish Germans do indeed tend to project onto Jews anxieties, qualities, and meanings that Jews themselves had no part in generating (Stern 1991). Today these often philo-Semitic meanings, which are not restricted to the German Jew but often are extended to the European Jew, refer to the Jews as guardians of memory, the conscience (and origin) of the West, and a litmus test for German democracy.

The production of meanings around 'the Jewish Question,' or the Jew-as-exception, has been accompanied in the last two centuries by a mass removal of Jews from Europe. Beginning in the nineteenth century large numbers of European Jews emigrated, or fled, to the Americas. The policy leading to the Holocaust not only eliminated approximately six million Jews but also forced the exodus of yet others to America and Israel in a pattern that continued throughout the Cold War. Indeed, this flight seriously undermines the possibility for future European contributions to Jewish identity, which, it might be argued, is now more centrally generated in Israel and the United States. And if most of the estimated three million Jews in the former Soviet Union leave the continent, as they threaten to do, the last remaining large group of European Jews will no longer live in Europe.[6] A lesser European contribution to Jewishness will not necessarily mean, however, a lesser Jewish contribution to Europe. And herein lies the potential significance of the German Jew. The 'missing Jew,' of which the living Jew is a constant reminder, may indeed be an 'open wound' and thus of even greater significance for Europe than the Jew who is present (see Caruth 1991). With respect to Germany, one commentator even argued recently that German postwar identity was constructed around 'the code of the Holocaust-nation and its transformation into a consciousness of the catastrophe' (Giesen 1993, 247). In this highly emotional and political field, the specificity of the German Jewish subject, particularly the German Jew who returned to Germany, has been blurred and confused, if not effaced.

It is commonplace in the popular media to assume that Germanness and Jewishness are mutually exclusive identities, to stress the cultural autonomy and timelessness of Jewish culture as distinct from the same aspects of German culture, and to think of the Jewish community as a homogeneous, never-changing group that practices traditions. We have inherited this conceptualization from German romanticism and nineteenth-century debates on cultural nationalism, and anthropologists have been perhaps the major carriers of this basically Herderian tradition. The German Jew has a historical and syncretic identity, fundamentally shaped in interaction with Europe. And Europe, as we well know, is indebted not only to Jewish religion and Greek culture, which predate 'it,' but also to a continuing relationship with Christianity and, at least ideologically, against Islam. To be sure, Jewish culture has its own history of interactions with ancient Greece, Christianity, and Islam, not to be collapsed with European history. The point I wish to stress is that twentieth-century Jewishness is not an autochthonous culture with properties exclusively its own but owes a great deal to the hybrid, derivative product that we call Europe (see Brague 1993). Even though much of contemporary Judaism is being defined in America and Israel, its constitution to date can only be understood with reference to Europe.

Thus, one does no justice to German Jewish identity by considering the Jews as always external to the Germans, by assuming that the Jews have always had to choose between cultural autonomy and assimilation into an unchanging Germanness, or conversely, that the Germans have to fear being Jewified, recalling the Nazi notion of a *zersetzender Geist* [a decomposing, perverting spirit]. Indeed, the very idea that the Jews could so easily pervert the Germans indicates a basic National Socialist insecurity, even admission of an inferiority complex, for it assumes that German spirit was itself incomplete and thus open to influence.

This kind of thinking is reinforced by the idea of a homogeneous nation, written into the West German statutory law, as well as in Article 116 (which defines expellee and repatriation rights) of the Basic Law of 1949—that Germanness is inherited, a matter of descent, that a German is necessarily limited to a single citizenship and hence must decide to which culture he or she belongs.[7] As is well known, this ethnocultural ideal of German nationality has never been realized. At least since the Middle Ages, Germans have resided in many competing principalities, each with distinct tribal identities. In the last several centuries, millions of ethnic Germans have been living outside any German state, while millions of non-Germans (primarily Slavs and Jews) have been living within the different German states. The ethnocultural ideal is further reinforced by an assimilationist model of the *Volk* that has traditionally assumed the Jews, alone with the Gypsies of all the peoples in Europe, to be nonassimilable to the major 'nationalities' on the continent. The inspiration for this idea is the nineteenth-century Mazzini formula, that a culture, nation, and state are isomorphically related, a program on which the Zionist movement also modeled itself (see Brubaker 1992; and Hobsbawm 1990). This model of an ethnocultural nation-state continues to inspire the leaders of the vast majority of the more than 190 states in existence as of this writing, even though in only a handful is there anything resembling a homogeneous nation.

The German Jews whom we studied do not fit neatly into this either/or categorization, for clearly they are either, neither, or both (all) German and/or Jew. In their lives culture, nation, and state are more often than not disjunctively instead of continuously related. In this sense they are a 'third' with respect to the binary German/Jew or native/foreigner, moving back and forth between the categories German and Jew, native and foreigner. The program of a continuous national history and bounded cultural identity expressed in a single language that realizes itself in a state was further complicated for these people, since during their periods of exile many had obtained another citizenship—Soviet, American, or British—and become fluent in another language. By migrating back to Germany, these German Jews have challenged and destabilized the assertion of the binary opposition German and Jew. In passing between and claiming multiple cultures, nationalities, and citizenships, they continue to vex those who want to assert a more stable opposition between categories of Germanness and its radical other. As the histories that follow show, however, being in between has been neither easy nor a constant state. Indeed, both German states and other interested actors and organizations have continually pressured people to choose, for example, between East and West, Jew and German, Israel and one of the German states.

German Jews today are not like most Jews who live in Germany nor most American Jews who visit Germany; they are members, or the children of members, of a very small group of people who share the characteristic of being part of the legendary so-called German Jewish symbiosis—unique within nineteenth- and early-twentieth-century Europe. They 'stayed in Germany,' writes Ruth Gay, 'because they had made a bet with history, and for more than a century it seemed that they were on the winning side' (1992, 479). Up to 1933 half a million Jews lived in prosperous communities in Germany. Many had integrated into the local economic, social, and cultural life, and many had committed themselves to communism or some version of a socialist utopia. They did not always experience these identities as mutually exclusive, nor did they feel the need to prioritize them. In fact many found themselves at home in communist and progressive, or cosmopolitan, intellectual circles precisely because so many of the theoreticians and prominent Party organizers were Jewish. For example, eleven of the forty-four Germans awarded Nobel prizes before 1933 were Jewish (Sievers 1983, 226–27). Indeed, if German culture was thoroughly infused with Jewish culture, especially in Berlin, it was in the intellectual, artistic, and economic domains, with large numbers of Jews also involved in law.[8]

This cultural symbiosis had its costs, however; in particular, German Jews in striving for respectability had to distinguish themselves linguistically and culturally from Eastern European Jews as a precondition for their acceptance in the German state. Between 1900 and 1925 the ethnic contours of the Jewish population changed rapidly, as the percentage of *Ostjuden* among the Jews in Berlin increased from 12.6 percent to 25.4 percent. According to Peter Gay, 'Berlin's Jews hop[ed] that the *Ostjuden* might go away or, failing this, that Berlin Jews might maintain their distance, and that Germans would continue to differentiate between them and the newcomers' (1978, 186–87). As we know, this distance from the *Ostjuden* did not spare Berlin's Jews from the same fate under the National Socialists. The lives of German Jews changed drastically with the ban on employment of Jews in civil service and other prominent occupations in April 1933 and the Nürnberg Laws of September 1935, which served to racialize German identity by forbidding marriages between Jews and Germans. State statistics suggest that in 1933, for example, about 60,000 Jews and Germans lived in 'mixed marriages,' meaning that approximately 250,000 people fell into the (Nazi) category *Mischlinge*. Mixed marriages were only one aspect of a more general fusion of cultural forms that revealed the Jews to be 'a part of the German nation,' writes Y. Michal Bodemann. 'This was apparent not only in the German but also in the Jewish part of the population, where one understood oneself to be a 'German Jew'; [or] a 'German citizen of Jewish faith,' in a unity of Germanness and Jewishness—to the [extreme] of right-wing Jewish groups [who maintained that] Jews were a German *Stamm* [tribe, root], much like the Bavarians or the Swabian' (1983, 28, my translation).

The fusion did not, of course, lead to any harmonious whole; as in any cultural interaction, there was continuous conflict. Nor did the fusion involve Jews from all social classes. More than likely, it was limited to professionals who became cosmopolitan *Bildungsbürger*, those who shared the Enlightenment optimism that acquired knowledge and self-development were more meaningful than religious or national heritage (see Mendelsohn 1993; and Mosse 1985a). Moreover, as Gershom Scholem has pointed out, the German Jewish symbiosis was never a dialogue, for the recognition and effort to communicate went in one direction only: from the Jew to the German. In this asymmetrical relationship, Jews were asked, and often were prepared, to 'liquidate their peoplehood.' Liberals saw their self-abnegation as a positive condition of integration, while conservatives viewed it 'as evidence of their lack of moral substance' (1976, 83, 76).

Regarding historical representations of Jews, Sander Gilman concludes that German culture categorized and stigmatized Jews as 'degenerate, masturbating women,' as Oriental and in particular female (1985, 267).[9] Gilman also stresses that these images were projected onto German Jews and should not be confused with their own self-conceptions. Nonetheless, he writes that Jewish interaction with these projections frequently resulted in self-hatred, 'an acceptance of the mirage of themselves generated by their reference group—that group in society which they see as defining them—as a reality' (1986, 2). Gilman is careful to distinguish between representations, with which he is dealing, and basic self-perception. Although there is much evidence that these representations contained commonly shared meanings, a strong argument could be made that they constituted an extreme version of the racialized Jew and thus were not universally shared. Recent historiography suggests that many Germans did not think and practice these anti-Semitic representations. There are also many indicators, some of which Gilman (1986) and Mosse (1985a) present, that Jews themselves widely resisted these projections as stereotypes. Indeed, many, if not most, German Jews believed that emancipation was possible in Germany and thus sought to integrate. In any case, it is impossible to decide how significant pejorative projections and German stereotypes of Jews were without knowing how German Jews talked about themselves. Their voice is privileged here because it is the one voice without which one cannot make any claims about their identity.

Unfortunately, very few German Jews remain who can give voice to this identity in both its pre- and postwar forms (see the documentation in Herzberg 1990). The vast majority of Jews living in Germany are Polish, Hungarian, or Russian Jews, along with a sizable number of American Jews, and most of these live in western Germany. Of the small number that remain in eastern Germany, nearly all are German Jews. The German Jews's singularity, both in the sense of being a 'third,' as described above, and in having returned to or, in a few cases, remained in Germany after the war, has not been widely recognized by other Jews living in Germany, most particularly American and Israeli Jews. Most other Jews in Germany expect them to drop the dual distinction and become simply Jews, part of an undifferentiated minority called 'Jews in Germany.' This universalist position, while perhaps understandable for strategic political reasons, obscures the specific ways Jews in Germany historically have constituted themselves. With regard to the German Jews interviewed here, it relegates their histories to either the heretical (by banning them to nonhistory) or the inconsequential (by seamlessly incorporating them into a universal history of the Jew).

♣ VOICE

The first assumption of our study was that German Jews are part of a living culture, not a dead one. We wanted to understand the peculiar circumstances in which living German Jews have fashioned an identity in postwar Germany. 'Visitors [to Germany] want to see ruins and ashes,' writes Ruth Gay, 'not kindergartens, rebuilt synagogues, or rebuilt lives.' Why is it, she asks, that the Jewish presence in Germany is most often reduced 'to a single epoch of twelve years'? She suggests that American Jews' antagonism toward German Jews can be explained by the fact that the 'overwhelming number of American Jews are of East European origin,' meaning that in the prewar period they were contemptuously referred to as inferior and unassimilable *Ostjuden*, juxtaposed to a putatively superior and more assimilated *Westjuden*. Thus among American Jews the word *assimilation* is still used as 'a reproach.' In her work, Gay recovers some of the history of the German Jew, who, she writes, remains an 'idea' in postwar Germany (1992, 470, 474). We have concluded that this hostility toward German Jews is based primarily on a denial of Germans' and Jews' mutual influence, on a refusal to accept that the 'assimilation,' or the making of the German humanist tradition, went— and still goes—both ways. We also go beyond the 'idea' of a postwar German Jew and record German Jews' own words, thoughts, and recollections about themselves and their lives.

If one pays close attention to German Jews' own representations, one gathers that the term *cultural assimilation* was not widely used until after World War II. The term *assimilation* was popularized by American cultural anthropologists in the 1920s to describe the incorporation of different ethnic Europeans into a postulated Americanness. Germans in American exile who returned to Germany after World War II took the term with them and substituted it for the more widely employed German term *Integration*. Most German Jews before the war thought of themselves not as assimilated but as emancipated—from traditional religion and from a growing national sentiment within Europe. Post-Enlightenment thought generally was more concerned with emancipation from religious dogma than with cultural purity and origins. Indeed, in his famous essay 'On the Jewish Question' Marx makes no mention of cultural purity or assimilation but is instead concerned with the limits of political freedoms (primarily citizen integration through representation in government and inclusion in a nonpolitical civil society) that are not accompanied by a critique of what we might today call 'ethnic essentialism.' For Marx, the Jew (he himself was one by heritage) would never achieve selfhood and equality within Europe unless he was freed of the stereotypes attached to Jewish culture—greed, money, haggling, commerce.[10] Emancipation, not assimilation, was his proposed solution to the Jewish Question.

That the Nazi regime, along with most of the rest of Europe and the world, ignored and even took advantage of this emancipation says more about the abuse of stereotypes than it does against the tremendous contributions made by German Jews to the renaissance in cultural and political life of this era. 'If their success was largely illusory in immediate terms,' writes the German-Jewish-American historian George Mosse, 'in the long run they presented an attractive definition of Jewishness beyond religion and nationalism' (1985a, 20). The overwhelming majority of German Jews whom we interviewed have remained loyal to emancipatory goals, though they are now sobered by the realization that self-emancipation takes place in a field of power where the assertion of a distinct Jewishness and the promised protection of a Jewish state may be two necessary preconditions for the further survival of Jewish life and culture in this century.

This said, obviously we do not solve any problems concerning the authority of our text by reproducing their and our words in the raw, unedited version (for such an attempt, see Dwyer 1982). A tape-recorded autobiographical interview is not necessarily more 'truthful' or revealing than a well-researched biography. In the academy, biographies have a much more esteemed place than do autobiographies, primarily because they are assumed to be more objective. Nor does the dialogic aspect—that we co-constructed protocols in a sequence of exchanges, that we submitted the interviews and our comments about them to our discussion partners for review—relieve us of having to defend and assume responsibility for the final product (see Marcus and Fischer 1986). Nor do we think that giving voice to German Jews is defensible as a project in reconstructing the German Jew in order to pluralize the sovereign German and/or Jewish subject. To paraphrase Gayatri Spivak (1988, 118–33), we are not merely adding another voice to the orchestra, for every voice is already inhabited by an ethnic differential. In other words, we understand the exploration and deployment of voice—who speaks and from what position— to be part of a critical exercise in understanding the making of ethnicities in twentieth-century Germany; we are not interested in constructing any particular ethnic identity.

Most, if not all, of our interviewees would admit that telling their lives is an extremely partial exercise, a form of self-justification, a defense of the way they lived and constructed an identity. Likewise, we began this project with a set of particular interests. Foremost among these interests, in my opinion, was to bring issues surrounding identity politics in the United States to bear on identity that is conceived otherwise in Germany. As I indicated above, in Germany the Mazzini-derived formula of equating culture with nation with state remains a widely shared axiom. My purpose here is to show that this formula is often descriptively untrue and, in today's world, prescriptively misleading and dangerous. I also wish to suggest that the consequences of thinking in these terms, evident in the many examples of *Ausländerfeindlichkeit* [hate of foreigners] and xenophobia of post-unity Germany, are most often extremely negative. Perhaps the first step toward a conscious change in identity is to envision an alternative that is already present (see Unger 1983). In this light, identity politics should not be seen as the export of a set of cognitive alternatives from America but as the (re)presentation of real people who are already Germans and Jews who present from within possible alternative identifications with cultures, nations, and states.

Our second interest was to conduct a study of ethnic identities other than our own. Studying the other is an anthropological commonplace, but most recently this has not been the case in the study of American ethnicities; and it has never been the case in the study of Jews, who tend to be studied only by other Jews. The importance of studying and being studied by the other, for Jews in particular, has never been stated more cogently than by Jonathan Boyarin in his study of Jewish memory: 'Jews will only be in a safe and healthy position when our self-image can be challenged and enriched by an informed critique from a variety of others. . . . the parochial isolation of Jewish thought is inseparable from a situation in which most self-identified Jews understand their collective security needs in ways that strike the rest of the world as narrow-mindedly exclusive' (1992, 104).[11] We hope to challenge what in my opinion is an extremely dangerous idea: that members of any group should have sole or final control over their own representations and that only they can, or can best, study or represent themselves. Representations are not pieces of private property that can be exclusively owned but goods that are always also simultaneously part of the public domain.

A third interest that we had in this study was to better understand the experience of homelessness and the conditions of repatriation. Contemporary scholars are devoting a great deal of attention to conditions of exile and marginality. Their studies, in particular those of diasporic (im)migrant populations and subaltern intellectuals, have contributed to the rethinking of such commonplace concepts as 'society' and 'culture.' But little attention has been paid to the possibilities for and experience of return or repatration of people to their country of so-called origin (for an exception, see Spitzer 1989). Those German Jews who repatriated speak to this complex of problems—marginality, exile, repatriation—and above all to what I would call a continuous politics of reconciliation. Some had no choice but to reconcile themselves to return and reintegration. Others returned willingly, by invitation, for pragmatic reasons, or because it was the lesser of evils. Yet others, loyal to an idea, returned searching for communism, one of the twentieth century's great utopia dreams. Whatever the reason, they have worked within both German and Jewish identities; they have balanced living for a great historical ideal with the need for belonging in a family or the comfort of a taken-for-granted home. Most have experienced existential insecurity as a way of life and have improvised accordingly. It is this fund of historical experience to which we were drawn and to which we wanted to give voice.

♣ MORALITY AND RETURN

Any study of German Jews must also confront the experience of the Final Solution, the Holocaust, the Jewish catastrophe, the Shoah—whatever we might call this event that defies exact description. We also assumed that the Holocaust has different meanings for different Jews and that German Jews who lived in exile and returned to Germany after the war must have a peculiar relationship to the Holocaust. For those who want to understand the experiences of the concentration camps, we have very little to offer. We can only refer the reader to the many excellent histories and personal journals of these events that already exist. These histories focus primarily, as Ruth Klüger writes in a remarkable contribution to this literature, on the meaning of death. For Klüger, who survived the camps as a child and now teaches German literature at the University of California, Irvine, 'Auschwitz was not a learning opportunity for something or another, and especially not for humanity and tolerance. Nothing good came out of the KZs' (1993, 72, my translation). Her own writing stresses the singularity, and not the universalizability, of the camp experience for its prisoners. Some of the peoples we studied also experienced the concentration camps; some experienced Stalin's gulags. We have concentrated on what followed from them: on the relations between reasons for and place of exile (not only from Germany but from the Holocaust and from death) to the situations that enabled Jews to return to and live in one or the other Germany. In trying to understand these relations, we further narrowed our study to three different experiences of exile—in the Soviet Union, the United States, and England, or the nations of the 'morally correct' following World War II.

The Jews in this study returned from exile within the morally correct to the land where the genocide took place. Those in the East justified their return in antifascist terms. They claim that they returned to eliminate fascism; they remained on the side of morality. For those in the West the reasons for return vary tremendously, few having anything to do with morality. Most returnees claim that they just got stuck in Germany and then made the best of it. But to the extent that some justified the return to Germany in moral terms, it was to build a democratic Germany. This difference between the condensed symbols of 'antifascism' and 'democracy' has been a major theme of debate in the unified Germany. And since the unified Germany is being redone according to the West German model of democracy, and since the 'morally correct' Soviet Union has dissolved, the antifascist subject position of people in the East, Jews included, has been criticized and severely undermined.[12] Indeed, the unification of Germany was never a major goal, or reason for return, of any of the Jews in this study. Those who returned because Germany was divided and because they thought that this division was right suddenly find themselves to be displaced peoples in a country not of their choosing.

The point I wish to make is that both place of exile and place of return, East or West, provided different positionings of German Jews with regard to the Holocaust. First, the Holocaust affected this group directly, but unlike those who survived the war in one of the camps or in hiding in Germany, they survived in exile, and exile is remembered as life, not death. Second, their memory of the Holocaust has been shaped by return, by being positioned as German citizens living in German culture, by direct confrontation with the site of Holocaust culture—place, people, sounds, sights—which other Jews remember from afar. Their return has entailed a different living out of the Holocaust trauma, a kind of working through condemned by most of the Jews in America and Israel. But this working through is different for those who returned to the East than it is for those who returned to the West. Devoting one's life to eliminating fascism, even if it is considered a failed project by some of the participants themselves, is not the same as dedicating one's life to rebuilding democracy (see Borneman 1995). Above all, over time the project of antifascism tended to displace concern for present crimes onto a criminal past, whereas the project of rebuilding democracy, while initially 'neutralizing' the past, tended to produce more vigilance about possibilities for crime in the present.

What a successful antifascist working through entails remains highly disputed. It would be simplistic, however, to claim that the East German antifascist policy was totally ineffectual or even, as some claim, counterproductive. An opinion survey done between 1 October and 15 October 1990 indicated that West Germans were much more anti-Semitic than East Germans. In response to the question whether Israel was a state like any other, to whom Germany had no special obligation, 57 percent of West Germans responded positively, compared with only 40 percent of East Germans. In response to the question whether the Jews instrumentalize the Holocaust, 45 percent of West Germans said yes, compared with 20 percent of East Germans. In response to the question whether Jews have too much influence in world politics, 44 percent of West Germans said yes, compared with only 20 percent of East Germans (Benz 1991c, 21). Despite the weaknesses of survey research data, the antifascist policies of the GDR should not be dismissed lightly, for they have had some influence on public opinion. How deep and how significant the changes in public opinion are and whether the changes in opinion reflect changes in behavior is a matter for further research.[13]

Lastly, given the end of the Cold War, is the Jewish returnee to Germany again repositioned? Certainly the dissolution of the Soviet Union, coupled with the unification of Germany, has dramatically affected who can determine morality. With the United States and the United Nations also unable to assert moral leadership on a world scale, it appears that what is right is increasingly being decided at a national level. Even if this trend does not continue, the Jews in Germany no longer occupy the singular space they did during the Cold War. Nor are they likely to reoccupy the phantasmic space they occupied in the nineteenth century, the space, as Marjorie Garber puts it, of an 'interimplication of the Jew, the homosexual, and the "woman" ' (1992, 232). The postunification increase in xenophobia and actions against foreigners in Germany has not been paralleled by a similar increase in anti-Semitism. German Jews appear to have lost their iconic status. Though they are not yet a mere sign in the forest of symbols, they are part of a forest that is being reassembled. It is still too early to speculate on their future form.

♣ ANTHROPOLOGY AND STUDYING GERMAN JEWS

Of particular relevance to this project are two practices of the discipline of anthropology that I will gloss as *reflexivity* and *deconstruction*. Neither is new to this kind of study, though they have been prominently argued for recently (e.g., Clifford and Marcus 1986, Marcus and Fischer 1986, Siegel 1986). A *reflexive* practice is one that understands knowledge not as describing an independent, isolable object but as mutually constituted in real-world interactions between the viewer and the object, the questioner and the interviewee, the researcher and the discussion partner. Because this is discussed in more detail in the final chapter, I will limit myself here to a description of how we came to do this project.

In 1988, while in Berlin finishing my dissertation research on nation-building, I ran into Jeffrey Peck on a street corner. He was about to return to the United States after a year of research in Berlin. We immediately fell into a discussion of what we had been doing, of my contacts and research in the East, and of German Jews in Berlin. At the beginning of my graduate study, eight years earlier, at the time in political science, I had enrolled in two of his courses—on hermeneutics and literary theory—at the University of Washington. Although we were in different disciplines, we shared many concerns about the relation of the human to the social sciences. We also shared an interest in the way Jews have taken on particular meanings in postwar Germany. We were well aware that Jeff's Jewishness placed him in an unusual and special position in Germany. Moreover, we are both gay, a contemporary identity that, given our own histories of the closet, has made us sensitive to the intricacies involved in creating a subjectivity, to the role of position, knowledge, and power in and outside the academy. Forced to confront how our own positions are the result of both extreme self-fashioning (no role models) and confrontations with external social stigmas projected onto us and over which we have had no control, we have been sympathetic to the trend toward increased reflexivity in our respective disciplines.

Following our brief encounter in 1988, we decided to begin this project. I set up preliminary contacts before returning to the United States on 2 February 1989. Eleven days after my return I received a letter of support for the project from Dr. Peter Kirchner, head of East Berlin's Jewish Community. Five months later we returned to Berlin with the support of an International Research Exchange Grant (IREX) that not only supported us financially but, more important, opened doors to official and unofficial contacts in the GDR. IREX sanctioned our project under an international scholar exchange program. We financed the two months in West Berlin from other sources.

Suffice it to say that a project involving a book and a film, two countries and two sets of bureaucrats (one of which was radically transformed four months into the project), two scholars and several universities, has not been easy to complete. If interdisciplinarity means merely a form of cooperation with little substantive contribution to the crafting of a common object, it is often easy. But this project was entirely collaborative, and at first we disagreed about many aspects—about commitments, expectations, modes of understanding, comparative contributions. Perhaps most of our disagreements arose because we were the products of two different traditions, Jeff a textual one and I an ethnographic one. In any case, neither of us could have completed this project alone. Among the commonalities that held us together throughout the project, the most significant, in my opinion, was the fact that we are both gay men who were then unattached. This status set us apart from most scholars, who are indeed or presumed to be heterosexual and often married, with husbands/wives/lovers and perhaps children who constrain the allocation of time and who care for them, and therefore represent themselves differently in research situations. We were asked frequently about our non-heterosexual status, though in the Berlin context this did not automatically lead people to assume that we were gay. It is my experience that the absence of a wedding ring or any of the other markers of heterosexuality, such as a referral to one's spouse immediately after meeting someone, creates a productive ambiguity in a fieldwork interaction. It creates the possibility for curiosity because others cannot automatically assimilate one into an identity with which they are familiar.

We felt uniformly well received, with warmth and respect, by both East and West Berlin German Jews, whether members or nonmembers of the Communities. In our interactions with people of our own age, we addressed each other with the familiar German form (*Du*), and the boundaries between our public and private lives often became fluid. With people of an older generation, references and questions regarding our private lives were mostly indirect, and we continued to use the polite German form of address (*Sie*) even with those individuals with whom we developed a more personal relationship.

An explanation of the contribution of the second practice, deconstruction, to our project requires a small excursion. Until the last several decades, American anthropology as a discipline unified around a so-called four-fields approach—physical, cultural, linguistic, and archaeological—that took as its object the primitive or primitivism. A suitable anthropological object was a people with a language, a deep or pre-history, and a distinctive set of habits and material culture. This culture was perceived as unchanging—in Claude Lévi-Strauss's pithy formulation, 'a cold society'—and as endlessly self-reproducing its social and ideational structures. Along with other northern Europeans, Germans have often perceived themselves to be a self-reproducing culture, and in this respect they differ little from most non-Western peoples. Yet they were rarely thought to be a suitable anthropological subject, for Germans were assumed to be 'a hot society,' modern and civilized, the very antithesis of the primitive. Additionally, to the extent that white northern Europe has been an anthropological site, the focus has been either on a village (which was considered colder: more bounded and traditional), on peasants, or on 'minority cultures' within a larger national culture.[14] The social evolutionism and ethnographic authority implicit in this typology of and relation to research objects obviously has more to do with Eurocentric categories of race (white and colored), time (modern and primitive), and place (West and non-West) than with any inherent qualities in the subject. This consensus about primitivism and the nature of the 'human subject' has been continually undermined, however unwittingly, by practitioners of the discipline of anthropology itself.

Some of the most notable anthropological studies have always been involved in both constituting and relativizing the human subject. For example, many early-twentieth-century studies that intended to prove the 'psychic unity of mankind' also stressed the distinctiveness and specificity of each human group; others that tried to prove a biological or environmental base to human nature instead demonstrated extreme variability in the relationship of environment to culture and arbitrariness in the cultural elaboration of putative biological constants. In focusing on heterogeneity instead of homogeneity, anthropology, like psychoanalysis, as Foucault noted, tends to both constitute and 'dissolve' man and in doing so undermines assumptions of the universality of a Eurocentric conception of the human. It follows that if the European conception of the 'human' is not universal, then the historical example par excellence of humanness—white northern European men—is also not universalizable. From this perspective, the anthropologist is placed in a difficult position with respect to his or her traditional subject. Not only does he not speak from a privileged, neutral perspective about other humans but he is not beyond being spoken about. The anthropological distinction between primitive and modern made sense only from a particular vantage point—from the modern one, of course— and it can no longer justify itself. In short, studying the primitive, or primitivism, has become impossible to defend. As Roger Keesing, an anthropologist whose major contributions have been in the study of Melanesians, has written, anthropology's findings illustrate that its knowledge has 'been fashioned in terms of European philosophical quests and assumptions, superimposed on the peoples encountered and subjugated along colonial frontiers' (1993, 301). This dissolution of the primitive initially resulted in a search for new objects, such as kinship, women, gender, or gift exchange, all of which, however, also soon came under attack and in turn were dissolved and displaced by newer objects, such as writing, modern medicine, the colonial subject, or the nation.

The sequential alternation between dissolution and displacement that characterizes much of anthropology is a mode of deconstruction. Although we tend to associate this kind of analytics with Jacques Derrida (1981), it was Lévi-Strauss, the father of structural anthropology, who initially told us that the 'ultimate goal of the human sciences [is] not to constitute but to dissolve man,' that 'properly scientific thought consists in decomposing and recomposing on a different plane' (1966, 247, 250). By positing this genealogy, I do not mean to deny the significance or originality of Derrida's contributions to the sciences or to minimize his differences with Lévi-Strauss, but to stress the fundamental similarity between deconstructive practice and much of anthropological practice. Deconstruction is not a destructive exercise that reveals imperfections (in need of correction) in the subject examined, as is often assumed, but an analytic one that focuses on the grounds for the subject's possibility. For example, instead of asking what the German Jew is or means, we ask, From where is the German Jew made? and How is this subject constructed as a particular difference? In the process of this kind of anthropology, the facticity of the objects being studied is undermined. Without a secure (timeless, fixed) object, anthropologists have been forced to find new objects or, in many cases, to be alert to the historical transformations of its old objects; they also now have to justify how they constitute their objects and how these objects constitute themselves (Fabian 1983). I would argue that the singularity and originality of anthropology lies in this continual critique of its object, in the fact that anthropology is at base a deconstructive science: it identifies its objects and assumes them to be nonfamiliar, describes these self-representations, and demonstrates that their constructions are arbitrary—a sign in a chain of signifiers—and thus could be something other than they are. This 'something other' is not an alien being but, to use the deconstructive phrase, an other that is always already there as a representation within the object or group being examined.

With this socio-logic in mind, we have resisted studying German Jews as a 'minority culture,' separate, nontypical, and outside the majority one. For intellectuals, minority groups within Europe function as the equivalent of the primitive outside of Europe: they become the exoticized other. Regardless of the nature of the minority difference (religious, political, racial, ethnic, linguistic, sexual, or gendered), minorities tend to lose their radical force when they become institutionalized in separate enclaves in the academy and elsewhere.[15] The danger in this sort of institutionalization lies in how it legitimates the study of 'majorities,' as an instance of the typical, as if majorities were a self-constituting subject. Minorities and majorities are not discrete groups but historically fluid indexes of difference writ large, of relations between unstable groups and measures of power differentials.[16] Minorities, for example, are extremely variable in makeup, being either numerically large or small, extremely significant or insignificant, culturally distinct or indiscriminable from the majority, the most powerful or the weakest group. The German Jews in this study encouraged us to approach the issue of minority from a different angle: Under what conditions in the 1930s were they identified as a 'minority culture'? Minority with respect to what majority? What were the stakes after 1945 in being identified a minority, and hence with the (to-be-) dominated and external, instead of with a majority (of Germans), who were then the dominant and internal? One of the historical functions within Europe of labeling Jews the unassimilable minority has been to reinforce a view of them as alien beings, separate from and outside the majority. This reasoning is, however, circular, for to define them as unassimilable and separate has tended to make them so, regardless of their own views on the matter.

Furthermore, to view Jews as a minority in Germany is a specifically Eurocentric way of dealing with differences that enables naturalizing ethnic differences without acknowledging the political functions of their generation. Thinking in terms of majorities and minorities was one of the corollaries of the growth of the nation-state and democratic government in the nineteenth century. As Boyarin suggests, 'The question of how "minorities" are exploited and excluded in the reproduction of domination is inseparable from the various conceptions they and the dominant group form of their integrability into the state' (1992, 30). Functioning democracies were legitimated by majority rule, and majority interests were equated with organic, unitary national ones. Equating the nation with an ethnically homogeneous majority has led down a slippery slope historically, often with disastrous results. Now, as Central and Eastern European nation-states, most of which wish to represent themselves as ethnically homogeneous, are in various stages of crises, either disintegrating or reconstituting themselves through either partition or 'cleansing,' it may be time to rethink the use of these terms. The breakup of Yugoslavia and the inability of Europe to formulate a workable policy around 'protection of minorities' within the nation-state is but the first boulder in an avalanche of problems imploding the Eurocentric (might we say ethnocentric?) vision of order. Not to be underestimated is another encounter occurring with people considered to be outside the nation-states of Europe—for example, refugees, former colonials, asylum seekers—who are now challenging their putative outsider status.

Because these old categories of belonging are no longer adequate for the task of establishing boundaries and justifiable criteria for membership in the post–Cold War period, current nation-states, such as Germany, are entering an extremely dynamic and tense period. Issues such as the right to political asylum, immigration law, social welfare rights and privileges, citizenship, and freedom of movement are now being hotly debated throughout Europe. In response to these challenges, many politicians are finding the idea that 'minorities' are forcing their way into 'old nations' to be quite useful in helping to create a sense of domestic solidarity, a feeling of 'us' versus 'them.' This mode of representation of politics assumes that a majority, called 'the nation,' is inside and already exists prior to the entrance of an ethnically marked minority. Yet, as I have emphasized repeatedly with regard to German Jews, who is inside and who is outside is entirely relative to one's position in a dynamic whole. The same history that has generated the Germans as normal or typical, as a majority, has generated the

Jew as an aberrant minority and the German Jew as virtually invisible, since he or she simultaneously embodies both histories.

In light of these frameworks, arguments, and positions, we hope that the documentation and study of these lives, of people who have dealt with the minority question from many different angles and over time, will contribute to a critical understanding of the perspective that considers certain subjectivities to be problems and others not to be.

From the Soviet Union to East and West Berlin

CHAPTER I. RUTH BENARIO

'I find nothing homey here. I am here to help, that is all.'

Born 1910   Berlin
1932   Leningrad
1934–1936 China
1936–1941 Moscow
1941–1943 Bashkirin (Siberia)
1943–1954 Moscow
1954–   East Berlin

Our way to Ruth Benario was through a labyrinth of contacts but well worth the effort. Our interview with her proved to be one of the most important, and she became one of our dearest friends. In the fall of 1988 we visited Ossip and Lili Flechtheim, the parents of Marion Thimm (see chapter 8), in West Berlin. Ossip Flechtheim had returned with his wife and daughter to teach at the Free University in West Berlin. Lily Flechtheim had known RB *before the war, and they had rediscovered each other in postwar Berlin. The Flechtheims suggested that we get in touch with her. Lily called and asked her about seeing us.* RB *gave an unequivocal no on the phone, so Lily made us strike her name from our list. Our friend Uli from East Berlin intervened, as he had done in other cases, and helped us arrange an interview. Unnerved by* RB's *lack of interest, we were hesitant about visiting her. But she received us with a lightness marked by a self-irony that was disarming. The planned two-hour interview lasted four hours.*

Since returning to East Berlin from the Soviet Union in 1954, RB *has lived alone in the apartment she received from the government in the Pankow section of the city. Her daughter lives nearby, and one of her two grandsons lives with her from time to time. Above all, she emphasized how lonely she was and how much she enjoyed our company. Appreciating her situation and even more her spontaneity, laughter, and curiosity, we continue to visit her often.*

RB I am in fact a real Berliner. I had a wonderful life as a young person, like in a fairy tale. My parents were very progressive and quite interesting. We always had artists and writers in our home, and because of this it was very [worldly].

J You mean they were very middle class [*bürgerlich*]?

RB No, They weren't. They were just very artistically oriented; for example, they had a very large collection of antiques. They were just very progressive people. So . . . now let's go to how I came to go to the Soviet Union. I had a friend who is now a world-renowned physicist. In fact, I just found him again after thirty-three years. It is really funny the turns lives take, especially in our generation. He was supposed to go to the Soviet Union. Perhaps you have heard of him—Viktor Weisskopf. *RB tells us that in 1932 Viktor was to lecture throughout the Soviet Union. She accompanied him and immediately began to travel, looking for subjects to photograph. Shortly after her arrival, she was detained by the police.*

Suddenly someone tapped me on the shoulder. It was a GPU man [secret police]. In Germany I was told that if you have anything to do with these people, you'll be sent to Siberia. I thought twenty-two years old was a little young to be sent to Siberia. *RB was cross-examined and finally released. She and Viktor went to Leningrad and then on to Moscow. In Moscow RB worked for a year as a professional micro-photographer and then found work at the research institute where the first color photos were produced. During this time she was introduced to a Russian man at a club for foreign workers. She corrects us when we ask if this was her first husband, since the German word* Mann *can mean both 'man' and 'husband.'*

I never had a husband. I never needed official papers to prove that I was married. I always said that as long as I want to live with someone, I will, and when I don't want to anymore, then I won't.

She interrupts her story here to say that she 'married' her second 'husband' when he was already dead. RB makes this point about her husbands again and again to emphasize her independence from the social conventions of bourgeois normality. Returning to her story, she tells us that she and the man she met in the club lived together 'like man and wife.' One day he told her that he was being sent to China as a consul, and she insisted on accompanying him. They decided that she would leave her German passport in Moscow and travel on his diplomatic passport. When she returned in two years, she would get Soviet citizenship.

Okay, I knew in any case that Hitler was there [in Germany]. I wouldn't be able to go back. That was completely out of the question. *This is the first time in her narrative that* RB *refers to her Jewishness, and even here the reference is not explicit. Strangely enough, this acknowledgment of how Hitler's presence in Germany changed her entire existence even seems incidental. She seems to be preoccupied with relating the positive events of her time in the Soviet Union.*

J Earlier, when you were talking about going to China, you said you knew that Hitler was in power and that therefore you couldn't return to Germany anyway.

RB Yes. That's the reason I had to stay in the Soviet Union.

J When Hitler came to power, you were in the Soviet Union. What did you know about what was going on in Germany?

RB Of course I had heard in the most general way that Hitler was beginning to be open about his plans for aggression. Of course one didn't think that the Soviet Union would be his target. We saw what happened with Poland and we were all shocked. Of course. But we never thought it would spread. But then it went so far that Jews should not return to Berlin or to Germany at all.

J How did you hear that Jews shouldn't go back? From your family or friends?

RB We heard about this, of course, on the radio, and then people came to visit and they told us about it.

J Was the man with whom you were in this first relationship Jewish?

RB All of the men I was with were Jews. I don't know, I probably have somewhere a special relationship to Jews. It just happened that way. They were all 100 percent Jewish.

RB *returns to her story. Her narrative is marked by these kinds of digressions, evoked by the many associations attached to what obviously was a rich and exciting period in her life.*

We were in China and we didn't hear very much. Naturally we heard from people who came to visit, and it was terrible. We were afraid of what was to follow and of this uncertainty. We were living there absolutely out of the way. I was living there as the consul's wife and was treated like a princess. Looking back, it was like a fairy tale. We came back after two years. I brought back with me Njanja, my daughter's nursemaid, who was a white Russian who had come to China as a young girl.

J   What year was it that you came back?

RB   Nineteen thirty-six, back to Moscow.

J   During the time that you were away, did you receive letters from here?

RB   No, of course not. Everything here was in a fog, and one didn't know about anything. Later, much later, when I was working at the radio station, I found out through the Red Cross about my mother, who was living in London. She got out with the last train. Our housekeeper and maid, whom she always especially liked, helped her. We got along with them very well. They really helped my parents before they got out. They had to sleep somewhere different every night, and then my father died of a heart attack in 1938. They wanted my mother to get out, but my mother didn't want to, because she wanted to take care of elderly Jewish people in Berlin. But that was out of the question, and they both helped her leave at the last moment for London. She was the only one who survived, except my brother. He went to Israel. All the others died in concentration camps or were gassed—all of them.

J   You learned about this during the war or after?

RB   After the war. Because during the war I was sitting in the Soviet Union, which was quite cut off from what was going on abroad. RB *tells about returning with her 'husband' to Moscow, where the four of them lived in a cellar room nine meters square.*

We had to fight the cockroaches at night. There were so many of them! It was awful. Winter was coming, and we were living out of our suitcases.

I got a job with the newspapers. At least I knew Russian, so I could make myself understood. I took over newspaper photos. I had a Russian passport after I returned from China. I photographed for newspapers and magazines—*Pravda, Iswestia,* and others.

RB *returns to the topic of her apartment and the year 1937.*

We were outside of Moscow in our dacha [which my husband built]. While we were there, my daughter became sick, and it got much worse. The doctor said that she would have to be taken to a hospital in Moscow immediately. RB *tells us that when they found a hospital, she was told that she could not stay with her two-and-a-half-year-old daughter. RB protested, and she was allowed to stay.*

And after six days my child died in my arms—in a foreign land, with foreign people and a foreign language. It was terrible. But what could I do? I had to get over it. I didn't work for three months. I just stayed home. I told my husband and Njanja they should take care of everything. During this time Ilse Münz [Kostja's mother (see chapter 11)] was with me with her baby. Her husband had just been imprisoned. And for three months I wandered around the whole day. When it was too cold at home, I went into stores. And then I would be the last one out of the cafes. Then home to sleep and back out again. For three months, [I did this]. RB *then began to work for the newspapers again. She kicked her husband out of the apartment since 'he didn't behave himself.'*

I didn't want to have to wash floors or wash dishes. I was alone there and had given up everything. And in the midst of all this we heard about the terrible events: Hitler had moved further ahead. It was awful. One just didn't know what one should or could do—how one could help. It was a terrible situation: Hitler had advanced toward Moscow; war had been declared.

Wait a minute—I'm getting everything confused. I reversed the order of things. I know what I want to say. I have to pull myself together. RB *has difficulty keeping to the temporal chronology of her story. Although she self-deprecatingly attributes this difficulty to her age, it is clear that she frequently experiences emotional trauma during her telling, particularly when speaking of the beginning of the war and the death of her child. She often is so moved by something she says that she starts to cry; she then stops herself, saying, 'One has to control oneself.'*

My husband was drafted. He was a communist who could speak good German. He had to go eight days before the war began. I was alone with the child and Njanja.

After we returned from China, he worked for the Central Committee. The secretary came to me outside the city and said we had to get out because Hitler was approaching the city. You could see Hitler's army with binoculars. I said, 'No, wait a minute.' I was in

Moscow after we came back from China. That was 1937 and my child had died. I had tried different things for three years. But then I said to myself, You can't live without a child. I needed someone who needed me, to whom I could give all my love. To work just in order to live for myself was no life for me. So I drove out to where my husband was living in the dacha. He was the one I had been with, and the one I had left for three years and hadn't seen. I told him I wanted to get pregnant and have a child like the last one. I got pregnant, and I worked up until the last minute. I kept saying to myself, I must have a little girl again, another little girl, but not Natasha. That chapter is over.

RB *relates the details of her labor. Her first child had been born in China; this one was to be born in a maternity hospital. All around her were Russian women screaming in labor. They took her in. As her labor began and became more painful, she could not cry like the others. She kept saying to herself that it must be a girl.*

It was a girl, and she was so like the first Natasha that I named her Natasha. And she is still alive today. She lives fifteen minutes from here. I spoiled her and treated her like a little princess, although it was very difficult in Moscow, and later on as well. She now takes great advantage of me. I myself am of course to blame. RB *speaks frequently about her child's apparent indifference toward her. She finds it particularly hard to bear in light of the sacrifices she made in those years.*

So, as I was saying, I had the child in 1941 and I brought her home to my nine square meters. Six weeks after she was born, the secretary from the office where my husband worked came out to the dacha and said that we had to get out. Hitler was on the outskirts of Moscow. I said, 'I am not leaving. I lost my first child. I am not in Moscow and I am not going anywhere.' Two weeks later she came again and said that the last train was leaving and that I should leave, at least for the sake of the child. So I decided to go, packed our things, and with Njanja and the child I left. We had to ride in cattle cars filled with people. RB *tells us that her child was infected with whooping cough and of their long trip to Bashkirien (Siberia), where they were taken to a village inhabited by old people and mothers with children. The men were all in the army.*

I didn't want to twiddle my thumbs, so I went to the Communist Party Secretary to get a job. I wasn't in the Party and still am not a member. I think people should do what they do because they think it is right for them, and for that I don't need a Party. But that is my own particular view.

In Siberia, RB *and her daughter were always hungry. They received one piece of soap per month and only 200 grams of bread each day. In exchange for a blanket* RB *obtained a sheep so she would have milk and sometimes butter for her child. The next year they grew some vegetables. In the winter they had to shovel the snow from the roofs, fetch water from frozen streams, and cut down trees for wood.*

After two years [the battle of] Stalingrad was over. We were allowed to return home because there was enough distance between Moscow and Stalingrad. *She returned with officers' wives and relatives, but without Njanja.*

J The whole time you were there, were you treated as a German or a Soviet?

RB As a Soviet citizen—necessarily so. But anyone who had looked at my passport would have seen that I came from Berlin. But basically I was a Soviet citizen. And what was good about that was that those who had 'Jew' printed under nationality could not go back. But in my case 'Soviet citizen' was printed. Jassi, my husband, had told me to write 'Soviet citizen,' and that allowed me to return.

J Were there other Jews there while you were there?

RB No one noticed such things. It was just like it had been earlier in Germany. Hardly anyone knew who was a Jew or not, except for the very pious. We didn't identify with the pious ones, although my father kept up the traditions, was a member of the synagogue. We had our regular seats in the synagogue on Fasanenstrasse [a Berlin synagogue destroyed before the war and now the site of a reconstructed community center for the West Berlin Jewish Community]. *Interestingly,* RB *compares her situation as a Jew in the Soviet Union to her family's typical German Jewish secularization in Germany before the war. She emphasizes that in both cases she was integrated into the society around her: just as she was not singled out as an ethnic Jew in Berlin, she was not singled out as an ethnic German in Siberia.*

J Your father had these seats?

RB   Yes, my father, my grandfather, my uncle—as one says, the whole *meshpuche*. Exactly. RB *seems to be proud that her entire family were regular members of the Jewish Community.*

J   And where you lived in Siberia, wasn't there an *Arbeitsarmee* [work army; the term was a euphemism for those interned by Stalin in the gulags]?

RB   Nothing, nothing, nothing. We weren't ordered to go there: we were evacuated. Because of this, it was quite a different situation. No, no. It was clear that we didn't have anything there. Also during the trip back to Moscow the circumstances were very difficult. We returned to our apartment.

J   That was in 1944, wasn't it?

RB   No, 1943—1943 was Stalingrad, and in '43 we came back. RB*'s life, like the lives of many Germans during the war, was marked by the battle of Stalingrad. But while for most Germans Stalingrad was a defeat, for* RB *it marked the point when she was allowed to return from Bashkirien.* RB *tells us about returning to an apartment without heat or furniture.*

[The apartment] was completely covered with mold. I slept on the floor on camel's-hair mattresses that I had brought from China, which laid down on top of newspapers. Natasha slept in an iron bed with legs. At night the rats began to run over me. I would grab an axe and a hammer, and whenever they appeared I would start to pummel them. I closed one hole with pieces of glass, but as soon as that one was filled they came through another. I fought against those things for three-quarters of a year. All the other people had been evacuated and were not allowed to come back. I didn't have anything to eat. I did get a family ration card, the lowest level, since I didn't work, and I got a child's ration card. I could exchange my card for milk and whatever else was available. Sometimes I could get a potato, sometimes a carrot, for Natasha. I only ate cabbage with water and a bit of salt.

Because of the mold, she and the child would leave the apartment during the day, returning only for two hours in the afternoon so the child could sleep and in the evening so RB *could cook for the next day. She had to put rocks on top of the pots so the rats would not get inside. Some mornings she would discover that a pot cover had been moved and she would have to throw the food away.*

It was terrible! Then I decided that I wanted to work. Even though I was a Soviet citizen, they simply said *nyet* because they were afraid that I was a spy, having been born in Berlin. I wasn't even allowed to wash a dish or clean the floor. Then always the terrible news that one heard from people who had more connections to what was going on. You were completely confused. You just didn't know what to do with yourself—where to go. It was a terrible time.

J   You mean the information about what Stalin was doing?

It was not clear whether by 'terrible news' RB meant the war, the genocide, or Stalin. Even for someone of her age living in the GDR in 1989, it is still necessary to speak circumspectly about some of these events.

RB Exactly. It was 1939 when everything began with Stalin. Then it was suddenly the turn of all the Germans and foreigners. Starting in 1939, the arrests came mostly at night. And it was terrible when the bell rang. We were in in an apartment with five other families, each in one room. They took people at night. One waited: How many times did it ring? Who is going to be next? Is it my turn? It was a very awful time. They took people when someone simply denounced them. There didn't have to be a reason. Someone simply said something, and you were taken away. You were really fortunate if you weren't taken away, especially between 1939 and 1941. So I had to live as I have described. I couldn't work; I simply vegetated. I met my friends from time to time and heard from them what was happening, since I had no connection to the outside—my brother had been in Israel since 1933 and my mother was in London.

I tried to help wherever I could between 1943 and 1945. In '45 a friend who was an actress came to me. She was working for Moscow radio at that time. The war was just over. She said, 'I want to go to Berlin, but I have to find a replacement. Come on, read something for me.' I had never done anything like that and I didn't know how. The problem was that my situation was difficult—I needed a kindergarten for my child, and I couldn't look for work. She told me that I would get the kindergarten that I needed. I went to the radio station, tried it out, and they liked my voice. I would have preferred to do still shots for films, but I took this job. I told them I wouldn't stay longer than two months—it was all too strenuous to have to talk into a microphone and to let the whole world hear me [RB *read news and spoke on political and cultural programs*], but I stayed ten years, until I left the Soviet Union at the end of 1954.

J   During the years that you were at the radio, your life must not have been so difficult as before.

RB   Naturally, it wasn't. I had my pay. But it was always nerve-wracking. Since we read everything in translation, you never knew whether you would end up at home or behind bars in the evening. It wasn't the original text. First, it was written in German, then the editors got it. Then it was translated into Russian, so the political editors had to look at it. Then it was retranslated again.

I came the first day, and I knew many people already. There was one man in the corner. I went to him and introduced myself: 'My name is Benario. I don't believe that we know each other.' He answered, 'My name is Hart.' He was, so to speak, my third husband. This is the way I got to know my husband.

J   What did he do there?

RB   He came out of the *Arbeitsarmee*. He had been in a concentration camp for two and one-half years and was freed by the Soviet army. He was in Romania and got into the *Arbeitskolonne* [work unit]. That's where Hans Rotenberg [who later worked in the *Volkskammer*, the governing body of the GDR] noticed him after he had written an article in the German-language newspaper. He was brought from the *Arbeitsarmee* to the radio.

J   Was he German?

RB   An Austrian, typical Austrian.

J   Was he Jewish?

RB   Yes, 100 percent.—Which of you two is Jewish? *She points to Jeff.*— I really went after him. He looked terrible after being in a concentration camp, then in the *Arbeitsarmee*. He had shoes that had cardboard glued on the bottom.

We worked together until he was fired because someone at the station was jealous and wanted him removed. He was out of work for four and one-half years. I took care of us both. We lived in the basement apartment in Moscow. It was a catastrophe. My other 'husband' lived in the dacha, outside the city. Of course, I had to figure out a compromise in this situation. We lived this way until we left. Then, through the Red Cross we asked for my repatriation. I had been in the Soviet Union long enough. I wanted to be in Germany again and help with the [rebuilding].

I wanted my husband Camillo Hart to come with me even though he had no papers. We came here [to the GDR] although they didn't want me to leave the radio station [in Moscow], since it would be difficult to find someone to replace me. Then a colleague who was in the *Abhörburo* [secret surveillance office]—we had two such offices in our building that listened to our radio programs—said that when I was in Berlin I should come by his office. He was the director of the radio, and I could get work.

I first went to the housing office, since we were put up right away in a very good hotel near the Brandenburg Gate, the Hotel Adlon. After two months I said, 'I'm tired of this hotel. I want to get my own apartment. I want to feel at home.' I was shown this apartment. They told me that if I didn't like it they would be glad to show me another. After living in a basement apartment nine meters square, I didn't need anything more. Naturally I was impressed. For weeks I walked in and out of the rooms here, in and out of the kitchen. In Moscow there were seventeen people using one kitchen. I now had a kitchen all to myself. I could do what I wanted. It really overwhelmed me. So then we arrived, and Lily Becher, the wife of Johannes Becher, said she would give us furniture since we didn't have any money. Then all the trouble began: my husband had a heart attack and had to have absolute quiet; he couldn't even think of working. We were in pretty miserable shape. Some people didn't treat us very well.

I decided to go to my colleague from the Soviet Union to get work. He sent me to the head announcer. Apparently he was afraid that since I had just come from Moscow, I wanted a very important position. He even said that I had a Russian accent. This was, of course, very funny. He sent me on to someone else, and that person also probably thought that I would take something away from him. So then I went to the television station and worked in the department that took care of Russian films. I decided which films should be translated, taken, not taken, with subtitles or dubbed, and so on. That was my job until 1965, when

I retired. I retired as a VDN member, one who has been persecuted by the Nazi regime. *The acronym* VDN *stands for* Verfolgte des Naziregimes *[those persecuted by the Nazis]. The* VDN *was the official organization for victims of the former Nazi regime, who were mainly communists and Jews. Members of the* VDN *were entitled to higher pensions, which they were allowed to take at an earlier age (fifty-five for women and sixty for men). They were also eligible for improved access to housing and preferential treatment at curative spas.*

J   When did you first contact the Red Cross about returning?

RB   Two years before [in 1952].

J   Why did you wait so long? Why didn't you return right after the end of the war?

RB   Because I thought I should first stay in the Soviet Union and help rebuild the country. Also, I had my job in propaganda and that was a very responsible position. We didn't just read texts; we were also responsible for what was going on the air. After that I thought it was the right time to return to Germany.

J   Does that mean that in the beginning you didn't plan to come back to Germany?

RB   No, I had the intention, but not right away, since I wanted to help there. Since I had been there the whole time, I knew how chaotic everything was and the kinds of problems the people had.

J   When you decided to come back to Germany, did you have particular ideas about how it would be here? And after you returned, was it indeed different than you had imagined? How was it?

RB   It was different than I had imagined. And I must admit to you that it was difficult to get used to living here. After being to so many places in the world—I had lived in China, and been in London and in Switzerland; I was here, there, and all over. When I arrived a friend said to me, 'You are here. How do you feel? Are you home again?' I answered, 'I don't feel like I am home at all. I have been away for twenty-two years. And I am sorry, but it is a different world. It is not what I am now used to. I was in the Soviet Union for twenty years and in China for two years.' I have to tell you that it has been the same up until today. [I cannot] call Germany home [*Heimat*], I don't have a home [*Heimat*]. I am home everywhere I go. And the most important thing is that I help wherever I can. *She begins to cry. We stop the tape until she is ready to continue.* RB *often loses her composure when she talks about caring for people.*

J   Do you think that you were Russianized, if one can say that, or were you just different?

RB I certainly wasn't Russianized. But the place and the people—they think differently than people here. I had the feeling that one had to switch gears here.

J   Did you think at first about going back to West Germany, or was it clear to you that you would return to the GDR?

RB It was clear to me. My husband had said, 'We won't unpack; we'll go right away to West Germany, to West Berlin.' I responded, 'Without me.' The people there [don't appeal to me]. Besides, I don't go along with what they stand for, but rather for socialist democracy. And more specifically, people had warned me about the concentration camps. I couldn't simply turn my back on that. I couldn't do that.

J   You mean the Soviet citizens?

RB Yes, the Soviet Union. Another reason, of course, was that my daughter grew up there [in the Soviet Union]. 'My God, West Berlin!' [people told me]. 'Your hair will all be cut off there. Be careful that you don't go over there and get a shock.' I didn't want to, and I still don't want to. I can go over as much as I want. I have permission, but I am now so old that it doesn't really attract me. What I see there, I don't have to have. You see, I had everything I wanted in my childhood. I had heaven on earth. I know all that. Those who have never had it lust after it. It's all the same to me. I don't need it. I want to grow old properly. I want to help where I can. That is the most important thing. *She begins to cry again.*

J   Didn't you have reservations about coming back to Germany, to a country where crimes had been committed against Jews and your own family? Didn't you feel estranged from the people here?

RB I never had reservations, because before I went away there weren't such things. There were just Germans, right? There weren't Jews, and Christians, and Catholics, and so on. When I came back I treated everyone the same, just as before. *Again,* RB*'s experiences in the twenties were in a secular milieu, in which racial, ethnic, and religious differences were unmarked. She emphasizes the socialist-*

*humanistic qualities that characterize her values. She is interested in
all people, irrespective of their nationality or religion, and feels a need
to help them all.*

J   When you came here with your daughter, could she speak German?

RB   No, my daughter had naturally rejected learning German in the
Soviet Union, although my husband and I spoke it with each
other. It was, admittedly, after the war. She was in school and
people told her quite a different story: 'Oh, the Germans, we
would spit on them'—things like that. RB *talks of Natasha's successes and failures in school and says that she finally completed high
school in the* GDR.

J   Does she still have relationships with friends in the Soviet Union?

RB   Certainly. Of course she has connections. That is obvious. She
doesn't know what her mother tongue is—whether it is Russian or
German. She now works as an interpreter and is always busy.
Natasha, like her mother and many other returnees, works in a profession that requires her to use her linguistic and communicative abilities. For RB, *these activities account in large part for her internationalist and humanitarian attitudes.*

J   Do you have any kind of relationship with the Jewish Community in East Berlin?

RB   Yes, I became a member because I think the tradition needs to be
maintained.

J   When did you become a member—from the beginning? or when
exactly?

RB   From the very beginning, after my return. *She means in 1954, upon
her return to the* GDR, *the beginning of her new life in a new Germany.*

But I must admit that I really didn't feel comfortable there. I
couldn't seem to make contact with these people. Now it is especially difficult because the meetings are in the evening and I can't
get there. I can't drive any more since I am blind in one eye. So my
children have the car, and I have to ask them to take me every
time. Or the meetings are in the afternoon, at three or half past
three, a good time for older people but that is just when we eat,
and I naturally want to be with my family. *Despite the tensions with
her daughter,* RB *seems to feel that having meals with her daughter's*

family is more important than taking part in the activities of the Jewish Community.

So I really didn't really feel connected to them, nor to the leader. I find that the things that are important to me are not emphasized in the Community.

J   Does your daughter have contact with the Community?

RB She doesn't, but strangely enough, my older grandson is interested.

J   Did you educate your daughter in the Jewish tradition?

RB Not at all, not at all, because I am not religious in this way. I mean, I am religious [*gläubig*], but without the outer trappings, like going to synagogue or things like that. Whenever there is a concert in the synagogue I go, and it is wonderful and I feel very moved. But not all the rites and rituals. I don't need that. All of these things are inside of me, in my heart. I deal with those things privately. Naturally I went with the children to Seder, so that they could take part and see what that was, so that they could experience these rituals and traditions. I went with them to the synagogue for Yom Kippur and Rosh Hashanah, the important holidays.

And the older one, it is strange. One day I said that it was too bad that the name [Benario] will disappear because I don't have any male heirs. Then the older one said, 'I want my name to be Benario.' I thought that was a good idea, and so we went to the city hall and I said, 'My grandson would like to take on my name, because otherwise it will disappear and the name has tradition.' After two months they called back and said that it was possible, although he would have to have a double name, that of his father and Benario. Right away he said, 'Probably after a while, the first name will be dropped.' The younger one went too.

It came time to get his identification card renewed, and his also had the double name. We hadn't said anything about it. We just had to laugh. The older one is very interested in Judaism. I had to bring him a book from West Berlin from which he could learn Hebrew. He would also like to go—of course we just don't know if it is possible—to Heidelberg, where there is a chair, I think, for Jewish teachers or for some sort of Jewish subject. *Even though they knew little about Judaism, the grandchildren recognized the signifi-*

cance of carrying on the name of RB *'s family. While naming is generally significant for carrying on family traditions, in Judaism it is
particularly important; for example, Jewish children have Hebrew
names in addition to their secular names. It is also interesting that the
grandchildren took on the name of their maternal grandmother,
through whom their link to Judaism is established. Clearly,* RB *'s
grandchildren are trying to establish roots to a Jewish tradition to
which they are connected through their grandmother.*

But [the opportunity to go to the West to study Judaism] is
only possible through an exchange with the GDR. I don't know
how this all works, but it is happening here now, which was not
the case before. Things are being done for the youth, which is very
interesting, and really at the international level. I don't know if
you know that or not, but here it is the case that only older citizens
are able to travel into capitalist countries, not younger people.
Suddenly the older grandson was approached to turn in an ap-
plication for a youth group that was to travel to Italy. This is
something quite new for us. I didn't believe that it would work,
but it appears to be happening in September. Very nice, very nice,
and I am very happy for him, because up until now that was
impossible. So we are opening our gates for the young people too,
and naturally that is a very good thing. *This issue became moot a
few months after we talked, since* GDR *citizens began streaming out of
the country in August and September. In November the Wall came
down.*

J   What is your relationship to Israel? Is your brother still there?

RB No, he is dead. I have been in Israel four times.

J   When was the first time?

RB These are all really questions of conscience. RB *'s comments remind
us that the relationship of Jews in the* GDR *to Israel was very complicated. Most of them felt positively about the Jewish state, and some
even had family there, while officially the* GDR *was critical of Israel
and a supporter of the Arab states.*

J   I mean, was it as early as in the 1950s?

RB Yes, I retired in 1955, and I probably went to visit him for the first
time in 1956. Naturally it was shocking. At that time he was still
living in the country. He had a farm with cows and hens. In fact
the cow that gave the most milk was named Ruth. I thought that
was wonderful.

RB goes on to say that he had to give up the farm and move into Tel Aviv. She traveled all over Israel and found it 'very interesting.'

The fourth time I went, in 1984, I had to move him into a German old people's home. And that was the second time in my life that someone died in my arms. Someone called to tell me that he had been taken to the hospital. They laid him on the stretcher for a heart operation, and I said good-bye to him. That was forever. I buried him, just as I had buried my daughter fifty years before, in a foreign country, surrounded by a foreign language, among foreigners. *RB's reference to death in a foreign country illustrates that she does not look upon Germany as foreign, that implicitly at least she thinks of it, if not as home, then as native or familiar. However, she has no word for this 'being in Germany' to correspond with the 'foreignness' of being elsewhere.*

That was very strange—that this situation repeated itself. That was that. So now I live here and take care of other people, worry about other people, old people and sick people, those who have cancer, who need a little cheering up.

J   Do you still have a connection to Israel?

RB   I don't have a relationship to Israel that I already haven't told you about. I still have two cousins there.

RB is reminded of how she discovered a whole new set of relations named Benario, when she thought she was the only one left. A painting by Kokoschka of her as a little girl was seen in Zurich by a woman who knew someone named [Benario] in Canada. Contact was established through a number of different channels, and the two cousins discovered each other's existence. Twice in the telling of this story, RB acknowledges that this could only happen to members of her generation, who were 'scattered [durchgeschüttelt] to so many places' and to whom so many 'crazy' things happened.

You wouldn't believe it: in the whole world 140 families. Now all of a sudden, after not having any family aside from my little family here—two boys, a daughter, and a son-in-law—I have 140 families for my relations. Isn't life crazy? And I am eighty years old. If I only were a little bit younger so that I could experience all of this! *RB returns often to this theme of time lost. She still has enthusiasm and curiosity and would like very much to experience more of the world.*

J   Just two more questions: Many people say they are German Jews or Germans with a Jewish heritage. How would you express this? When you describe yourself, what do you say?

RB   I am a German Jew.

J   You don't find this whole thing to be contradictory or—

RB   Burdensome?

J   Burdensome or—I don't know.

RB   Hmm. No. My God, one notices, sometimes there are [burdensome aspects] in some corners. Where doesn't that exist in life? That doesn't matter.

J   You mean when people perhaps . . .

RB   Yes . . . are not 100 percent enthusiastic when one says one is a German Jew. But I will tell you: This is what I am and this is what I will stay. I will always be a Jew. And 'Jewish heritage'—that sounds so funny in my opinion. I am a German Jew. So, anything else?

J   How do you deal with the entire war experience, the persecution of the Jews? Are these events part of the same story?

RB   First of all, the fact that I came back from the Soviet Union to the GDR is obvious. What would you like?

J   I am only looking.

RB   Turn [the tape recorder] off. We don't need it any more.

J   No, we still would like to record what you have to say.

     RB *becomes bothered by our tape recorder. It may be because the topic evokes complicated responses that involve criticizing friends.*

RB   It is like this: It is obvious that when one comes out of the Soviet Union one cannot go right away to the Federal Republic. It is just the opposite there [of what one knew]. And at that time it was the Cold War, when the situation was much worse. There was a much greater contrast between East and West. The situation created unpleasantness for those who returned from the East. For me it never was a question whether to go to the West. I did not need to do that. And above all, what people had to go through and then to go to those who perhaps wanted to celebrate after they had lost [the war]! No, that was not for me. I still feel the same way today. There are very few people with whom I feel comfortable who live over there. The majority of the people there don't suit me—their attitudes, the way they present themselves, they way they talk, what they are interested in. That's not me. I am not like that and don't like that. For these reasons I don't go over there that often. But I cannot get used to being with these people. I would ask them, 'How are you?' 'What did you have to do to survive during the war?' She [Lily Flechtheim] answered, 'Nothing. I had an easy time. We were in Zurich.' She went from London to Zurich. I was so perplexed by the fact that she didn't experience anything in the period when we had to deal with Herr Hitler and Comrade Stalin and it was so hard for us. They really didn't understand that people are really shaped dramatically by these experiences. Then I spent a long time dealing with that until I could understand the difference [between experiences such as her own and experiences in England or America during the war]. They just couldn't experience the way we did what had happened to us, what our life was like. This was very strange for me until I came to recognize that they have a very different life than we are able to have because we see life from a very different perspective. This was all very interesting for me. I just discovered this in the past year. These people are very nice, but they simply don't understand what has gone on inside of a person [who had the experiences that I had]. Period. End. That's it.

It was difficult to convince RB *to read, correct, and comment on the typescript of her interview. She was suffering from serious eye problems, had already had one operation, and was expecting another. After unification I had arranged for her to see an ophthalmologist at a West Berlin clinic, who finally told her that her East Berlin doctor had done a bad job on her eye and that it would be difficult to correct his mistakes. As if to invoke Western medical superiority as a metaphor for political domination,* RB *became even more frustrated with her condition than she had been before.* GDR *medicine had failed her!*

She resisted doing anything with the transcript we had sent her. She wanted to destroy it—she couldn't believe that she had said all those things. It took considerable persuasion to convince her to meet with us for a second video interview. I realized that we could use the transcription of this second interview for a second response to postunification events, since I could not convince her to write a response to her interview.

The meeting was initially postponed because of her health. Finally, on 2 February 1992, we met, this time at my apartment in West Berlin. For some reason, the idea of conducting the interview in a different environment than her apartment or in East Berlin had appealed to her. She said she didn't want to wait for the cameras, lights, and sound equipment to be set up. When she arrived at Eisenacherstrasse, everything was ready and we could proceed. John was in the United States at this time, so I conducted the interview alone.

J We talked over a year ago—before reunification, before this great change. How do you see all of these events? How do you feel about them?

RB How do I feel? As it all happened, on 1 July [the beginning of the currency union, the date that marks the first official step toward unification], I went into the street to see what was left in the shop windows. I went by a store around the corner and the window was empty. I looked at the shelves and they were empty. The only thing I saw was a pair of men's slippers, otherwise nothing. It was a total selling out of the GDR. Naturally, at the beginning that was difficult to comprehend [*begreifen*], and second to swallow [*verdauen*]. But it probably had to be that way, even though in my opinion the whole thing should have moved much more slowly, so that people wouldn't have gotten such a shock as they have now. Now you see, wherever one looks, unemployment, [people] waiting for the pink slip; they wait for their offices to be closed, their businesses to shut down. It goes on and on. The people who at first were so enthusiastic about unified Germany—of course this is ultimately something wonderful—[are realizing that it is difficult]. *Although* RB *was never explicit about why unification was 'ultimately something wonderful,' it is likely that she realized how the* GDR's *repression and corruption limited human potential.*

It was all too hasty, too quick. These people only saw money, the chance to travel, all the comforts. But the rest—the other side of the coin—has gone all wrong. Now it is emerging slowly, and people notice. We are on a downhill course that will last a long time. There is nowhere that people can take a breather, that they can say, Now I am starting a new life and everything will work out for the best. We won't see that for a long time. And the older people have it harder. We had Herr Hitler, we had Comrade

Stalin, then Honecker on top of that, and we're only really finding out now all that he did to us in the past forty years. Now it's suddenly back again in the Gulf. *This interview took place during the 1991 Gulf War.*

I must say, we have had nearly enough, and it is very difficult to point to anything positive, but one must. Because we are not living just for ourselves. After us come the children, then grand-children, and they will have it again, so that whoever works a bit and studies a bit will come to something.

J   What has been lost, so to speak, through this reunification? What has been lost of the GDR that you valued?

RB   Oh, we have lost the easygoing nature [*Gemütlichkeit*] of the GDR. It was a very easygoing country, much more peaceful than it is now. Everything is terribly tense, terribly hectic, and I must also say that produce tasted better in the old GDR. Take spinach or wurst: it tastes Western and chemical. [On the other hand,] the butter never tasted great. Now, I like butter, and when I was a child we always got Danish butter, and now we have [good butter] again. I am delighted with the butter, but otherwise, no. RB *often expresses differences between political systems and grand ideologies in terms of everyday experiences, as in her comments on food.*

J   Besides food and a gentler life, what else is lacking?

RB   Oh God, hold it a moment! You are overwhelming me now. I really don't know now what I should say, but there is so much. Things that one felt were good before, and now one wonders why they don't exist anymore.

J   Do you feel personally threatened in this new, postunification situation? Do you have fears that you didn't have before?

RB   Look, as a very old person, I am no longer afraid. But people are very fearful about not getting jobs. There is already mass unem-ployment. The older people have no prospects.

J   There is reportedly more anti-Semitism and xenophobia. Do you think that is the case, and are you afraid of that?

RB   Again, I can't be personally afraid, because I am so old that I am beyond that. But anti-Semitism is really such an ugly thing, and it is again being stirred up by so many people—and xenophobia too. This happens because there are simply more people than work; indeed there is, of course, a certain sector of people who are narrow-minded, who believe it is German to be like that. Some feel that there is no work and we don't need foreigners taking our jobs away. We don't need any Jews, who could also perhaps take something away from us, who might get better pensions.

J   In the former GDR there was officially no anti-Semitism. Now it exists in the new federal states [the former GDR].

RB   Excuse me, we had it too. Obviously, it was kept quiet. Officially it didn't exist. But of course one often noticed it in different ways in how one was received, how people spoke to you. Let's not kid ourselves.

J   Are you disappointed by what has happened in the GDR in the last forty years?

RB   We were spoon-fed and made to toe the line to such a degree, and lied to. It is remarkable what people did to us. No, no, it was terrible what happened—that nothing was brought to light. The people who did this must be made responsible and shouldn't get off the hook by saying they are sick or ready for retirement. RB *is referring here to the revelations about corruption by the highest leaders of the* GDR, *who were believed to feel solidarity with* GDR *citizens. That they were living 'the high life' in luxurious surroundings and with material benefits far beyond what anyone expected demoralized many faithful Party members and average citizens.*

J   Do you think that it would have been better had people spoken out earlier against what was going on in the GDR. Perhaps the GDR would have changed and would still exist.

RB   Look, of course the GDR had to go and there had to be a united Germany. Forty years was enough, but the problems with the GDR are always emphasized. Only the bad things about the GDR are talked about, how the high officials benefited. But although it is good that it has come to an end, everything is painted with the same color—all bad—and the good we had is condemned along with it.

J   What were the things that were so good in the early years?

RB   Oh, there were various things . . . oh God, I just told you . . . oh what can I tell you?

J   Ok, I'll ask another question. When you returned to the GDR from the Soviet Union, you purposely came to the GDR, not to the Federal Republic. Now you are living in the Federal Republic, the country you expressly wanted to avoid.

RB Look, I quite consciously wanted to go to the GDR, as I told you, and now I find it remarkable that I am in the Federal Republic, since all we heard during the Cold War was how horrible it was over there. Suddenly we are part of them. But we just have to keep going, to try to stay decent and honest. How far one can do that in such a place, I don't know.

J You came from the Soviet Union, and now Soviet Jews are emigrating to Germany even though the World Jewish Congress, for example, has encouraged them to go to Israel. Do you think they should come here?

RB Where should they go? They have to go somewhere. The Soviet Union is very anti-Semitic and the people suffer. Life is hard there, and yet it is not for fun that they leave their country and start from scratch here. That they come here is remarkable, since they are only too aware of how it was under Hitler. But they want some ground under their feet, and they know that this is a civilized country. They probably want to work here with the rest and start afresh.

J Do you think that it is important for the future of this new Germany that Jews live here?

RB But of course. Absolutely. But work must be found for people. No one should get preferential treatment; then you get anti-Semitism all over again. That is the question that has to be solved. Because even without the Jews there isn't enough work.

J When we met last summer we spoke about the question of identity, whether you saw yourself as a GDR citizen, a Jew, or a German. Now, after reunification in this new Germany, how do you see yourself?

RB I don't feel German—I feel Jewish. I am not a German. I don't have anything in common with the whole German people. Granted, I was born here. I lived here for a long time—twenty-two years. I also came back here very consciously, but not to my homeland. I don't call anywhere my homeland. I am at home where I have people with whom I can get on. But otherwise I can't say that I am German. I was in fact rubbed the wrong way when I returned from the Soviet Union. At that time a friend asked me if I wasn't happy to be back in my home country again. And I said I was sorry that I came back. I find nothing homey here. I am here to help, that is all.

J   We will stop soon; just another short question: Do you think that in Germany there is no solidarity with the Jews in Israel?

RB   Much too little. The Jews aren't well-liked in Germany, and the idea of a Jewish state is even more unpleasant. It is difficult to explain to them that other people want to live just like the people here.

J   You have experienced many different things here over the years. What would you like to see for this new Germany or for the country in the future?

RB   One can only wish for the future that East and West, which still exist, will really grow together so that one no longer feels that there is an East and West. Now there are the Ossis and the Wessis. The wages are different and there are two camps where there should be one. But this will take time. Everything is more expensive—rents, public transportation—and the wages haven't equalized. It will take time.

J   You believe that things will come together?

RB   I am convinced of it.

J   In all that you say, the human ideal [*das Menschliche*] always comes through: one should stay human and treat others humanely. You believe this after all you have experienced?

RB   Absolutely. That is the most important thing.

'Berlin is home for me.'

Born 1903 Berlin
1935   Prague
1936–1939 Vienna
1939–1971 Lithuania
           (1942–1944 Uzbekistan,
           1944 returned to Kaunas)
1972–1979 Israel
1979–   West Berlin

W*ith his full head of white hair and sparkling eyes, Albert Klein makes a lasting impression even today, at eighty-six. AK was, however, sensitive about his age and even felt disadvantaged because of it. He emphasized that after his return from Israel to West Berlin he had to be very aggressive to get the attention he thought he deserved. Now AK heads the Office for Foreign Journalists and remains active in international journalism. A filmmaker both in Berlin and during his years in the Soviet Union, AK focuses in his own work on actors and directors who left Germany and lived in exile during the war. Speaking with a heavily Russianized accent that is often difficult to understand, AK obviously enjoyed talking to us about his accomplishments in film and journalism and his acquaintances in the theater. It was clear that the people he mentioned—few of whose names we recognized—were still quite alive to him. His joy in telling stories (both in his films and during our interviews) often proved frustrating as we tried to follow the events of his life.*

AK identifies with the film and theater world and with his position at the head of an organization to which he belonged before he had to leave Berlin. We conducted all of our interviews in his office on Hardenbergstrasse, where AK seems to spend most of his time. I sensed that his life at home is dedicated to his wife, to whom he often referred in our interviews. The fact that he lost his first wife in the 1930s under tragic circumstances and met his present wife under circumstances that were not much better apparently accounts for their closeness. In fact, the following interview is based on the transcript from tapes of our interview with him and a revised, somewhat edited version produced by his wife, who in her very gentle way seems to speak for her husband.

AK Many emigrants who lived for twelve years outside of Germany had it very difficult. All of us asked ourselves, how will it be when the war is over? During this period I met many famous exiles: Erwin Piscator, Leon Feuchtwanger, Bertolt Brecht, and many others who made plans about how cultural life in Germany should be rebuilt. It was a similar situation in the Moscow exile, where a committee was organized in order to rebuild Germany. The emigrants were happy when the war was over [since] Germany's capitulation meant liberation for them. However, for the majority of the Germans, especially those who had secretly fought against Nazism, it was a catastrophic defeat. What now?

The exiles, who had dreamt of building a new cultural life, were not involved in it. There were hardly any invitations for them to return [to the West], for example, to the theater. In what was then called the East Sector [the Soviet zone, which would become East Berlin] it was a different story. The director Gustav von Wangenheim returned to East Berlin, and from there he sent out a circular everywhere with the call, 'Come back! We can't promise you a lot, but you can work here.' Many came back. They all worked again in theater and film. Brecht also returned, perhaps sooner than he would have liked, because he was persecuted in the United States as a communist. He didn't return directly to Germany, but first to Austria, where Helene Weigel got back her Austrian citizenship and Brecht also became an Austrian. After that he returned to East Berlin.

J Could you tell us about your story, how you came back?

AK It took a long time for me. The idea to come back was a kind of duty. In 1935 I left Berlin with my first wife. She was a German [not Jewish]. *He explains that she had learned a lot about Judaism and was allowed to convert even though it was very difficult to do this at the time. Although his father was not Orthodox, they were married at his father's request in the Oranienburger Synagogue, where the rabbi was more sympathetic to such situations.*

In 1935 we emigrated to Czechoslovakia because of the racial laws here. In 1936 we went to Vienna, where our son was born. You might ask why we went to Austria. The whole world said that Austria would remain neutral. England would protect it; Italy would protect it. Within two weeks it was sold out, and we weren't prepared for this. During those days of the Anschluß [the official German term used to describe the accession of Austria by Nazi Germany in 1938], there were terrible street battles, and there I lost my wife.

We lived in a very nice section of Vienna—Hitzing—where there also were a lot of Nazis. Next to us lived a Jewish lawyer and his German wife. He had defended communists and many others. You can't imagine what it was like! This was an election period and everyone had voted for Schuschnigg. And suddenly, as the Germans came in, everybody became a Nazi. You just can't imagine how it was! Within hours everything had changed, although they all say they didn't know anything about it. All the streets were filled, and simultaneously Jews were dragged out of their apartments, beaten, ridiculed, and arrested. It was completely chaotic. Groups of Nazis went through the streets, especially young ones, and they attacked people and they attacked this family. My wife, as a typical Berliner with a sharp tongue, tried to help them. I was not at home. When I got home I heard that a group of young Nazis had attacked my wife. She had tried to protect herself but was brutally beaten. Perhaps they really didn't want to do that, but they were so caught up in all this and didn't know what they were doing. I found her in the hospital, but she never woke again and died from her injuries. I sent my son Mark to relatives in Riga. I couldn't leave since my papers had been taken away and my house was being watched.

J Did you still have relatives in Austria?

AK No longer at this point. At this time my relatives had left Germany and gone to Latvia. My mother and brothers and sisters later were in the Riga ghetto. All of them were killed. After the war, when I was with a Russian film team in Riga, I received the official confirmation that my mother was shot in November 1941 with a group of women in the Kaiserwald. My son had been taken to a camp for children and I tried to find out where he had been, but [I learned about his fate] only to a certain point and then he disappeared. Since the lists of these camps were kept with German precision, I found where my mother's name was listed, when she arrived, when she left, when she was shot. That was absolutely terrible.

But let me come back to the problems of getting out of Austria—that was very difficult. I was essentially under house arrest; I had no documents. The times there were difficult, but it lasted only four or five months. I got to be friends with a family who lived on the other side of the Austrian-Hungarian border and succeeded one night to go over with them. I didn't stay long in Hungary. Czechoslovakia was not yet occupied, so I went back to Prague since I had good friends there. The city was full of emigrants and I ran into many film people, journalists, business people, and also writers. I got an offer to work on a film in Sweden. Since I didn't have a passport anymore, friends of mine arranged for a captain whose ship went daily between Stockholm and Memel to take me with him. With detours through Poland and Lithuania, I finally got to Memel. However, a few hours later the German army marched in. That was 23 March 1939. At the last moment I got to Kowno [Kaunas]. There I met university and professional friends, among whom was the journalist Paleckis, who later became the president of the Lithuanian Republic. Meeting these people helped me get established, and I was introduced into the right circles.

A year later, on account of the Hitler-Stalin Pact, the Soviets occupied the Baltic States—Lithuania, Latvia, and Estonia. The Lithuanian film studio had already produced the first documentary films. A group of film people came from Moscow to help with the work. The borders were closed and one couldn't leave the country for abroad. Right before the outbreak of the war, in 1941, the Soviets arrested and exiled [deported] masses of emigrants, foreigners, and so-called capitalists. That is how I wound up in a deportation column. On the way I escaped with a group of men, and instead of getting sent to Siberia, I succeeded in making it to Uzbekistan, where I worked in the theater. Then I was involved in the beginning of the Lithuanian division, which I freely joined. At that time there were such national divisions. It was made up of Lithuanian citizens, 40 percent Jews, who could manage to flee before the German invasion. Many Jews died.

J   What language did you all speak with each other?

AK   They spoke Lithuanian and Russian. Yiddish was used to communicate with each other. The leading commando of the division was, of course, Russian.

J   You learned Russian in the twenties?

AK   I had already started studying it in Berlin. Between 1920 and 1930 you could hear more Russian than German on the Kurfürstendamm. They all came here then, and I got to know these emigrants. Then I was also with a Russian film team in Lithuania at the end of the war, August 1944; on exactly 2 August I returned to Kowno. When the Germans were retreating, they planted *Brandbomben* [incendiary bombs] in individual houses in the ghetto because many people were hiding in bunkers and cellars. They were all incinerated. Those Jews not killed in the ghetto were transported to extermination camps. We filmed interviews with people who had hidden under the ruins of the ghetto and were able to save themselves. It was not always possible in the last days to save yourself, and you needed help from someone who took a risk to do such a thing. You had to pay them something, gold or whatever, to find a hiding place. There were also some Lithuanians who just helped for nothing.

I had the chance to go to Berlin with the army film team, but I stayed because I hoped to find out something about my family. In Kowno I met a girl who, as if saved by a miracle, had survived the ghetto. Life takes it course, you know, and the girl told me that she had studied in an art school. And this girl grew up and became a well-known painter, and suddenly she was my wife. That is fate. She had been in the ghetto for three and one-half years and had suffered terribly, and I thought maybe I would find out something about my family. [That was the way it was]—people found each other after one or two years.

At the beginning of 1946 I had gotten a letter from Odessa that revealed the fate of my sister. As a suspicious foreigner, she was interned for six years by the Soviets in 1941 in a work camp in Karaganda (Kazakhstan). She was supposed to be taken to Austria on a transport train. I got to Odessa a few days later, but too late. The train had already left. She didn't yet know that her husband had been killed in the Riga ghetto. I didn't see her for thirty years. She was in Austria, alone—she didn't have anyone. We corresponded. I had been alone, I had lost my wife and my son, and now I had a new family.

J   In 1944 you came to the Riga ghetto, where you met your wife. What happened then?

AK   I stayed in Kowno and worked in the rebuilt film studio. When the Lithuanian film studio moved to the Lithuanian capital of Vilnius and I wanted to stay in Kowno, I took the position of director of the philharmonic for three years.

J   Weren't you forced to demonstrate your political orientation— antifascism or pro-communism?

AK   That is a very good question. First of all, I was known as a political émigré, and second, I had worked with a Soviet army film team at the end of the war and fought against the Nazis in this Lithuanian division. But since I was not a member of the Communist Party and didn't want to become one, the career chances of my wife and me were limited. I wanted to go back to Berlin. Everybody knew that I was just waiting. My father-in-law was also from Berlin, and we both wanted to go there. But I could have maybe become minister of film, and she could have had many more commissions or become a professor of art, but we didn't want those privileges. It was difficult for us, but we managed. We weren't forced into the Party, as many people think. They simply offer you the privileges, and many people take them. So for political reasons I was not appropriate for directorial positions, especially as anti-Semitism grew before Stalin's death. So I founded a film journal at the state film distributors, although censorship allowed us no journalistic freedom. We had to be critical of Western films. We did have contact privately, in our apartment in Vilnius, with intellectuals from Moscow and Leningrad. People came to our home who were more free-thinking—progressive foreigners, journalists—although this was very dangerous. In the last years of Breznev's rule I no longer had any official positions. *Like those whose life is marked by political events in the two Germanies,* AK*'s life is marked by his experiences in the countries from which he was forced to escape and then, in the Soviet Union, by the freedom he had to practice his profession under various Soviet leaders.*

J   Weren't you asked to return to East Berlin?

AK   No, we were not allowed to travel abroad since one had to ask for permission from the union [*Gewerkschaftsbescheinigung*] and had to get a *Führungszeugnis* [certificate of good conduct] from the Communist Party. Aside from that, only one family member was permitted to travel at a time. We were allowed to travel twice to other socialist countries. When there was a political thaw in 1969, my wife was able to organize an exhibition of her work in Vienna. The Soviet Union needed PR. At her own risk, she took advantage of her two-month permission to travel abroad and went to Israel. When this became known in Vilnius, she was no longer permitted to travel.

J   How did you experience restrictions?

AK   As a film critic I had to give public lectures. Every one had to be reviewed first by the city Party organization, whether one was a member of the Party or not. They censored the lectures, and it was often the case that the texts contained political mistakes. Earlier on, citations from Stalin were expected to appear on nearly every page, Breznev's statements, and naturally Marx and Engels had to be cited as often as possible. The Party secretaries scrupulously copied from my lectures. Oh yes, you wanted to know about East Berlin.

I was correspondent for the Polish magazine *Film* in Warsaw and *Filmspiegel* in East Berlin. In these magazines I could express myself somewhat more freely. Around 1959 we learned that it was possible to be repatriated to Germany. I sent proof of my German citizenship to the appropriate [East] German authorities. I thought, This Germany is as good as any Germany. The main thing is to go to Germany. The GDR embassy recognized my citizenship. But from the Russian side I was told that I had taken these steps too late and that the GDR embassy had been informed that Mr. Klein really didn't want to emigrate, but only to make a visit. I was ultimately invited by *Filmspiegel.* That was 1970. We stayed almost a whole month, and we were treated very well. It was difficult for me to see the divided city. We visited Leipzig, Halle, and Dresden. The parallels to the Soviet system were evident everywhere.

At this time we also applied for permission to emigrate to Israel. This was the time that Jews began emigrating there. It was possible to go if one had an invitation from relatives.

J   Why was that necessary?

AK   In the Soviet Union it was only possible to get permission for immigration for the repatriation of Poles from the area of Vilnius or in individual cases to go to other countries for purposes of bringing families together. At the end of the sixties there were the first emigrations for Jews who had families there to go to Israel. However, for those who were educated it was difficult to get permission. At the end of 1970 we applied. It was almost two years before we received permission, and this would probably not have been possible if American friends hadn't intervened. We had many problems with the KGB, who wanted to know why America should be interested in people like us. It was the period of coexistence. The United States sent grain to the Soviet Union, and the people joked about 'Jews for Bread.' We could hardly talk in our apartment since we were being bugged. After we had actually applied, it got worse. We were held in suspicion for 'betraying our country.' Anyone who has never experienced this cannot imagine what it is like.

That was in November 1972, and our immigration did not take place without difficulties. The border control confiscated our silver, my wife's gold watch, and her doctoral dissertation in spite of the permission we had from the Lithuanian cultural minister. As we finally jumped onto the train to Vienna as it was leaving, we breathed a sigh of relief after all of these chicaneries that were put in our way to make our departure so difficult. While my family went on to Vienna, I stopped in Warsaw in order to finish some of my business with one of my editors because I needed the money. I traveled on, toward Vienna. I wanted to go into the city in order to see my sister; however, this was only possible through the American embassy. Our friends from the United States helped us with this, and a limousine was sent to take my daughter and me to Vienna. And I finally saw my sister Rea again after more than thirty years' separation.

J How was this reunion with your sister?

AK You can't imagine what it was like. We cried because we were so happy. We hadn't heard anything from each other the whole time. Until this moment she had had no idea about what had happened to her husband. As the widow of a successful doctor and without professional training, she had to work as a seamstress. *Although life was much more difficult for émigrés in the Soviet Union than in the United States, in both countries many worked at menial jobs or at jobs far below their qualifications.*

In the beginning she didn't get any reparations or compensation for her sufferings in a Soviet work camp and the loss of her entire family in the Riga ghetto.

AK talks at length about his stay in Israel. He emphasizes the feeling of coming home. The satisfaction in finally ending his wanderings quickly disappeared, however, when he had to deal with the difficulties of integration, the new language, the climate, and the basics of everyday existence. He founded the Israeli Film Institute in Tel Aviv and helped Russian immigrants to integrate culturally in Israel. His wife exhibited her work and taught in art schools. In 1973 she was invited to America to show her work and was there as the Yom Kippur War broke out. Their daughter integrated much more quickly: she learned Hebrew, served in the army, and studied theater at the university.

J When did you come to Berlin?

AK In 1979 I was invited to the Berlin Film Festival. I went to the Berlin Senate [as part of the city's cultural programming] and they said, 'You are a German citizen. Why are you just coming back now?' and I responded, 'It was my fault.' I got my passport back. I have to tell you how it was then. I didn't get any help from the Jewish Community. Nowadays they say how much they helped everyone. I experienced quite a bit here that was not very pleasant. *According to AK, the West Berlin Jewish Community did not serve all Jews. For various reasons, many Jews felt left out. Compare the case of Jessica Jacoby (chapter 10).*

I wanted to become an active member of the Foreign Press

Association in Berlin, and some of them were not so interested in having me there. I was too old—that is, I knew too much. I thought I could do without them, and then two days later they asked me to be honorary head. They were afraid that I might talk too much. I saw what was going on very quickly, and I really had to be aggressive. But I went where I belonged [*hingehöre*].

AK's identity is tied both to a place—Berlin—and to his profession. He wanted to return to Berlin not only because he considered it to be his home but also because it was where his professional identity was founded. In the following discussion he repeats the word belong *[gehöre, hingehöre].*

As a young man in Berlin I belonged to this organization; it had existed since 1906 and was eliminated during the war. I came here and I belong to it. There are some of the old ones left, and they were happy to see me. I was elected to be treasurer and then president. We really began to work, and we incorporate journalists from all over the world—from the East, Russians and French, English, and the Arabs too, or Iraq, Iran. We are all together. And still at the elections I represent Israel.

J   What do you see your role to be in coming back to Berlin? You said earlier that when you were in the Soviet Union you often thought about coming back to Berlin. You went to Israel. Was it difficult to leave?

AK   I wanted to come back. I tried. I was in Israel for six years and it just happened that way. I didn't go to Israel in order to stay in Israel. *Today the World Jewish Congress still encourages Soviet Jews to immigrate to Israel rather than to Germany. This attitude is reminiscent of the years directly following World War II, when it was assumed that most Jews would not want to stay in Germany and would move on to Israel or the United States.*

Naturally I was interested in Israel, and my whole family and I took part in Israeli life. But I wanted to come back to the city where I had grown up, and I thought that I could fulfill certain tasks that I had set for myself. I wanted to show the youth here what had happened. AK, *like Ruth Benario, sees his return to Germany as a chance to teach young people about the past.*

When I came back in 1979 many people didn't seem to know what had happened or acted as if they didn't know. They just didn't *want* to know. People didn't want to be reminded of the past. Then as we got to know more people, there were some who told us about their experiences. But it was difficult here financially as well. We came back with very little except our talents. I worked in the Soviet Union, but that is not recognized here for pensions. Those who came back from America had it different than we did. AK, *again like Ruth Benario, emphasizes this point about the difference between emigration experiences in the East and the West.*

They had money and could live, and one has to say that in the case of the Americans one didn't ask so much what they had done there. All the doors were open—not right away, but in the last few years. But if one came from the East and from Israel, it was difficult. But you see, I made my way here. I am now making my fourth film.

J   Then how do you feel about the Federal Republic since you have come back?

AK   As a journalist, I judge events objectively, based on facts, whether I like them or not. I try to forget that those who belong to the German people killed my family. You can approach this situation in different ways. You can't come back—back home, so to speak—and think, That one there killed my son or That one there may have killed my wife. If you're going to do that, then you shouldn't come back. I didn't come back to take revenge or to have a worry-free life. I was in the Soviet Union and I worked there to make what happened here known; but there I always had to think about what I could say and what I couldn't say. They would tell me that I had gone a little too far, and that is the single thing that bothered me and my wife. Because of this [censorship], we wanted to come back, and because I wanted to return to where I had grown up, where I could also feel freer.

One could interpret AK's commitment to return to Berlin, which he repeatedly calls his home, as evidence that he favored his German Jewish identity over a more all-encompassing, universal Jewish affiliation, which Israel would undoubtedly represent. That he still represents Israel in his organization, however, reflects his dual allegiance.

I also came back because I felt that I had certain duties here. I wanted to present in publications and film what happened during the Nazi period. Many people really don't seem to know that much about it, and many act as if they didn't know. AK *returns again and again to the fact that people do not know what happened. To inform the Germans is clearly his goal.*

J   What tied you to Germany in the years that you were gone? Did you continue to speak German?

AK   I tried when it was possible to speak and to read German. I was born in Germany, grew up here, and felt connected to German literature, German songs, and German images [*Bilder*]. For this reason, the question of a lost home [*Heimat*] really disappears, because one can't lose what one really never had, or because places in which one felt oneself foreign can never be described in this way. Certainly this word brings to mind associations of my youth.

J   Since the German language is so important for you, do you think that you have a connection to the GDR Germans through language?

AK   No, it has nothing to do with that. I know many German journalists from over there. We all speak the same language, but either we are colleagues [*Kameraden*] or not. We meet at festivals and conferences and talk about our work, but there were taboos regarding talking about political systems, just as in the Soviet Union. That's what I didn't like about this regime. There were so many people in the GDR tied to the party that one couldn't say or write what one wanted. At that time I felt the same in East Berlin as I did in Moscow.

In AK's *wife's transcript, a passage from which follows, she speaks for him about the notion of home and the Holocaust in ways that he didn't express himself.*

However, with every trip or move the feeling diminishes of having lost something that is tied geographically to a particular place. It gets dimmer and dimmer. There remain only abstract contours of images of people and landscapes. The question that comes up over and over again—'How can you live in Germany after all that has happened here?'—answers itself. I had to survive the trauma of the Holocaust in Lithuania in order even to live on. I didn't suppress it, much less forget it. However, I have learned to differentiate between the indifferent and those who just went along with it and those who actually did it [*Tätern*]. So the feeling that I have to live among murderers rarely leaves me, even when I am not sure about the people. My intuition helps me here to find liberal and tolerant people and to protect myself from imaginary enemies.

J   Do you associate with Jewish people here in Berlin?

AK Of course, I am a member of the Jewish Community and go to the High Holiday services in the synagogue in order to preserve the Jewish cultural tradition. But I am not happy with the cultural politics of the Community. Once I went to a Passover seder in the Community. There was no feeling of community, but rather a very cool atmosphere. I said to myself, I am not going back.

J   When you say 'I am a Jew,' is that the same as saying 'I am a German'?

AK No, it is not the same thing. It is not easy for me to say whether I am a Jewish German or a German Jew. AK *refers here to the complicated historical discussion about German Jewish identity: should those who are Jewish living in Germany be called Jews in Germany, German Jews, or even, as it was during the war, German citizens with Jewish beliefs?*

I can very easily put two worlds together. I grew up with the good and the bad of both cultures, and since then I have been in the German and international cultures. But just as I reject any lumping together of Jews, I reject any generalizations of other ethnic groups as well. It leaves me cold to hear people in Germany talking about 'the Russians' and other schematic generalizations, such as 'the Poles,' 'the Turks,' and so on. Likewise, I cannot accept this lumping of all Germans together. I try hard to discover what holds people together, and not what separates them. This is the only way a pluralistic society can develop.

J   So does that mean you don't feel closer to Jews?

AK Of course, it's natural that Jewish problems and Jewish suffering are closer to me. However, intellectually I want to remain open for cultural multiplicity, as long as it is liberal and tolerant. I have always been interested in Jewish topics. This subject is especially interesting because I am familiar with the mentalities of different Jews. Among the German Jews there were those who rejected the Eastern European Jews. They thought that they encouraged the anti-Semitism in Germany. In contrast to these Eastern European Jews, they wanted to assimilate. That those who came from the

East named their children Schlomo or Chaim shocked those German Jews who had themselves baptized or named their sons Siegfried. I am also a German Jew, but I never thought that baptism or complete assimilation was a means against anti-Semitism. One has to remember how the German Jews stood by as the Polish Jews were driven out of Germany back to Poland and to certain death in 1938 and 1939. In those years many German Jews thought that nothing would happen to them—they had been good Germans.

J   Did you ever think that?

AK   I experienced with my first wife the Jewish boycott, the Reichstag fire, and the book burning. We never could believe how not only the simple people on the street but also the German intellectuals accepted the persecution of the Jews. We first went to Cologne and then to Düsseldorf, where I could write my articles since no one there knew me. During a trip to the Black Forest in July 1934 we heard Hitler's voice on the radio. He was screaming, 'We will eliminate them all.' Then we heard how the SA and their leader Röhm was killed, and then General Schleicher was shot. Then we realized how dangerous it was to be a Jew or an opponent of Hitler in Germany. Many of our friends suddenly disappeared, and many escaped with only a suitcase to Paris.

My wife and I said our good-byes to our relatives in Berlin. I remember still how my wife said, 'Before we go we should say good-bye to my mother's grave.' Even before we got to Vienna she had the feeling all of this Nazi activity would lead to catastrophe, to a war, and then to complete disaster. And if we survived we would come back here. She never experienced the end, nor did my son. Neither returned alive. Only I did, all alone.

J   Tell us more about your exile in the Soviet Union.

AK   As I said, we always wanted to come back, but it took a long time. In Lithuania there were many refugees, different waves of emigrants from different countries. There were discussions about where one should go. Some went to Shanghai, but I stayed because my son was with my mother and I was waiting for him to be brought to Kowno. You know I met my present wife in Kowno—I found her in a camp—and we also always said we would return to Berlin.

J   Since there was so much anti-Semitism in the Soviet Union, the Stalin era was particularly bad—the Slansky Trial in Czechoslovakia and the Doctors' Plot in the Soviet Union. How was it among the Jews in the Soviet Union? Was there a sense of community?

AK   Perhaps one could trust Jews more, but that was not always the case. There were many unwritten rules and regulations that concerned the Jews. There was never an official quota for accepting Jews into the universities, or granting of scholarships, and so on. It was mostly those Jews who had relatives abroad whose mail was checked and had their telephones tapped. At the KGB there was a department for Jews called Jewish Questions.

J   How was it, then, living in Israel among Jews? Did this change your idea of what being a Jew was?

AK   We went to Israel with open hearts. So we sold everything in order to pay the fees. We were happy to be free and have not forgotten this until today and haven't regretted it. But what we didn't like was the sloppy bureaucracy and the lack of punctuality in Israel. *It is interesting that* AK *criticizes Israeli traits whose opposites are stereotypically identified with Germans.*

The inefficiency was the same as in the Soviet Union. The Jews there can be unfriendly and impolite but exhibit in a time of crisis a wonderful solidarity, with sympathy and understanding. I saw this during the Yom Kippur War. But many Israelis treat other Jews, Oriental [Sephardic] Jews, like second-class citizens. Many Israelis are racists and discriminate against the so-called Blacks. The anti-Semitic excesses of the Soviet Union make one sensitive to all kinds of discrimination. To be among Jews in a country where there was not anti-Semitism was a good feeling. However, it was strange that Jews fought so aggressively among themselves. Regarding the Palestinians, I was shocked to find that the hardest work and construction was performed by them and that there were such crass social divisions, aside from the religious and ethnic ones. I know that it is difficult to find a way for Jews and Arabs to live peacefully, but the problem has been swept under the rug too long.

J   Let us come back to Germany. You live in Germany but work here for the foreign press.

AK   But as I told you I am also a member of the German journalists'
organization, which is a piece of home [*Heimat*] for me. I joined it
as soon as I came back.

J   You used the word *Heimat*—do you mean Berlin?

AK   Yes, Berlin is home for me, and I started very young being a
journalist. But here I was young and here I began my life. I
learned a great deal here, good and bad. When I had to leave, that
was very hard for me. You know, every remnant of that life,
whether a book, a shirt, or a memory, a person I once knew—that
all disintegrated. Emigration, exile. Some people left and could
take money or possessions with them. We didn't. I came back with
nothing. You got a room, or lived somewhere and then you had to
leave again. I mean, I never thought about staying in the Soviet
Union. These were just the circumstances, and it was a great trial
to get out of there. But you see, I have strong survival instincts
[*lebensfähig*]. I have had many difficult times, but I get back on
my feet again every time. How long that will continue, I don't
know. I belong to that generation, to those families, whom you
had to kill to keep down. We don't die so easily.

♣

We received AK*'s response dated 23 May 1992:*

I was deeply shocked the first time—after thirty years—that I
experienced Berlin as a divided city and as the capital of the GDR.
During the war I had seen many cities that had been reduced to
rubble, like Orjol, Smolensk, and Minsk. Here, however, not only
was a metropolis cut right through the middle with a dividing
wall but also two worlds collided irreconcilably. For hours I sat at
the window of a cafe and stared at the cordoned and guarded
Brandenburg Gate.

The life of a journalist in West Berlin was all the more fascinating because of the special status of the city, and so I accepted the
complications of traveling and the entire absurdity of the divided
city. However, I avoided traveling into the Eastern part of the city
as much as possible. I did this not only because of the unpleasant
formalities of getting permission, a transit visa, compulsory exchange of money, but rather because of the hostile atmosphere
that one was confronted with.

Thus the fall of the Wall was also for me a reason for euphoria. Also now, after more than a year, I am still amazed when I can drive by the Brandenburg Gate to Unter den Linden [the main street of the former East Berlin, which runs into the Brandenburg Gate]. It is all like a miracle.

The sudden transition from a centralized, so-called communist system to a market economy has brought disappointments, and aside from those of the market, it has also created a lack of self-confidence. This has meant, especially for artists, writers, and other intellectuals, who have dreamed of creative freedom, that they have had to reorient themselves to a capitalistic system. Occupation rather than unification, being told what to do rather than working together, and above all, the expectation to become the 'poorhouse' of Germany—these are their fears, which to some extent I also share.

For me as a Jew, marked with that terrible phrase 'damaged by the Holocaust,' having fled from the Soviet regime, the German reunification elicits an ambivalent resonance. On the one hand, I am happy to live in a democratically 'normal' country, one that is not divided into two states. I especially wish for the East Germans that they will learn to live in a free country and to use this freedom. I am happy about the breakdown of all the socialist democracies in Europe, which were neither socialistic nor democratic, but rather totalitarian and controlled by Soviet structures. On the other hand, I share the fear of those who see Germany developing into the most powerful nation-state in Europe. Also, the different historical developments of these two German states have become quite obvious. The GDR regime took too long to face its responsibility for the Nazi period. One searches in East German history books to no avail for signs of guilt as executors and collaborators. They made it easy on themselves, by establishing that all the 'evil Nazis' lived in the West, whereas there were only 'good comrades' in the East, where, naturally, all the resistance fighters and anti-Nazis lived.

Actually I should have satisfaction about the fact that I saw the collapse of the rigid GDR regime earlier than was expected. However, that such a terrible economic crisis would be the result was hardly expected. Having a Soviet army three hundred thousand strong in a unified country is a difficult extenuating circumstance.

That the rebirth of right-wing radical elements, with their anti-Semitic and nationalistic excesses, makes me worry is obvious. The hostility toward foreigners, with attacks on Polish tourists and black asylum seekers, destruction of Jewish cemeteries, Nazi and ss meetings—all of these outbursts are often minimized by the press or seen by citizens with indifference as the price of democracy.

From the United States to East and West Berlin

'I was deported by the Americans. I am a GDR Jew.'

Born 1912   East Galicia (father Austrian Jew,
             mother German Jew)
1912–1914 Antwerp, Belgium
1914–1937 Frankfurt, Germany
1937–1941 Poland, Czechoslovakia, France
1941–1949 New York City
1949–   East Berlin

When Hilde Eisler was born, East Galicia was part of Austria (it later was part of Poland and currently belongs to Ukraine). When she was six months old, her family moved to Antwerp, Belgium. When World War I broke out two years later, her father was drafted into the Austrian army, and her mother, labeled an enemy foreigner by Belgium, moved to Frankfurt, Germany, where her parents lived. Although HE grew up in a fairly integrated, wealthy family—her father was a banker in Poland, and her Belgian relatives were in the diamond business—because she was an Ostjüdin by birth, she was never fully accepted in Germany by the Westjuden. HE spent a year in prison for underground activities against the Nazis and then was exiled in 1937: she was deported to Poland, then fled to Czechoslovakia and France before landing in New York in 1941. She was deported from the United States during the anticommunist hysteria of the McCarthy purges in 1949 and resettled in East Berlin.

A friend of ours who knew HE from her activities as editor of the monthly cultural journal Das Magazin persuaded her to grant us an interview. We returned several times to film interviews with her. Jeff did a final interview with her in 1991. We always met in her roomy, third-floor apartment on Karl-Marx-Allee. The day of our first interview was extremely hot and muggy. HE, in a fashionable dress and eyeglasses, served us chilled grapefruit juice, coffee, and pastries. Jeff

*briefly explained again why we were there, and she responded in
English, 'You don't know the Eisler story?' and began to tell us, still in
English, about her husband in America. At our request, she began
again in German and conducted the rest of the interview in German.
When she reviewed my translation, she suggested several corrections,
all of which I made.*

J   Can you start with the conditions under which you and Gerhart
Eisler, your husband, left the United States?

HE   My husband was in prison in the United States. [They wanted to]
prevent him from assembling people outside the prison to let
them know who he was, an antifascist, a German who only
wanted the right to return to his home after the war. His sarcastic,
accusatory speeches, which he made everywhere, did not at all
please the American authorities. Therefore they again put him in
prison, along with a few of the leading Communist Party members—Erwin Potasch, for example, and various labor union organizers who had lived their whole life in America but because of
their political orientation could not get American citizenship. For
eight days [Gerhart] went on a hunger strike, which attracted a
great deal of attention because using the hunger strike as a weapon
was still unusual at the time. It was a very unusual event, and there
was a huge demonstration in Times Square.

J   Where was this hunger strike?

HE   In the prison on Ellis Island. In New York. Gerhart Eisler and the
American communists had agreed to return all the food they were
given in their cells. This did not prevent the hostile press from
maintaining that they had hidden their food. [But] they didn't
have a single crumb; rather, they scraped by for eight days. The
authorities released the hunger strikers on a Saturday afternoon,
something quite out of the ordinary. Just then I was with friends
at the home of my brother-in-law, Hanns Eisler. We turned the
radio on and, coincidentally, heard that the hunger strikers would
be immediately released. First they were examined by a doctor,
and then they had to learn to eat again, little by little.

    In any case, a short time after the hunger strike he was arrested
again. They didn't want to let him out because they wanted him as
witness against, for example, Harry Bridges on the West Coast, as

well as against other leading communists. He repeatedly refused [to cooperate]. One day he said to me, 'They will never let me out. If I am arrested again, I'll have no more chances. I have to leave.'

He decided to visit some friends on a ship going to Europe, to wish them farewell. That was customary. It was permitted again after the war. One evening he told me, 'Listen, tomorrow I will try to get on a ship, a Polish ship, that is returning to Europe with friends of ours [aboard], other German emigrants.' He bought a folding toothbrush—that was his entire luggage. He took a bunch of flowers, put on his hat, [and left].

I have to add to this: We were watched by the FBI day and night. Six men—two sat above our apartment, two sat in front of our apartment, and two sat in the car with the motor running so that they could always be with us. Wherever we went, they were there. If we were eating, they always sat at the next table. We thought that we would show them a beautiful Russian film. They came with us into the cinema. I wrote about that in [the journal] *New Masses*. This article was very popular at that time. Everyone found it funny, because I portrayed [the spying] with humor.

We direct her back to the story of her husband's exit.

So, in the early morning he left the house. I thought that he'd be returning home for lunch, that it wouldn't work out because he was so [vigilantly] observed. He took—I don't know how many different undergrounds, or how often he switched trains, or how many taxis he took. In short, he arrived at the docks, went on board, lay down on a deck chair, pulled his hat over his face, held the flowers in front of him, and acted as if he wanted to rest on his way to Europe. Then the ship left. Shortly thereafter, he saw a police boat come up to the ship. He thought, Damned, now they've noticed that I've left and they're coming to get me. But it wasn't even meant for him; rather, a pair of drunk Americans on the ship hadn't heard that they were supposed to get off before the ship left. The [police] boat picked them up.

Then he had to make his acquaintance with the Polish captain. He had money with him to pay for a ticket. He asked the captain not to betray him. He would go as a stowaway. [The captain] accepted this. But someone on the ship sent a message back to New York [about Eisler being on board]. In Washington this caused an incredible storm, a howl of fury and rage that Eisler had escaped.

When the ship arrived in Southampton, an American airplane was already waiting to take him back. The Polish captain had given him asylum on the ship, but in the harbor of Southampton he no longer had that authority, for [the harbor] was not Polish national territory. Under the direction of the Americans, the English authorities—four men—dragged him from the ship. He purposely had [let] them drag him. He did not go freely. An American correspondent, I think from the *New York Post*, who witnessed this telegraphed it back to the United States. In response the Hearst Press sent a cable: Eisler should sell his story to them; he could write a blank check for it.

In short, he was at first imprisoned in London, then went before the court. The English judge—he was defended by Pritt, a leading defense attorney [in England]—decided that Eisler had broken [no laws] that would justify his extradition. There were large demonstrations for Eisler in London. 'Let Eisler free.' [The English] were outraged by the Americans, who had arrogated to themselves [the right] to arrest a man on their [English] territory and then to return him quasi-secretly to the United States.

Then [Gerhart] took a plane to Czechoslovakia.

J This was '46?

HE The spectacle lasted three years. It was '49. On the Czech-German border, then part of the Russian Occupation Zone, he was picked up by friends. [During this episode] I was arrested and spent six weeks in Ellis Island [prison].

HE *then returns to 1941 and tells us that she had already spent three months on Ellis Island when she and Gerhart arrived in the United States as refugees. They had an invitation from the Mexican President Cárdenas, but an American law forbade Germans to travel through U.S. ports on their way to Latin America; this law was applied universally to all Germans, with few exceptions.*

J Can you tell us more about your time in the United States after Gerhart left?

HE There was a large campaign for me, a solidarity campaign. After Gerhart was arrested, the Civil Rights Committee asked me to go on a tour throughout the United States. I was in Boston. I was everywhere—from New York to Hollywood and San Francisco. I called upon the people to show solidarity and to give money to help [for his defense] in the trial. It was incredibly expensive. You have to be a millionaire to [defend yourself in] the American courts. I organized many meetings and went to many assemblies throughout the United States, from coast to coast. Many large gatherings, some in private apartments, where [we] collected money. For example, in Hollywood a well-known screen writer, Salka Viertel, who had also written scripts for Greta Garbo, a very courageous woman, invited me to her house, along with other artists, to whom I then told the whole story once more.

J   What was the purpose of this trip?

HE   The purpose was to explain to people about Gerhart Eisler. He was blasphemed as a spy, an atomic spy. The Hearst press couldn't make up enough fairy tales about him. I said he was a German antifascist who wanted to go back home.

I must [also] say that I was deported by the Americans. I was not allowed to pay for my trip myself. They took me from Ellis Island, in a night-and-fog action. I was supposed to leave without the public knowing. But the entire press was there. Indeed, they found out about it, about when I was leaving. I made a statement [to the press] in which I expressed my gratitude for the hospitality of the United States and the solidarity of the American people, which we had experienced, but [I said] that I also had a bitter feeling toward the American regime, which had treated my husband so shabbily.

J   Let me get the sequence correct. When did you make this trip through the States?

HE   Nineteen forty-seven. My husband and I exchanged letters during this trip. Some have been published. I would tell him in prison about the gatherings, how well they went and how well attended. In Boston the media organized a big campaign against my coming, a virulent campaign, so that my meetings were overflowing. People were simply curious.

J   Were most of these people academics, or from other classes?

HE   Many different and also ordinary people. For example, people like Thomas Mann, who also issued a statement in support of Gerhart and characterized the atmosphere in the United States as anti-working-class and reactionary. He denounced the [persecution]. Many well-known people protested, especially when my brother-in-law [Hanns Eisler, who wrote much of the music for Bertolt Brecht] was called before the House Committee on Un-American Activities, [where] he was named 'the Karl Marx of Music.' Yes, the stupidity knew no limits.

J   You were deported directly to the GDR?

HE   Via London, Copenhagen, and Warsaw. We had to avoid places where the Americans were—West Germany—for example, because perhaps [they] would try something once more.

J   But this entire trip was organized by Americans?

HE   I had a Polish passport. I was born in Poland but grew up in Frankfurt, in Germany. I had nominally a Polish passport, and [after the war] the Poles renewed my [old one].

J   Did you have a Polish passport when you first came to the United States?

HE   I had absolutely no passport. I came on the visa of my husband, as his quasi-engaged woman. I didn't receive a Mexican visa from the people [in France] who had organized [my trip into exile]. To this day I don't know why. [Gerhart] therefore asked that I be put on his visa. I had, after all, worked in the German resistance. I was in prison there. I worked illegally, passing out illegal literature against the Nazis. I was arrested, spent a year in prison, was [first] deported to Poland, a foreign country for me, then went to Czechoslovakia, and [finally] to France, where I was supposed to work for the radio station 29.8, an antifascist station. I first met Gerhart Eisler in Paris working for the station 29.8. He introduced me as his engaged woman in order to put me on his visa.

J   Were you actually engaged to him then?

HE   No. I was not. We were friends. We married in America, in Connecticut. Because I was in such danger—first as a resistance fighter and communist, second as a Jew, which was enough to take me to Auschwitz—in order to escape this fate my husband requested that the Americans, above all the Mexicans, put me on his visa. They also did that.

There was an extremely unusual incident that happened before we took the French ship [to America]. My husband had just come from Les Milles [a French concentration camp that held many

Germans who had fought on the side of the Republicans in the Spanish Civil War], where Leon Feuchtwanger and others also were, and he was allowed to travel to Marseille to get a visa. It was very difficult to get a visa to leave France, for you didn't have most of the necessary papers. In Marseille [where he and Hilde had agreed to meet], on one Sunday morning we noticed a famous American film, *You Can't Take It With You*, was running. We definitely wanted to see the matinee performance. I said to him, 'You know, you should take off your KZ jacket.' At my place he had another suit—he always changed his clothes at my place—and he put on another jacket and other shoes. When we came back to the hotel later, I noticed already at the door that something wasn't right. He had forgotten that all of his papers and money were hidden in the jacket he had worn before he left—at that time Marseille had clothing thieves—and everything was stolen. We had nothing. The American visa, the Mexican visa, the ticket for the ship: gone. In eight days the ship was leaving. Can you picture this? We went to the police, and they reviled us from top to bottom as 'sales boches.' This misfortune was our fault, [so] they kicked us out. Then we sent a telegram to America, and Gerhart went back to all the embassies. In the end we were successful in getting the papers together, and the tickets, and in getting on this ship. It was like a KZ ship—surely you've heard about such ships.

J   What was the ship called?

HE   The ship was called *Winnipeg. She took our question too literally— we had meant to ask about KZ ships. Such ships were really made for the transport of freight, not people. And since the ship owners transported refugees only for the profit involved, the passengers, as HE wrote me in a note later, 'were treated quite shabbily.'*

J   What kind of relations did you have to enable you to pull this off?

HE   You could always get money sent by cable from America. We got money from the refugee committees and with the money bought a new ticket in the office of American Express in Marseille. A woman who was sympathetic to refugees worked at the police station in Marseille, and she gave us the visas once again. The Americans also gave us a new transit visa.

J   What year was that?

HE   Nineteen forty-one.

J   Did you know others on this ship?

HE   Yes. Albert Norden [later a member of the Central Committee in the GDR] was there, Bruno Frei, and various others whom you will not know. Anna Seghers [a leading writer who resettled in the GDR and headed the writer's union] with her family—they came from somewhere in Africa.

There was another incident. HE *tells us that the* Winnipeg *was a French liner and that on the order of the British it was captured and forced to land in Trinidad, a British colony, instead of Martinique, a French one. They were again imprisoned in a 'concentration camp,' where a search was conducted to discover whether any Nazis were among them.*

It went like that. I'm telling you telegram style.

She goes on to explain that their goal was to go to Mexico but that the Americans prevented them from going.

J   Were you particularly disappointed that you had to remain in the United States?

HE   I wasn't at all disappointed. I felt quite content in the United States. I was happy to be in the United States. I also have many relatives in the United States. My mother's brother, who in any case died, many cousins—all Jews.

J   Did you remain in New York?

HE   Yes, in Queens, metro station Bliss Street. We lived in a development house, very cheaply. I found various jobs. First in a kindergarten in order to perfect my English. You learn well with children. Then I did various other things. I worked in a factory making optical lenses and frames, in an office for the New York Clothing Workers' Union, where I did payroll, at the Unemployment Fund Agency, for Yugoslavian War Relief. In '46 all hell broke loose and I couldn't work any more.

J   At the end of the war what did you already know about [what had transpired in] Germany?

HE   Above all, I heard about the concentration camps. My parents and my sister were killed there, and many of my relatives. I have not been able to find anyone. It was very difficult [then] for me to go back.

J At that time, did you already think you would return?

HE Yes. It was already clear to me that I'd return. I didn't have a permanent visa.

J Did you ever think that it would perhaps be nice to remain, or did you want to go back?

HE The Americans made me an offer to stay if I would betray him, [reveal] how my husband had left. But I didn't do that. Under no circumstances did I want to give the American government the satisfaction they would get if the widow of Gerhart Eisler stayed behind.

Although HE *did no political organizing in the United States, Gerhart founded a newspaper, the* German American, *which agitated against the Nazis and was used to reeducate German* POWs, *and he also wrote for the* Daily Worker. *This antifascist and pro-labor work was what led to Gerhart's being suspect to the American political authorities.* HE*'s position on the war, and that of her husband, was to encourage the United States to start a second front in support of the Soviets. She asserts that finally it was the Soviet Union that defeated Hitler.*

J In America were you primarily together with other Germans?

HE We had many American friends. I am still in contact with some [of these] friends in America. I would be extremely pleased to travel there again, but I was deported. I am not allowed [to return without the threat of arrest].

J Not even today?

HE I haven't tried to. I won't let myself say [a final] no. But I don't trust them, especially the Reagan administration, this reactionary regime you have there now. But I'd really love to come and visit my friends, to see New York again.

J Did you receive support from other Jews or from the Jewish committees in New York?

HE Actually not much from the Jewish committees, but more from the rescue committees [who worked with political emigrants].

J Could you explain your relationship to Jews in Germany before the war?

HE My father was very areligious. Naturally he was a Jew, but totally nonreligious. My mother held to the Jewish traditions, in which I also grew up. I went to a Jewish lycée in Frankfurt and also took part in a Jewish youth organization. *Her parents had left East Galicia, then part of Austria, for Belgium in 1912 and then settled in Frankfurt in 1914.*

My mother was a kindergarten teacher, [quite unusual because most women of her class did not work back then]. In 1938 my parents were deported to Poland along with all [other] Jews who originally came from the East. They were put out of their apartment. There were many such actions—perhaps you know about them—against *Ostjuden.* I was already in Paris.

J   Did you discover their deportation through a letter?

HE Yes. I was able to correspond with my parents up to the beginning of the war. They were then in Lemberg. My sister should have gone to the United States. We even had an affidavit for her, but the Americans boycotted it. 'The affidavit is not strong enough' [they wrote]. That cost her her life. The Americans committed many crimes.

J   Did you appeal to the Jewish committee in New York?

HE No. [I had appealed to] a rescue committee for political emigrants. The Civil Rights Congress had been very concerned [about these emigrants]. They also sent me on this trip, this tour [to raise money for the trial of Gerhart Eisler and] to beg for solidarity with him.

J   You said you went to a Jewish lycée and that you were also a member of different organizations. Which organizations?

HE For example, the Jewish Pathfinder [similar to Girl Scouts], the Kadima.

J   Kadima—we have that in America too, but it is progressive, left-oriented.

HE Yes. It was also a bit Zionist and a bit left—quite mixed. In addition, [I belonged to] an organization called Kameraden. They were, how should I say, German nationalist Jews. They also existed. I didn't feel so good [about taking part] in this group. I didn't like them. They were too German somehow. In America it's not that way, but in Germany it was the case that the German Jews and the Polish Jews [lived in] two different worlds— *Ostjuden* and *Westjuden.*

J   When you lived in New York, didn't you notice this divide at all?

HE No, not at all. It played absolutely no role there.

J Did you experience being a Jew in New York differently from the way you experienced being a Jew in Germany or a Jewish emigrant in Paris?

HE No. I couldn't maintain that I experienced it differently. It didn't play a role. We didn't make the distinction whether one was a Jew or not a Jew. This pointed Jewishness, the conscious return again [to the Jewish], was after the Holocaust. It is not true that many did not recognize their Jewishness back then. I have always said I am a Jew. I have never concealed it. But this conscious Jewishness [*jüdischsein*]—the Holocaust created that, enlarged it.

J When you said before that your Kameraden group was too German, what did you mean?

HE Too German nationalist. There was also an organization—what was it called?—Germans of Jewish Belief. They were even more German. They emphasized their Germanness. For these people, after what the Nazis did and how they were treated, the world broke in two. They were, after all, Germans. By law we were never Germans at home. We never became Germans. It was very difficult for *Ostjuden* to become citizens.

J Although you identified with Austria?

HE No. Not that either. Actually German in the sense of culture, speech, and environs—I have never denied where I came from and what I am. Already in the school, the lycée, I sensed [among the students] children whose parents came from the East, even though there were only a few of us. The difference was already considerable. I became conscious of this only later. As a child you aren't so observant.

J Were your parents economically and culturally integrated in German circles?

HE Yes, especially my mother, who came to Germany as a small child with her parents in the last century and went to German schools. My mother was as German as you can be. But she also never denied that she was Jewish. She respected the Jewish traditions, much to the pleasure of her father. My grandfather was a very well-known man in Frankfurt.

J Were you and your mother kosher at home?

HE   Yes. My mother upheld the traditions. My father didn't make a big deal of them, but he liked Jewish food, especially on Jewish holidays.

We asked HE *to go into more detail about her decision to return to Germany.*

HE   We left Queens because the people there pursued us. When my husband became [the object of] this large media campaign, the people among whom we lived, despite otherwise good relations, [suddenly turned against us]. My husband had even received an award [for civil-defense service in the community]. Then suddenly that was all transformed. Many Irish Catholics [lived in our neighborhood], and they heckled us: 'You are not Catholics. You should be hung.' It was a fascistic situation. We had to leave. Then a schoolmate of Franklin Roosevelt, a very bourgeois man, took us in, into his apartment, because, well, our lives were in danger. People threw stones through our window, and once one just missed my head. There was a huge smear campaign. It was unimaginable. I don't know if you can imagine what went on there.

J   Hadn't this campaign begun already during the war?

HE   No. Then it was all butter and wonderful. There was absolutely nothing in Roosevelt's period. It all began with Truman, with the Cold War.

J   Can you pinpoint the exact point when it began?

HE   It went as follows: We had tickets on a Soviet ship to Europe that would bring us to Germany through the Soviet Union. It was 1946. Before that we could not leave. It took this long to get permission to leave.

J   You tried immediately after the war?

HE   Yes, a hundred times. Even during the war my husband tried to go to Mexico. Each time [his petition] was rejected. Then after the war we all tried to go back home. It took a year. Then [the authorities] gave us permission. All of our things were already on the ship [when] the campaign against my husband began. We had to take everything off again. Our apartment was already a third empty.

J   You say that you wanted to return home.

HE   Return to Germany.

J   Even though you knew what had happened in the KZs, you still wanted to return?

HE   I had no choice. I had no choice because, first, I was married and my husband definitely wanted to return—he was a politician. Second, I would have found no understanding from my American friends, if I would have, so to speak, deserted. There would have been a huge political fiasco if I had remained. The Americans would have cannibalized us. They would have made such a story out of this.

HE's *two reasons reveal much about the constraints and choices of women of her generation: they most often followed their men/husbands, and they, like their men, were more motivated and constrained by ideology than by material considerations.*

And I didn't want to answer [to this media campaign]. But it was very difficult for me, given what had happened in Germany.

J   When did you first learn about Stalinism and what had happened in the Soviet Union?

HE   The trials and all that—naturally, we knew absolutely nothing about what was behind them. We had received no information. For us it was important that Hitler had been defeated, regardless of how. That was the [prime motivation] of our life, our fight against Hitler.

J   You had no information? For example, you didn't know Arthur Koestler's [work]?

HE   No. Arthur Koestler? No, not personally, only by name. We spoke with so many other emigrants, and always asked what they knew. I cannot say to you now on exactly which day [I found out]. We learned soon. When the first reports came—at first you really didn't know. What Hitler ordered, we knew. But about Stalin, we sometimes asked ourselves about the trials against Jewish doctors and the rest. But the whole truth—that came much later, at the Twentieth Party Congress [in February 1956], when Khrushchev revealed [Stalin's crimes].

J   Okay, your husband was already here [in the GDR] when you arrived?

HE   Only a few months. He was greeted as a hero, with great fanfare, as someone who had defeated the Americans, single-handedly, so to speak. People had been betting: Will he be sent back to America from England or not?

J   What kind of work did he do here?

HE   He was head of the ministry of information. Later he served as chair of the State Committee for Radio and Television, up to his death.

J   And you?

HE   I worked as a journalist. I was able to pursue my dream profession—that was my consolation. I was editor in chief for *Das Magazin*, a much cherished magazine here. I worked there for twenty-five years.

J   When was that?

HE   That was 1954. I [had] also worked for the *Wochenpost* [a newspaper], for a year.

J   When you came back, were you shocked to see Germany as it was?

HE   Well, I knew how it would look. I wasn't shocked, not at all. But I feared the Germans, [I feared] going on the street. It took a long time before I got used to living with these people. But there were many who I already knew: antifascists like Anna Seghers, Arnold Zweig. And my work was a joy to me. The career opportunities I had here I would never have had in America. That this was an antifascist country was, naturally, decisive. Here [fascism] was truly totally eradicated, every root and branch. In any case, the Nazis all ran away. And those that one caught were given a death sentence. The war criminals and those [who had served in positions of] authority were [put] in prisons or concentration camps for a long time, in contrast to the Federal Republic.

    These two claims are much disputed. Although it is true that most of the leading Nazis went to the West, not all did. Furthermore, the stringent sentences for Nazi war crimes in the immediate postwar years in the GDR *were often meted out without proper respect for due process, and sometimes the term* Nazi crimes *seemed to be used as an excuse for dealing harshly with political opponents.*

J   Did you have any other feelings toward the Germans besides fear?

HE   Actually, disrespect—loathing and disrespect for what they tolerated, if they weren't themselves all criminals, but [primarily] for what they tolerated, and [that they] didn't help. I am not speaking of those who helped, but I believe that was, among the sixty million or so people in Germany back then, a minuscule number. My greatest disappointment was, naturally, that there was never a revolution against the Nazis. People did not revolt against the Nazis, but rather fought [with them] until five minutes before midnight. There was no general revolt or resistance movement against the Nazis as there was in other countries, though there was, of course, [individual] resistance and some very brave people. The concentration camps were, after all, full.

J   After your return, did you associate mostly with other emigrants?

HE   You know, that just grew out of the situation. Occupationally, mostly young people. Naturally, also, we were friends with Arnold Zweig, Anna Seghers, Johannes R. Becher, with Brecht and, above all, Helene Weigel, and other less well known people.

J   How do you differentiate yourself from the Germans today? Or have you been integrated, so that you feel German today?

HE   I feel I am a [female] citizen of the German Democratic Republic.

J   With regard to your Jewishness, do you have close contact with the Jewish Community here?

HE   Yes, close contact.

J   Are you a member?

HE   I went to the Community as early as 1949 and registered with them. I also asked them back then to help me find out about my relatives. Then I went to Poland and through contacts discovered that a brother of my father had gone to Israel after he fled to the Soviet Union. When I finally got his address, I received a letter: 'He died four weeks ago.'

J   What had he done in those years in between?

HE   He and his family went to the Soviet Union with the Red Army, before the Germans marched in. He was evacuated to Samarkand or somewhere, where they [German exiles from Nazi Germany] were all sent, and suffered the same fate as the Russians—hunger and all the rest. After the war [these German refugees] gathered in the former German territory, in Schlesien, Breslau [now part of Poland], and from there they went to Israel.

J   Do you still have contact with his family?

HE   Nobody is living. They are all dead, all. From my mother's side, from my father's side, no one is still living. They all lost their lives.

J   You said you joined the [Jewish] Community in '49. Many Jews did not join the Community. Do you think it's important to be a member of the Community, to give witness to the fact that one is Jewish?

HE　My God! You know, for me it was only a formality to postulate that one was Jewish. *She sharply reprimands us for assuming any kind of primordiality in her Jewishness.*

　　In actuality it plays no role. No one asks you, Are you a Jew or are you not a Jew? That in and of itself does not play a role in life here. But there is solidarity and the feeling of belonging, especially after the Holocaust, [so that] Jewish life will not perish. Our Community has many young people, children of the elders, who themselves often are not in the Community. But the children are in the Community.

J　Do you still fear anti-Semitism as you did earlier?

HE　No. Absolutely not. I am not so naive as to believe that perhaps there are no anti-Semites here, but it is a criminal act. We have a government that criminalizes anti-Semitism and racism, and there are cases where that has happened [i.e., that violators have been penalized]. To present oneself as an anti-Semite here—no one dares do that; and if he does it, he'll be held accountable. That is the difference.

J　Do you have a relationship with Israel?

HE　I was there once. I went to give the names of my parents and my sister, for a certificate. But as I said, my uncle isn't living anymore, and the others—no, a very distant relative, I visited him there. But they've all been dead now for a long time. [The family] is dying out.

J　Do you feel personally affected by what is going on in Israel now?

HE　Yes, naturally. I find, when I read, I mean . . . I know the history well. *With great difficulty she struggles to position herself on this issue.*

　　I know that at [the time of] the foundation of the state the Soviet Union was exceptionally active, in the positive sense. The Arabs didn't recognize this division, that the Jews should [also] have a piece. Right away they waged war against Israel. But I am saddened and appalled, when I see pictures on television and when I read, by the brutality the Jewish soldiers, the Israeli soldiers, use against the young Arabs. Everything repeats itself. How to solve this problem is a mystery to me. Who knows? Who knows?

J　Are you sorrier about what they are doing because you are Jewish?

HE I am particularly sorry because we have ourselves been persecuted and have suffered and now in part are forced to go ahead with such means. Naturally, the Arabs have a right to live and to their territory, but the Jews also. And the Germans have to say, 'If you had not brought Hitler to power, then this problem wouldn't exist.' Many Jews went to Israel who never in their lives had thought about emigrating to Israel. It was their last chance [to save themselves]. And if there had been a Jewish state, there would have been no Holocaust.

J Can we switch to your history in the GDR. Did this history stamp you in some way?

HE You know, the GDR gave me the feeling for the first time in my life that I am a citizen with equal rights. For the first time in my life I can vote in the GDR. I feel I am an absolutely equal member of this society. I feel secure and safe. I don't know what all will come next. Please, that's all. I'm not a prophet. *She makes a veiled acknowledgment of the GDR's political crisis at this moment, surrounding the mass exodus of East Germans to the West.*

In any case, that's the way it is now. And as I said, my work as a journalist was very fulfilling to me. I sit on the board of the committee of antifascist resistance fighters, and I am thankful for the care, the way we are dealt with as antifascist resistance fighters here, also for the social welfare.

J Can you be more specific about the relationship between the antifascist resistance fighters and the state?

HE This is expressed in, for example, special privileges. We have special homes, vacation places, sanatoriums. We have a special pension, a higher pension. We don't have to pay for public transportation within the GDR.

As for us resistance fighters, there aren't many any more, unfortunately: more and more are dying. Approximately fifteen schools are named after my husband. Often I've been asked to go to the schools to tell about resistance and about my husband's life. They should know who Gerhart Eisler is—they carry his name! *All of these schools, of course, have been renamed since unification.*

Many resistance fighters go into the workplace and schools and to the youths to explain the resistance to the Nazis, but not only [that]: also how the idea of antifascist resistance can remain relevant. The youths here are regularly sent, about the time of the *Jugendweihe* [the state confirmation ceremony, at the age of fourteen], to the concentration camp, and [they] have to look at it.

J　My last question: Do you travel often in the FRG?

HE　Yes.

J　How is it for you there? Do you have a relation with the FRG?

HE　It works very well. I have a cousin in Frankfurt who has returned. We lived next to each other as children. We grew up together. I travel often to Munich. Friends from my youth live there, all men around eighty years old whom I have known for over fifty years. So I maintain these connections and travel as often as I want. I have a visa for the entire year.

　　Here HE *does not mention that travel in the* GDR *was restricted mostly to pensioners and a small group of approved citizens or, by the late 1980s, for emergencies or certain kinds of family reunions.*

J　Do you feel okay there?

HE　In the circle in which I move, with the people who I know there. But I must say, now I am worried about the development in the Federal Republic, exceptionally worried. Not only may the neo-Nazis again [engage in their] insolence, but such support [for them] exists in the government of the FRG. *It is curious that* HE *ignores how her own state is crumbling, preferring to concentrate on the more distant Federal Republic. She is answering, in her own way, our question about how the* GDR *has 'stamped' her in her forty years there. After carrying on for a few minutes about the neo-Nazis, she sees the writing on the wall and speaks with unusual perspicacity about her real fear: unification.*

　　This entire revanchist band there, which wants to have a Germany in the borders of 1937, a *Großdeutschland.* This exceptional economic power that the Federal Republic again brings with it, inevitably political power, which [the FRG] again wants to have in Europe. I mean, unofficially all of them do not want a united Germany—neither the French, the English, nor anyone else. This demand that the American president always repeats is made without reflection, without knowledge of the consequences. They chant about this [unification stuff] as if in a Tibetan prayer circle. It has to be. It's become a routine. You should stop a second [and think]. Who said, 'I love Germany so much that there cannot be enough of them'—De Gaulle or Mauriac or some other French-man?

J   With regard to your conception of democracy, I know that you have had negative experiences in the United States at precisely the time that democracy wasn't functioning well, but I'd like to ask if you learned something from American democracy? *I was thinking specifically about a criticism that is often heard within the* GDR, *that the lack of democracy was the system's greatest problem. Critics often blamed* HE*'s generation for the current problems because they were skeptical of democracy.*

HE   Under Roosevelt I had the feeling that [America] was a demo-cratic country. For me democracy does not necessarily mean that I can say, 'The president is a swine.' This is always used as an example, to be able to say whatever you like. That's not critically important to me, absolutely not. There are two sides. On the one hand you leave people completely free to do what they want; on the other hand you say, 'To hell with you,' and leave them free to perish on the street. [There are] two sides to the story.

J   Is there anything else you would like to ask or say that you find important?

HE   I seem to be exhausted. If you are satisfied with my story, then I am also satisfied. I don't know what else I [would] want to say. One can talk for hours on end, but first, I am already tired, and second, I've told it all already a hundred times. You can imagine that.

In response to our request to respond in a short letter to the changed situation since unification, HE *wrote the following on 7 April 1991:*

I would gladly discuss with you my thoughts concerning the *Wende* [change, turn of events]. Basically, I cannot stand to hear, read, or say any more about this topic.

She then refers us to an interview she gave to Manfred Engelhardt in March 1990, which he edited and published in Deutsche Lebens-läufe. Gespräche *(Berlin: Aufbau Verlag, 1991), 27–48. In this inter-view, she describes in more detail how her husband was fired from his job and 'declared a nonperson' in 1953. These actions 'broke my hus-band,' she says, though only temporarily. The years 1953 to 1956, before he was rehabilitated, she describes as 'bitter years, very bitter.' She lays the blame for the collapse of the* GDR *on the scandalous leadership of the* nomenklatura. *Her letter continues:*

What I am so appalled by is that the leaders in the Party isolated themselves. [They] had no idea what was happening among the people. They had forgotten everything, although they themselves suffered under fascism. They let themselves be corrupted. They took over structures from Stalin in the Soviet Union and installed them, blindly copied and changed in minor details. That our chance was wasted and we now must live through such a decline, that the people don't want to hear from us anymore, did not have to happen.

In September 1989 we had interviewed HE *before a camera again, posing very similar, though more directed, questions. On 30 April 1991, a full seven months after formal unification of the two Germanies, Jeff returned for a follow-up interview, also filmed.*

J   How do you feel about all these events [since 1989]?

HE   Very divided. Naturally, I am happy that the Wall has fallen, for I have always had my reservations about how long one can imprison a people. That is very positive. But there are also many negatives. *Among these negatives, she lists a 'general insecurity' about the future, unemployment, rising criminality. She also mentions the singular and virulent anti-Semitism that has 'broken out' in Germany, which she also finds threatening.*

J   After the war you came back to the GDR. Now you are sitting in the Federal Republic, a country that you never really wanted [to be a citizen of]. How do you feel about that?

HE   I must be honest [with you]. It doesn't really matter whether I am now a citizen of the Federal Republic or was a citizen of the GDR. It's simply that it doesn't concern me.

J   Do you have a stronger feeling about being Jewish now than you did before?

HE   I don't feel any more Jewish now than before. I understood myself to be Jewish before; that is my primary identity. It was always important to me and it will remain important.

Since our first interview, the way HE *sees herself has changed significantly. No longer able to reference the* GDR *as part of her identity, she also seems to have lost her nationality. In the united Germany she is merely a citizen and a Jew. When she says she is disappointed by the 'perversions' of East German socialism and by this 'great fiasco,' the failure to realize socialism in the* GDR, *Jeff asks her if she is sad.*

Of course I am sad that it has come to this. We had indeed had the idea to build a democratic, better, actually more just, humanistic Germany. That was the reason the people returned. That was the great hope of the people who came out of the KZs, who were persecuted as antifascists. Naturally, it's a great defeat, a defeat we have suffered. We have to live with that.

In the eighteen months since this final interview, HE *has appeared in public forums many times, in addition to giving other interviews, which have subsequently been published. Although she continues to be wary of the resurgence of anti-Semitism and xenophobia in the united Germany, she now says that she unequivocally supports the elimination of 'the dictatorship in the* GDR.'

CHAPTER 4. ERNST CRAMER

'I never stopped being a German Jew.'

Born 1913   Bavaria
1913–1938   Bavaria and other parts of Germany
1938   KZ, Buchenwald (six weeks)
1939–1942   Virginia, then Mississippi
1942–1945   U.S. Army (1943 U.S. citizen)
1945–1954   Germany (military government),
              United States
1954–   Frankfurt, Hamburg, West Berlin

After spending six weeks in Buchenwald, Ernst Cramer arrived in America in 1939. He returned to Germany first with the American army and later with the United Press. Thereafter he became the righthand man of Axel Springer, one of the most powerful newspaper magnates in all of Germany. With Springer dead, EC is now a top executive of the Springer publishing house. EC speaks with conviction and enthusiasm about West German democracy and the significance of German-American relations. He describes himself as a liberal conservative. His American experience clearly convinced him of the benefits of America's politics, its style, and its ethos. And America's influence on Germany in the postwar era showed him that the Germany to which he had returned was on a different path than the Germany that had driven him away. Exile in America benefited him.

We made an appointment to see EC in his offices on the top floor of the Springer building, a few blocks from the infamous Checkpoint Charlie, the checkpoint for Americans and other foreigners entering East Berlin. The Springer building is stately and elegant, with corporate suites, wood-paneled libraries, and restaurants with excellent service. EC has obviously done well in his new life in Germany.

We began our interview by asking about the relationship between EC's personal life history and his political position.

EC   Ah, yes. You know, a great deal in life is coincidence. As a child, I never dreamed that I would emigrate. Then came Hitler. I left much too late because I thought we could wait it out. That was 1939. Three weeks before the war began, I arrived in America.

     Most German Jews left in 1938 or 1939. During those two years alone 120,000 fled, compared with 150,000 in 1933 and the first half of 1938. Those who waited either thought that the Nazis would not be in power long or did not want to leave their parents or other older relatives. In addition, getting a visa often took a long time (Berghahn 1988, 74).

J   How old are you?

EC   I am an old man, born in 1913. I belonged to a Jewish youth group. There were many such groups, with different orientations [e.g., toward Germany or toward Zionism], and I belonged to the one that never thought about emigrating. In the summer of 1934 leaders from various Jewish youth groups met in a youth hostel near Köln. We could still do such things at that time. The bad times didn't come all at once. We all felt that those around us were telling us that we didn't belong anymore and we questioned what that meant for us. One group decided that if they were treated as 'foreign' [*fremd*] they would leave, and many in this group went to Israel and started their own kibbutz. The other group called themselves the Fellowship of German Jewish Youth [*Bund deutsch-jüdischer Jugend*], and they felt that they were still Germans [*unser Deutschtum bleibt*] no matter what others said. Of course I am oversimplifying this, but in any case I belonged to this second group. I didn't want to emigrate, and because of that I left too late and couldn't help save my parents or my younger brother. Only my sister made it to America. *Other refugees who left late have also admitted feeling guilty for waiting so long and inadvertently condemning their relatives.*

J   And how did you save yourself?

EC   I rejected many offers to leave, to go to South Africa. Then after the Nürnberg Laws were instituted in 1935, I realized that it was no longer possible to live here. I was involved in setting up agricultural job retraining and I went to one of these sites in 1937. But this particular group purposely didn't want to go to the ones for Zionist youths, because we didn't want to take spots away from them. They needed certificates to go to Palestine, and there were so few. Since we weren't Zionists, we were looking for another place so that the entire group could stay together—South America, for example. But that never happened, because then came 1938, Kristallnacht, what I would call the largest state pogrom, and we had to save ourselves.

I had the chance to go to Kenya or to America. I went to the United States, and I was very lucky because there I learned what I know now about democracy. When I got to America, I worked on farms and then went to Mississippi State College. I waived my deferment, went into the army in February 1942, was naturalized in March 1943, and was in the army until October 1945. From 1945 until 1954 I was in the military government and worked on a German-language newspaper published by the occupation authorities as an assistant editor. I returned to America: I had married and had children. We first wanted to stay in the United States, but the jobs I was offered there were not as challenging as what I could have in Germany. I felt I could do more there, and I was offered a job with UPI. *Like other Jews we interviewed who returned to West Berlin, EC emphasizes that he could have seen himself living in America. Professional opportunities in America or the lack thereof in America encouraged his return to Germany.*

J   How did you meet your wife?

EC   My wife and my sister went to kindergarten together in Augsburg, Germany. Her parents and mine were very good friends, and we came from the same city. We both belonged to the liberal wing of Judaism equivalent to a mixture of the American Conservative and Reform movements. EC *explains the difference between the meaning of the word* liberal *in America and in Germany. He apologizes for what may have seemed to be pedantry, but he wants us to understand that he did not marry his wife because she was Jewish: they simply liked each other. He goes on to talk about how they brought up their children.*

We raised our children to be Jewish, but that means that they always knew that they were Jewish, why they were Jewish, and knew about the family's history. *He has twins, a daughter, who lives in Norway and is married to a non-Jew, and a son, who lives in New York and is married to a Jewish woman. He emphasized that his son and daughter-in-law raise their children as Jews and live in an environment that is more Jewish than that in Germany.*

My wife's family was saved. EC*'s reference here to the Holocaust and his wife reveals that he defines his Jewishness in connection with surviving the Holocaust in Germany. He returns to the subject of his children.*

We did not give our children any formal religious training, although we raised them consciously as Jews. My wife and I found the type of religious training provided at that time not satisfactory. EC*'s remarks illustrate something that becomes obvious in these interviews, namely, that German Jewry, like American Jewry, is neither monolithic nor homogenous.*

J How do you feel about being Jewish?

EC I have always, my whole life, acknowledged my being Jewish, been involved with Jewish organizations, but I am not one of those Jews who think that Zionism or the Holocaust is a replacement for the Jewish religion.

J Was the decision to return difficult?

EC It was not really a decision per se, because I didn't just one day make up my mind. I never decided to live here; rather, it just happened [*das hat sich so ergeben*]. When I was a soldier in the army I assumed there never again would be Jewish life in Germany. I couldn't imagine that after the entire Nazi period there were enough people who thought differently [were not Nazis]. Then I came here and suddenly noticed [otherwise]—that, as it often is in life, things are not black and white. I found old friends of my parents' from before the war and made new acquaintances. A very important decision was to be part of the military government. I thought I could use my knowledge and my relationship to both cultures. I hope I was successful.

J Living between two cultures, being part of the American government and then helping to institute a free press, free institutions, in Germany—amidst all of this, did you still feel yourself to be a German Jew?

EC In contrast to many others, I never stopped being a German Jew. Only a few people might want to say that. Many of the Jews who live here have a bad conscience. They say, 'Yes, we are here, we were driven out of the East, could not go any further.' Many were sick and got stuck here. I understand their position. Other friends I have say they won't set foot on German soil. I don't feel this way, but I understand that someone can have these feelings. Hitler said that I am not a German Jew, that I cannot live here. I say that I am a German Jew, I want to live here. I don't want to give him the satisfaction of having even this point. But my answer is emotional, not rational. Do you remember that I told you about this meeting of youth leaders in the 1930s where we discussed when one is a German Jew. When are you an American Jew? *He asks this question in English.*

Is it when you want it or when others want it?

I get upset with things that happen in Germany as a German, just as I get upset with things in America as an American. These reactions are completely independent of whether I am a Jew or not. Is that enough? Or does one have to be completely accepted by one's peers as such? I don't have an answer. You probably could talk to many Germans and most of them would say that the Jews who always lived here and those who want to live here again belong here. Then there is another group who say, Sure, they can live here, but they do not belong with us. Essentially the question is whether belonging is a notion that depends on me or that depends on the others, or is it only real if it comes 100 percent from both sides?

J When you came back, what were your feelings? or what did you imagine it to be like? Were you afraid after what happened in the Third Reich?

EC For me returning was different because of the circumstances of my return. I arrived with the army, so I was the boss, if you want to call it that. That sounds arrogant. Of course, I hope I never behaved that way and didn't feel like that. But suddenly, after leaving Germany as the underdog, I returned as the top dog [so to speak].

Let me tell you, I have friends here, few enemies, but when I meet people who are of my age I naturally think about what they may have done during the Nazi years and I don't feel completely comfortable. I don't want to say that I think about this period incessantly, but no day goes by when I am not confronted with this memory. If I didn't react this way, I would be ashamed of myself, because all of my work for Jewish organizations and other such things come from this experience.

[Speaking] as a Jew, especially when one has had these experiences—lost parents, lived in Germany—there are two very important historical events that we have experienced that earlier generations did not. The first is the most negative that one could imagine: the Holocaust; the other, the most positive: the founding of the state of Israel. These are the most significant Jewish caesuras of our time. And if you would ask me, What goes deeper for you? then I would say Israel, because it has given meaning back to the lives of so many people. I personally didn't suffer as much as others. *He acknowledges here, as did Ruth Benario, who came back from the Soviet Union, that some refugees had a much easier life than others.*

What torments me is how Germany, a cultivated nation [*Kulturnation*] of the first class, could let itself be taken in this direction. But I don't say, How could the Germans do this? I say, rather, How could *we* Germans do this?

EC *goes very far here in identifying himself as German. In his use of the term* Kulturnation *he echoes many other émigrés, like Ruth Benario, who, having grown up as assimilated secular Jews in Germany before the war, believed in this particularly German notion of culture or cultivation. This ideal united the German people, especially the German Jews, who were highly represented in the professions, the arts, and culture in general.*

J   You have emphasized the importance of these two experiences for you as a Jew in the twentieth century. But what about the evolution of the new German state, the Federal Republic? What does that mean for your identity, career, and biography?

EC I spoke first as a Jew. From the German perspective, or, better, from an international perspective, the entire world was lucky that there were politicians after the Second World War—unlike after the First World War—who had a broader world-view [and thought] to establish a democratic Germany. In 1945 it was not so clear that this would happen. Stalin wanted a communist Germany, and if he had been successful the world would be a different place today. We are very lucky that Germany as the Federal Republic is a state where people can be freer than at any other time in German history. People are better off. They have more freedom, more possibilities. They can be taught freely and go to free universities. We have a social welfare system that the whole world envies.

J   How do you see the division of Germany and the fate of German Jews and other Germans in the GDR? Were they a necessary sacrifice? Were they sacrificed?

EC   Wait a minute. We have to be very careful with this term *sacrifice*. I don't think the question has to do with that. I am now talking about, not the Jews who are living over there, but the people in general. For the Jews it is an entirely different problem. In retrospect I almost want to say that any other decision than the one in 1948—namely, to build here in the West our own state, our own economy—any other decision made by the three occupying forces would not have led to a viable or democratic state, but rather to disorder. What we built here was substantiated by the developments in the Eastern European countries. I am of the opinion that things in the Soviet Union would have evolved quite differently if the fate of Germany hadn't developed the way it did after the war. Now you are probably going to ask me about reunification.

      In the context of postwar German politics before unification, it is not surprising that EC *brings up the issue of reunification, which was always a goal, at least in principle, for the West Germans. Many people felt that some of the politicians who had preached unification were caught off guard when the Wall came down and German politics moved so quickly in the direction of unification since they had never really imagined that it would take place at all, and certainly not so soon.*

      I think it will be a long, arduous historical process. There are two sides: the one about freedom—this cannot be abandoned—and the other about active and pragmatic politics. At the moment there is no unified perspective in Germany. What is important is what I brought back with me when I returned to Germany, what we brought with us. *We* means the army.

J   I actually wanted to ask about that *we*.

EC   That is why I tried to clarify my point. Freedom is the point. If there is someday in the GDR a society that enjoys similar freedoms as [the ones we enjoy] here, that the citizens can travel where they want, read what they want without fearing that the neighbor might inform on them, that someone will be standing in front of the door to bring them to court, then there will be no need for a Wall. But we are very far from this point.

J Regarding the German Jews over there, you said that is a different problem?

EC Here in the Federal Republic only very few former German Jews returned. Those who came back returned for very different reasons. Some Jews from East Germany didn't have any reason and simply got stuck here, live here, and do quite well. But most don't identify with being German. I don't know how it will be with the next generation—the children of these who returned are like their parents. But the next generation, I don't know.

   In the GDR there are very, very few Jews, maybe seven hundred, almost all former German Jews who are just waiting out their life. After the war in the West zones, as they were called, the Jewish Communities were initially built as transitional institutions for those who would emigrate out of Germany and for those who were old. This is not the case anymore; we are here and will stay here. If the situation doesn't change in the GDR, the Jews will dwindle to nothing.

J Do you feel connected to the Jews in the GDR, or does politics divide you?

EC I will have to say again, I am not closer to someone just because they are Jewish. Of course, as a Jew I am interested in Jewish problems, and when Jews don't conduct themselves properly [it bothers me more] than when a Turk does, because the Turk interests me only as a person, but the Jew is a representative [of my people]. One is very sensitive when someone from a group that one belongs to doesn't conduct himself properly.

   It is interesting that EC *chooses a Turk as an example when talking about the behavior of individuals in minority groups in Germany. At the time of this interview the Turks, who were not generally accepted by the German population, had not yet become the object of aggression and violence. Now, after attacks that have killed Turks residing in Germany, Turks and Jews are often compared.*

   EC *goes on to talk about America's significance for him, which, interestingly, he expressed in terms of his wife and of his relationship to the English language and to his children. Both children were born when he was part of the American military establishment and attended American universities. He says that he has one friend who went to America who continued to speak only German, while another would never set foot in Germany again. 'Avoided it like the plague,' he says.* EC, *on the other hand, says, 'I love the German language and speak it better than English.' He moves from talking about language to declaring his attachment to Germany.*

I think Germany is one of the most interesting and beautiful countries. I like its history, its arts, the architecture. Of course, one can like all of this and still not feel that one belongs. *Like Albert Klein,* EC *feels connected to Germany through language, cultural artifacts, and particular places. This is not atypical for German Jews of their generation, who felt themselves to be so German.*

Our next interview took place a few weeks later, again at EC's *offices high above the Berlin Wall. This time he seemed to be more relaxed with us. Having noticed at the preceding interview the attention given to Israel in the library of his offices—books, pictures, Jewish memorabilia—we decided to take our questioning in that direction.*

J Perhaps we can now begin with the postwar period. We didn't have much chance the last time to ask about Israel, your relationship to it. Have you been there? What do you think about the political situation?

EC I could answer this question quite simply by giving you two folders filled with articles that I have written about Israel. As I explained [when speaking of] my membership in German Jewish youth organizations in the 1930s, I belonged to the group which did not want to go to Israel, but I was neither anti-Zionist nor a Zionist myself. EC *grounds many of his contemporary positions in his membership in a youth organization with strong German Jewish ties. At this point in the discussion he certainly doesn't want membership in a non-Zionist group to make him appear to be anti-Zionist.*

In 1948 the Jewish state came to be. Jews had dreamed of this for centuries. As a result of the terrible things that had happened in Germany, such a state became even more significant. Naturally, there had always been Jews in Palestine, but I am convinced that there would not be a Jewish state today if the Holocaust had not occurred. I support the existence of Israel without reservations. I have many friends there and have been there many times, and I passionately defend the rights of the Israeli people, of the Jewish people, to live there in secured borders. But I do not belong to those who would apply to Israel the English expression 'My country right or wrong.' I reserve the right to disagree with the official policies of the government.

J   If you don't mind, let us push this point a bit. Some of the Jews with whom we have spoken have compared what the Israelis are doing with the Palestinians to fascism. Would you take the point that far?

EC   This comparison is wrong and stupid. The rebellion of the Palestinians in Judea, Samaria, and the Gaza Strip is only possible because money and ideology continue to be brought in from outside. The Israelis have to resist this. This is completely understandable, a necessity. However, I know that they have at times used excessive [means] that should not have been employed.

J   You emphasized the importance of the American influence in bringing the democratic press to Germany after the war, and you stressed your participation in that process. But many people in Germany have had difficulties with the Springer Press. They don't consider it as democratic as you do and call it a boulevard press.

The term boulevard press *is used in Germany to describe newspapers that tend to sensationalize events. The* Bild-Zeitung *is the Springer paper referred to here. The German student movements of 1967–68 and the years following identified the Springer Press as one of their main enemies. In the students' view, it was a monopoly media concern that tried to manipulate people's perspectives toward conservative and even reactionary positions.*

EC   The Axel Springer publishing group has many papers. My contribution to the *Bild-Zeitung* was very minimal. The spirit of all our papers is liberal-conservative. We have boulevard newspapers and also newspapers that are quite serious. Especially in the years when there was a serious confrontation between Left and Right, our position was very unappealing to many people; they even called us fascist. My political position was never different than [that of] the Axel Springer Press. If I ever had influence on [the Press], it came from my American experience.

J   Could you discuss the position of the Springer papers based on a concrete example—the building of the Wall, for instance, or the attempted murder of Rudi Dutschke? *A 'student speaker' for the Students for a Democratic Society (*SDS*), Dutschke was a leading German leftist active in the anti–Vietnam War movement. He was*

severely wounded when he was shot in April 1968. This provoked
demonstrations and riots in many German cities.[1] In these cases
some of the Sixties generation reproached the Springer Press for
their involvement.

EC In the sixties it was claimed that our reporting popularized the idea
of fleeing from the East. On the other hand, that would have
meant that we had compelled the communists in some way to
build the Wall. I have also heard this year that the reporting of the
West about the refugees fleeing through Hungary would probably
compel Honecker to introduce stricter measures. I know that
among the people whom you have interviewed there are many
who politically are quite different than I and who hoped that West
Berlin would become a single political unit, separated from the
Federal Republic. The events of 1989 are, of course, a great disappointment to them. In the sixties and seventies Springer was the
bad guy. I am happy that I could stand by him during that time.
Was our position correct at that time? I think so. Now we have
been proven correct.

EC discusses at length Springer's reporting of the Dutschke case and
the accusation that the press had encouraged the kind of behavior that
led to the attack on Dutschke. Similar accusations were made against
Springer regarding the death of the student Benno Ohnesorg [on 2
June 1967] during the violent demonstrations in Berlin in response to
the visit by the Shah of Iran. EC asks pointedly, 'Is reporting agita-
tion?' and goes on to say that there were investigations concerning the
Springer Press's involvement.

Looking back one always knows more. One has to judge the
reporting from the standpoint of that time, not from the standpoint of today. We certainly made mistakes, but the question is,
however, whether there was a political directive at Springer or
whether news was manipulated. Naturally, there was no such
thing. At that time Springer Press was a kind of bulwark against
defeatist tendencies, which, fortunately, did not succeed.

J   What do you mean?

EC In regard to the official policies toward the GDR and East Berlin.
The question of the Federal Republic's recognizing GDR citizenship. We were of the opinion that there was only one German
citizenship. By recognizing the other citizenship, we would be
supporting the division of Germany.

J   What were the democratic processes that Springer supported?

EC   Axel Springer formulated four essential tenets for which we all
worked: first, the reunification of Germany in freedom, prefera-
bly in a free Europe that supports NATO; second, the reconciliation of Germans and Jews, as much as it is possible, including the
right of Jews to have the state of Israel; third, the fight against
political extremism on the Left or Right; and the fourth point is
the support of the free social market economy. Aside from these
basic points there were never any rules to follow. Our editors are
producing papers to sell, and they serve the public for whom they
are produced. Since it began, the *Bild Zeitung* has always been
attacked by the Left, [although] more of its readers leaned toward
social democracy than toward any other political orientation. We
want to reach a broad base of people.

    EC *returns to his discussion of the army press and its influence and
then to his involvement in the denazification of the media after the
war.*

J   What about the reproach leveled against Springer that denazification contributed to the repression of the past?

EC   I am talking about the years that I was working for the Americans.
At that time the main question was whether it was worthwhile
and possible to bring the Germans into the Western alliance and
to introduce democracy. We needed people. It would have been
wrong to say, You, or your father, shouldn't have done that. Fortunately, we didn't fall into the same situation as after World War
I, when nationalism rose again and led to disaster. In short, let me
say that the rebuilding of the Federal Republic was successful
economically, culturally, and morally only because people with
criminal records were excluded and, on the other hand, those who
were Nazi Party members without personal guilt were included.

    EC *is referring to the postwar situation in the Federal Republic,
which was criticized for not excluding all former Nazis from positions
in the German government. In the decades after the war there were
two major scandals involving former Nazis in high positions. In 1950
it was discovered that Hans Globke, a state secretary in the chancellor's
office, in the Nazi period had been a ministerial adviser in domestic
affairs and had helped to write the Nürnberg Laws. In 1978 Hans
Filbinger, the minister president of Baden-Württemberg, was forced*

to resign because of questions arising from his activities as a military judge during the war.

If one had excluded all of these people [i.e., former Nazi Party members], then we would not have been successful. Today it is so easy to say that we should have handled it all differently. Certainly, I would agree that in the schools in the 1950s and 1960s more information about the Nazi period should have been disseminated, but it was not possible. There were no teachers; either they were too young and didn't know what happened or they were older and were themselves burdened with the past. And it is difficult for a man to teach about his own awful deeds. That was a problem.

We closed with a question about Germany and its immigration problems, which at the time of this interview had not reached the proportions nor the violence that occurred in 1992, 1993, and 1994. Since the time of this interview, the asylum law in Germany has been changed to make it more difficult to obtain asylum in Germany.

J There is a question about Germany as a 'land of immigration,' as the official terminology goes. If one wanted to make a comparison, it could be said that if other countries had not taken in German Jews, this group would have disappeared. Perhaps one should react the same way about those who want to come to Germany. Do you think Germany should be a land of immigration?

Germany traditionally has not recognized itself as a country for immigrants, although up until 1 July 1993 it had one of the most liberal asylum laws in the world. Germany has no immigration— unlike the United States, Canada, and Australia, which are internationally recognized as potential sites of immigration. The debate in Germany over asylum—that it was misused and therefore had to be changed—raises significant questions about who should be admitted to Germany and who is or should be a German.

EC Germany cannot be a country of homeless people. But here I have to be political. This old question about immigration can easily lead to demagoguery. What is important is that people who are threatened, really threatened, should be taken in. No one disputes this. But what has happened is that people from Sri Lanka, for example, whose life there is not so good pay someone who promises them that they will get them to Germany as a refugee. If they were to arrive as immigrants, this would be a different category.

But another question bothers me: Take a group of people from Sudan who are oppressed and say they want to go to Germany. Is it all right to bring these people here, to take them out of their own environment? This is a very complicated question with no easy answer. But I don't think you can say, Since Germany threw the Jews out, it should take all others. It is not that simple. I am just not convinced that people from the Sudan, to go back to my example, will find a homeland [*Heimat*] here in Germany. On the other hand, for centuries various population groups have moved through Europe. There is no 'racially pure' country on this continent.

EC *is always very busy. When I did not receive a response to my request for an evaluation and comment on his earlier interviews and to the recent political events in Germany, I made an appointment. On 30 July 1991 he answered me in person:*

When I was interviewed two years ago, I did not expect reunification of Germany to come so quickly. As a matter of fact, I did not expect the changes in Eastern Europe to be as fast and as final as they turned out to be. I think I underestimated Mikhail Gorbachev.

Living in Berlin, living in Germany as a Jew, means for me a new challenge since I believe that reunification has brought new problems to Germany that have been unknown to the Western part since the end of the war. The problem again is one of the underdog versus the establishment. Unfortunately, all too many West Germans—private citizens, companies, corporations, and government representatives—behaved like colonial officers in the British imperial period or like the carpetbaggers after the American Civil War. On the other hand, people in East Germany expected too much too soon. All this created a new climate. A new wall developed, this time in the minds of the people. It is a big challenge for everyone concerned to tear down this invisible wall, and it may prove to be more difficult than tearing down the wall of bricks and asbestos.

I don't think that Jews in Germany have a specific task in connection with this. They have their own problems. As before, the large majority of Jews living in Germany today have no real ties to this country. They are not successors to the German Jews who lived in Germany before 1933 or before the Holocaust. But they did contribute quite a bit to establishing democratic institutions in West Germany. Whether they will have to take on a similar task for the new territories, the former GDR, I have my doubts.

An added problem for the Jewish Communities in Germany are the Jewish immigrants from the Soviet Union. These are mostly people who, for one reason or another, do not want to go to Israel, but want to stay in Europe. They have no prejudices against Germany but also no special love for Germany. Also, most of them are 'ethnic' Jews and have little knowledge of what Judaism is or should be. This will provide the Jewish Communities and Jewish organizations with a large task, one for which they are ill-equipped due to the lack of qualified personnel.

In conclusion, I would like to say that I believe that despite present difficulties which the reunification process has brought, democracy will survive strongly in all of Germany. Unlike in the Weimar years, the German people have accepted democracy. There will be social tensions. There are outbreaks of right-wing manifestations, right-wing hooliganism, which in some ways remind me of similar happenings in the end phase of the Weimar Republic, but the situation is quite different today. Despite economic difficulties, there will be no recession of the type that we went through at the end of the twenties. And even if there were a political Pied Piper again, he would not find financial support among German industry as Hitler did sixty some years ago and would not find the masses to support him.

From England to East Berlin

'My friends, it is already after ten.'

Born 1904 Berlin
1926–1929 United States
1929–1936 Berlin
1936–1945 England
1945–1950 West Berlin
1950– East Berlin

*W*e *met Jürgen Kuczynski, professor emeritus in eco-nomic history at Humboldt University, at his large villa in the Weißensee district of East Berlin on 17 August 1989. His secretary took us into his study. Seated at his desk with his back to us, he rose theatrically, turned, smiled, shook our hands, and removed a clownish doll from an arm-chair, where he said one of us could sit. JK is a tall, charming, elegantly dressed man. He smokes a pipe, which he continually lights and relights.*

JK's life is extremely well documented, for he has written several accounts of his life. Understandably, then, he had no desire to repeat what he had already recorded elsewhere. He did not want to provide a narrative, but demanded of us a constant exchange. I have eliminated a few of our questions in an effort to reduce the choppiness of the story. The exchange also seemed to be shaped by the fact that JK was older, better educated, and wiser than either of us. He had been interviewed hundreds of times, at the time of our interview nearly daily, in many different languages. We were not able to overcome his sense of having done this all a hundred times before.

JK was born in 1904 in Berlin, where he was raised in a wealthy, leftist, Social Democratic family, which he described as 'not very wealthy, but wealthy' until 1918. In 1913 they built a fine house at Schlachtensee. 'But already during the war I often went hungry,' said JK, 'as my father worked at the ministry of nutrition [Ernährungs-

ministerium *] and forbade my mother to buy anything on the black
market. After the war, during the inflation, my parents lost their
fortune. People like my parents were called* Villenproletarier *[pro-
letarians in a beautiful home].' In 1926 he went to the United States
on an academic stipend at the Brookings School in Washington* DC,
*then founded and was head of the Research Institute of the American
Federation of Labor. In 1929 he returned to Germany. From 1933 to
1936 he worked against the Hitler regime in Germany before leaving
for England, where he resided until 1945. He returned to West Germany in 1945 with the American occupation forces and resettled in
East Berlin in 1950. He still maintains a lively correspondence with
friends in France, the United States, England, and West Germany,
where his three sisters and parents continue to reside. We conducted the
interview in German. I sent him my translation in 1991, which he
promptly returned with comments, nearly all of which are incorporated in this final version.*

J   Why did you leave Germany?

JK The Party threw me out because with my profile I endangered
    every blonde, blue-eyed *Genossin* [female Party member] with
    whom I might meet. JK *has a stereotypical Semitic profile.*

    There's also a very simple reason: Walter Ulbricht [First Secre-
    tary of the Central Committee of the Communist Party, 1950–71]
    had said to me earlier that I should go to England, where my
    parents and siblings lived. So I went to England.

J   You knew Ulbricht here?

JK Yes, of course. I met him in Moscow in '35.

J   And when did you emigrate?

JK Early in '36.

J   How long did you remain in England?

JK We tried to return to Germany at the end of '44. Then came the
    Ardennes offensive, and we were called back. [We returned] to
    Germany then in April '45. I was with the United States Strategic
    Bombing Service, which had asked me to reenter Germany with
    them.

J   Why not with the British?

JK They weren't interested in me. I was too dangerous for them. The
    Americans had a whole row of leftists, including many *Genossen,*

in their organizations. It didn't matter to them so long as we were useful. I worked for the Americans until August '45. In September I returned to England. I had extreme difficulties in returning to Germany and then came back [working] for the American Occupation, in November '45, to Berlin. I worked with the [American] administrators until April. It was a way for me to come back. I lived in West Berlin. My family was there. That's all in my memoirs.

J K repeats the phrase 'all in my memoirs' three times during the next five minutes. We wanted some details of his life before exile, but from his present perspective. But this proved to be impossible, for he could only repeat what he had already written down—rehearsed, rethought, reflected upon, rewritten—which he obviously did not want to do.

In his Memoiren: Die Erziehung des J.K. zum Kommunisten und Wissenschaftler *[The education of J.K. to communist and scholar] (Berlin: Aufbau, 1981), he states that his goal is 'to make more understandable [for young scholars in the* GDR*] the history of the Party, of German intelligentsia, of Marxist science' (418). The autobiography makes clear how often his own life story intersects with the history of the* KPD*, the German Communist Party. In addition, it is a cosmopolitan history, constrained by but not imagined within the borders of nation-states. Until 1936* J K *worked for the Party leadership. At that time, incidentally, he wrote stock market reports for the* New York Herald Tribune *that were similar to the reports Karl Marx had written eighty years earlier.*

J   Because I do not know all of these details, I may ask you to repeat something that you have already written in your books. After 1946 did you simply switch from the American to the Soviet occupation forces?

J K   No, not to the Soviets but to the Party. *He wanted to emphasize that he worked for the German Communist Party, not directly for the Soviet authorities.*

J   Weren't there any problems?

J K   Absolutely none, no. No, the Americans weren't angry to get rid of me, and the Party was happy to have me.

J   When did you begin to teach at Humboldt?

J K   Somewhat earlier, already in the winter. I recall that I had to wear a winter coat for my first lectures in the ice-cold lecture hall.

J   During your time in exile in England, were you always sure that you would return?

JK   Of course.

J   Did you know what to expect on your return?

JK   We had a pretty accurate picture but naturally didn't believe that the building of socialism would [go] so slowly and be so difficult.

In response to questions concerning his circles of friends in emigration—German, Jewish, English?—and how he mixed academic and political work, he tells us he has already written that in his memoirs.

J   Did you also describe your activities in the GDR?

JK   No, the memoirs go only to '45.

J   People have told us that you influenced the regime as an intellectual, that you had constant discussions with Ulbricht and were friends with him. How did you balance your two hats—as academic or intellectual and as a political consultant?

JK   Yes, that wasn't difficult. Before '33 I was a functionary in the Party. I was economic editor at the *Rote Fahne* [The Red Flag, the Communist Party newspaper]—this is all in my memoirs. So the relationship wasn't one between someone from the intelligentsia and the Party leadership, but one between an old functionary and another functionary. *Did he avoid the question?*

J   Would you characterize your role the same after the war?

JK   Yes.

J   What kind of role did you play in the development of the GDR after the war?

JK   Not any special one. At the university in the social sciences.

I was incredulous at this answer. Either I, and many others in the GDR, were totally misinformed, which certainly could be the case, or he was avoiding the question.

J   You were no longer a functionary? What about the Party? You played no role in the Party?

JK   No. I was in the central leadership of the Party at the Academy [of Science] for two years. Before that I was president of the German-Soviet Friendship Society. Then I was a representative [in Parliament], but I did not have any high Party function.

For an avowed Marxist-Leninist, JK was separating theory (his intellectual work) from practice (his Party work) in an untenable way. Lenin had assumed that the two were inseparable. And JK's writings had led us to believe that he remained a follower of Lenin. If I took his answer seriously, then his relationship to the Party leadership after the war was no longer one between functionary and functionary, as he claimed was the case before the war, but one between intellectual and politician, which was the point of our initial question. He had, I think, avoided answering it.

J   Were you friends with Ulbricht before 1933?

JK   No. Naturally, we knew each other.

J   Did you know other people who played an important role in [the development of] the GDR?

JK   Yes, of course. Many were also good friends of mine. *We seemed to be making headway again.*

J   How would you appraise the influence of Stalin or Stalinism in the 1950s?

JK   Immense, of course. Immense. The only [difference between the GDR and other Stalinist systems] is that no show trials were carried out. But it was bad enough.

He had responded abstractly to the question, in terms of a relation between two systems, whereas we were interested in his assessment of his own role.

J   How did you experience this yourself?

JK   I was a true believer until 1956, until the Khrushchev speech.

J   You were a true believer. Didn't you also experience some personal limitations?

JK   Continually. I mean, I was always again falling into disfavor, especially after 1956 but also before. There is this saying: 'The helm of an old *Genosse* is full of boils, and some of these come from an enemy.'

By this he means to defend himself, we suspect. The implication is that some of his disfavor was undeserved, coming from comrades and friends in the Party who blindly followed the Party line of the day.

Knowing that his economic advice in the late fifties indicated that he still considered himself somewhat of a true believer, I wanted to know when he experienced his first doubts.

J   When were you first informed, for example, about the gulags or the work camps in the Soviet Union?

JK   I would say that some of this I learned after 1956. I had a brother-in-law who was in a camp. But I only learned of the extent of the terror after Gorbachev.

J   How about the Twentieth Party Congress and the Khrushchev speech? Did that play a role [in altering your belief]?

JK   Yes, a definitive role. I mean, with that I quit, insofar as one can when one has lived so long as a Stalinist. For me the whole thing ended with Khrushchev, without my having a complete presentiment [of what this meant]. But because of that, I was again in disfavor in '58.

J   How was that?

JK   I was always, repeatedly, in disfavor. And presently again. No, for me today what is happening in the Soviet Union . . . [reminds me of] youthful memories of the time of Lenin and his great students. JK *doesn't say the words, but he seems to be referring to the reforms in the Soviet Union.*

   I speak—I give talks at over eighty assemblies a year—very openly in favor of *perestroika* and *glasnost.*

   Sensing his absolute comfort and sovereignty with more abstract themes, I decide to risk a move away from the concrete.

J   What do you understand *glasnost* and *perestroika* to mean?

JK   *Perestroika* is a type of revolution, comparable to the bourgeois [revolutions] in France, say, after 1789, 1793, 1830, 1848. It's high time that socialism also had a second revolution.

J   Is there presently a country whose system for you corresponds to [your conception of] socialism, or how socialism should develop?

JK   There is none, because one has to be always dissatisfied with the development, both constantly optimistic and dissatisfied.

J   Is there a country that comes close?

JK   I would say, regarding the superstructure, meaning the cultural and intellectual life, the Soviet Union developed tremendously. With respect to the economy, horribly bad. In the period after the war about which we are speaking, General Tulpanow played a very large role in the Occupation Army. A few weeks ago his wife visited me, and I asked her how it was in Leningrad, and she said, 'Unbelievable amounts to read, little to eat.'

J   Back to the history of the GDR. How would you periodize it?

JK   Not at all, not at all. That's silly. I have never spoken of developed socialism, rather, always of its developing. One should reconsider: You can say that capitalism in England began in 1560, then it took two hundred years before the machine came, and one can [now] speak of a developed capitalism. And we want to dispose of that in a few years? Isn't it so? That is absolute nonsense.

J   But I mean something else. Are there certain dates in the history of the GDR that are very important for you?

JK For me personally, no. Naturally, the seventeenth of June [1953, a worker uprising], then the thirteenth of August [1961, the building of the Wall]. Those are two very decisive and extraordinarily important days.

J   From your present perspective, how do you evaluate these two events?

JK The seventeenth of June was a real blow to me. *He seems to have just reversed his position.*

At that time I was dean of the faculty of economics, and after two years of a lot of bureaucratic rubbish I had had enough. I wanted to do more scholarly work. The Party was extremely angry about my wish to resign. It demanded that I remain one more year as dean. But then they passed a resolution that on account of my good behavior on the seventeenth of June, I no longer had to serve as dean. *Of course, his reference to his 'good behavior' is ironic.*

J   That was very personal, was it not?

JK Yes. No. At that time, it was of course a difficult time. We were good friends with Brecht and Helene Weigel [Brecht's wife] and Anna Seghers. *It is not clear why he mentions his friends, or these particular friends, in this context.*

J   And [your relationship] to 1961?

JK 'Sixty-one was an absolute—very sad—but an absolute necessity. We were being bled dry [*ausgeblutet*] without the Wall.

J   Given what is happening in the other socialist countries today, do you still see that as a historical necessity?

JK It's absolutely necessary, in order to make progress, that socialism appears more attractive, which in part has nothing at all to do with the economic relationships. The Soviet Union, or Soviet Russia, was very attractive for the whole world in 1919–20, regardless of the very depressing [economic] relations. An American engineer worked there at the time, and before he left he had an interview with Lenin. He told Lenin that he would convince a whole group of American engineers to come and help. The first thing that Lenin said to him was, 'But you must make clear to them how difficult the economic conditions are for us.' But that was the attractiveness [of the situation], and that is missing entirely here in the GDR.

J   Can you say more about what this attractiveness is when it is not economic?

JK   It is the spiritual or intellectual life. [Here] we lack critique and exchange of opinion. With regard to literature, everything is fine here. Recently a bourgeois newspaper in America published an essay that said that our literature was more attractive than in the FRG but that the social and human sciences were quite miserable. The press is boring, the media is boring—if I say it politely.

J   Do you see this as a generational problem to overcome?

JK   There are generational problems everywhere. Children are different from their parents, and understand their grandparents much better than their parents, everywhere in the world, just like us also.

J   But are these problems more intense in the GDR?

JK   Yes, of course, for two reasons: because the schools and universities are endlessly boring and there is little to do in the leisure time.

J   Do you think that old men are able to change?

JK   What? Excuse me?

J   Are old men able to change?

JK   Yes. I just wrote a book about that, a monograph, eighty pages, about old learned men and their peculiarities and changes with respect to other times.

J   How is it possible for them to change. Don't most old men find themselves incapable of changing?

JK   *Ach*, they change really wildly. I mean, you just have to look once at a dry, boring, stupid Party functionary. As soon as they become emeritus, they become reasonable people.

J   Why do they have to retire in order to become reasonable?

JK   You know, they have to leave their old tracks, get out of the daily atmosphere. This exercises great pressure on them without their being aware of it. Instead, it is the atmosphere in which they are at peace to live, without noticing any form of pressure. Then they come out to the people, from the desk to the people.

J   Was there an experience that took away your belief, or did that happen slowly.

JK It was the Khrushchev thing; [it set in motion] a thaw, a great big sigh. I wrote the critical Stalin chapter in '77—you know, *Dialog mit meinem Urenkel* [Dialogue with my great-grandson]—which wasn't published until 1983. I would formulate the negative side of Stalin even more sharply today but leave the positive side exactly as is. When I am with Soviet friends, we are in agreement about the positive and negative sides, but they have [suffered] such horrible losses in their families and with their friends, [which means] they have a heavier weight on the negative than the positive. But naturally for me the victory in the war and the existence of our country is bound with the positive side, the radical construction of heavy industry and with that the arms industry. We are then always agreed that our grandchildren will decide whether the positive or negative is more important.

J   When you returned, did you think the GDR would develop differently than it has?

JK Yes. First, I had never thought that the economy would lag so behind the Western countries. Second, I believed that—no, you must see it as follows: The critique and freedom of opinion were more widely and more strongly developed at the end of the forties and the beginning of the fifties than today. One cannot say that [this period] was boring. You can truly say [that] about the media also.

J   The reason for this [stagnation]?

JK The reason is that we [bask in] self-satisfaction, because we are the best-functioning socialist country.

J   Are you also of the opinion that the people who steadily resettle in the West represent a great loss in creativity?

JK Yes, of course, a very serious loss. The biggest blockheads and idiots are not the ones who are leaving us.

J   Do you see a possibility for a federation in the near future?

JK No, not at this moment. That doesn't come at all into consideration. *Wishful thinking!*

    I mean, I always say that I have not given up my childhood dream of a socialist Germany. But I know that it can take many more decades.

J   Is a [divided] state structure necessary?

JK   Yes. Adenauer [the first West German chancellor] realized that right away. Therefore he began a division. And weren't the Allies enthused about it? Listen, what kind of difficulties would appear for the other West European countries [should Germany unite]!

J   May we go back to your childhood? What does it mean for you to be a Jew?

JK   Absolutely nothing. It has played no role in my life.

J   Neither as a child nor as a youth?

JK   Absolutely not, neither in school nor elsewhere.
     Were we talking about the same thing?

J   Your parents?

JK   No. They were also not devout. No, I am not at all suited to be a Jew.
     Now it was clear that he was addressing Jewishness as a religion, and only as a religion.

J   Did you feel endangered at all by the developments in the thirties.

JK   No. Naturally, I was, objectively, doubly endangered after 1933, doubly endangered as communist and Jew. But after twenty-four hours you forgot about that—except when the Party reminded you, 'Be careful that you lay off the blonde *Genossin.*' JK *expresses this a bit less idiomatically in German:* daß Du schnell die Verabredung mit der blonden Genossin beendest. *I initially thought he was referring to racism in the Party, but in his written comments to me, Professor Kuczynski corrected this interpretation: 'There was not the slightest racism in the Party. I refer to the dangers under fascism for a blonde* Genossin *to be seen with a Jewish-looking person.'*

J   You mentioned that you were friends with Brecht and Seghers. There were many Jews among the intellectuals who returned. Was that an accident, or do you think that the Jews in the twenties and thirties were special?

JK   That's very simple . . . indeed among the intelligentsia who returned, the great majority came to us and not to the West.

J   You mean particularly among the intelligentsia.

JK   Yes, in the general [intelligentsia], whether they were bourgeois or Jewish. Only one university professor returned to West Germany.

J Who?

JK Rotfels.

J But how do you understand the fact that so many of the intelligentsia and communists were Jews?

JK *Ja.* Naturally, many Jews were distressed by the dominant anti-Semitism and felt drawn to the Social Democrats and communists—or they were free-floating leftists.

J How do you define anti-Semitism?

JK That the Jews are seen as inferior and Semitic, in particular as a race, not as a religion.

J Do you see Jews as a religion now?

JK Now here? As a religion, of course. *He is referring to the official definition of the East German state.*

J In Israel [Jewishness] is not only a religion. There are also many [people] there who are not believers, much like yourself.

JK But even the people who have converted to Reform Jews are in a difficult situation. The entire drive of the rightist Likud block is [to mandate] conversion to Orthodox Jew.

J But there is a choice there?

JK Yes, yes.

J Have you experienced any anti-Semitism since 1945?

JK Yes, of course. I mean, it went with the situation after '45. The population was raised that way, wasn't it? But I will tell you another story. As my friend [Johannes] Becher [head of the East German Writers' Union in the 1950s and 1960s]—are you familiar with his name?—drove through Mecklenburg in the fall of '45, he asked a female farmer, 'What astonished you the most as the Soviet troops marched into your village?' He hoped that she would say that they had behaved respectably. But the farmer said that they didn't have any horns. And now you are asking me about anti-Semitism.

J What is your position toward Israel?

JK Toward what?

J Toward Israel.

JK Like toward any reactionary state.

J Did you also have this opinion immediately after the war? Did you oppose the founding of a state for Jews?

JK I have nothing at all against that, nothing at all. Why [should I]?
    But they are a very reactionary society, racist and arrogant. I am
    speaking of the state, of the regime.

J   Did you not think it was necessary back then, that the Jews
    needed their own state?

JK I have absolutely nothing against that. Why not? They even had
    their own republic within the Soviet Union. No, I have absolutely
    nothing against that. The Soviet Union was one of the great
    supporters for the founding of an Israeli state.

J   What is your relationship to the present Jewish Community here
    in the GDR?

JK No relationship at all. None. But I am happy that they come
    together and carry on their religion and culture happily with each
    other.

J   There are very few Jews in the GDR today. How do you react when
    someone says that perhaps in twenty years there will be no more
    Jews in the GDR?

JK I don't believe it.

J   There will always be some?

JK Yes, certainly. They will be devout and they will multiply. *He is
    being facetious.*

J   How do you view the development of the Republikaner [a right-
    wing, xenophobic political movement] in the Federal Republic?

JK That's something that can be very dangerous.

J   Would you describe it as neo-Nazi?

JK When you belong to a Hitler cult and don't protest against it, then
    I would call that neo-Nazi.

J   Are you surprised that this [movement] is now happening in the
    Federal Republic?

JK I am surprised that it is so large.

J   Would you be surprised if it developed to the same degree in the
    GDR?

JK No, not surprised, but it will not happen here.

J   Are you sure that it will not happen?

JK Yes.

    *Within a year of this interview, the neo-Nazi movement had ex-
    panded in both parts of Germany.*

    When we compared the neo-Nazis to the skinheads in the GDR, JK *claimed that the problem was due to lack of real communication with the youths.*

J   How should one carry on with the youths?

JK   Give them some other possibilities. In school [here] they are expected to be model students. And at the university the schooling goes further. I always say, Marx and Engels would never be allowed to take the *Abitur* [the German high school graduation examination] here.

     My friends, it is already after ten.

J   May I ask one more question? With respect to Germanness, have you always seen yourself as German?

JK   Yes, of course.

J   Because of fascism, did you never fear coming back?

JK   I knew it was a huge task to transform the people. I held many assemblies in the workplace, where there was wild anti-Soviet [sentiment], especially during the time [we were paying] reparations.

J   What does it mean for you to be German?

JK   To have been raised in the German culture. Obviously, today I am a member of the German nation. Because of a few years before '45, which are quite separate, you cannot forget the preceding thousand years.

The following text is from a one-page letter JK *wrote us on 2 May 1991 reflecting on the events since our interview:*

     Today, eons since the summer of 1989, I would above all work out two aspects [of my analysis] much more clearly and sharply: Stalinism in the Party and the superiority of capitalism in the FRG, especially with respect to labor productivity and democracy.

     One must recognize clearly the following: The social formation of the German Democratic Republic was a mix of socialism, capitalism, and feudal absolutism. Socialism found its expression above all in a net of social security—in contrast to the Federal Republic, here there were no unemployed, no homeless, nobody needed to go hungry, not even for a single day.

     And despite this, there was no emigration out of the FRG into the GDR of millions of unemployed, of 10,000 homeless, of

100,000 who were still hungry every day of the year. The entire societal atmosphere, the lack of democracy, the authoritarian system, the constant surveillance, repelled the people in the FRG.

Today the people in the former GDR feel especially the loss of the extensive social net. To them, the worst aspect appears to be the enormous unemployment. But also, the penetration of criminal and racist elements from the FRG has led to insecurity among the people. Anti-Semitic telephone calls astonish no one any longer.

We can now ascertain in the former GDR not only an economic, but also a social and cultural catastrophe. Without a doubt, the relationships have become more democratic than before.

Since this last statement, Professor Kuczynski has continued to publish books and articles that elaborate, question, criticize, and above all historicize the various positions he has taken in the past. His most recent books are Kurze Bilanz eines langen Lebens *[Brief account of a long life] and* Frost nach dem Tauwetter *[Frost after the thaw], both published in Berlin in 1993 by Elefanten Press.*

'I feel stranger than ever in my former country.'

Born 1945   England
1947–   East Berlin
             (1968–1969
             Moscow)

*W*hen we entered her office at the prestigious Henschel publishing house, down the street from the large Oranienburger Synagogue in East Berlin, in September 1989, Susanne Rödel was speaking by telephone to a friend in the Soviet Union in rather loud Russian. After finishing her conversation, she greeted us warmly, although not without caution. She let us know that she did not want the interview to last more than two hours and that it must be kept anonymous. Her further interactions with us were also characterized by frankness and a straightforward manner. She was an articulate and strong person who reflected on what she said and presented her ideas coherently, clearly, and forcefully. She moved through the questions smoothly, answering them completely and concretely. One had the feeling that she knew what she thought about everything. SR was independent-minded and developed her own positions on individual issues, never resorting to generalizations.*

SR My mother comes from Frankfurt am Main and my father comes from the former German city of Breslau, today called Wroclaw. My parents managed to get to England with the help of the Quakers in 1939. My mother was fourteen and my father, sixteen. My mother comes from a good, middle-class family. My father's family was somewhat better off. After Kristallnacht my grandfather was sent to Buchenwald for a few months. *Around thirty thousand Jewish men were rounded up in the days after 9 November 1938 and shipped for weeks or months to Dachau, Buchenwald, and*

Sachsenshausen. They were to be released when a real possibility for emigration became available (Benz 1991a, 25).

[He was, however,] then released. The English had limitations for immigration and really only wanted to take relatively unqualified people. Since my grandfather worked as a lawyer in a ministry, he didn't get travel papers to England. He was only able to get papers to go to Shanghai. The English really had very stringent limitations, especially for men. My grandfather was a man who could think and play piano but couldn't boil an egg. He was terribly afraid to go to Shanghai and decided to stay here. After trying to hide a few times, he wound up killing himself the next time the Nazis came [for him]. Actually, we just learned a few weeks ago exactly when this happened. A friend in Frankfurt found the information in a Jewish chronicle.

My grandmother bought a passport for my mother and went to England through the Quakers, as I said, where she [her mother] was taken in by a Jewish English family. My grandmother arrived with the last airplane from Germany to England on the day before the war began, 30 August 1939. In England my mother met other German immigrants and became acquainted with the communist youth organization, which was already called at the time the Free German Youth. Other people probably have told you about this. In my mother's memories, this was, I think, a very good time there. As antifascists, these people identified with the Soviet Union, of course. My mother became a communist in England. They believed that they could build a blooming communist paradise in Germany. That is the reason they came back in 1947. I think that it would have been impossible to come back if one didn't have this faith. I have an aunt who went to the United States and still lives there. She wrote us just last week that she now is prepared to come to Germany in order to see us. She will be seventy next year. She could never before take the step to come back to Germany. My parents were active communists here. My father also came back in 1947, and in 1949 he became the head of the Free German Youth.

J And when were you born?

SR I was born in England in 1945, my sister in 1947. My parents came back to Germany with these two little children. My father was fatally injured in an automobile accident in 1949. Now we have all the important dates.

My mother was always of the opinion that the single obligation of the Jews was to react with sensitivity to all manifestations of nationalism and for this reason not to advertise our being Jewish. When I was about fourteen or fifteen I was very interested in where I came from, who I was. I was looking for my identity. My mother reacted very aggressively when I tried to find my Jewish roots. She always told us we did not do anything for it, that in the war we were on the other side. We were born into the position that put us on the other side [i.e., being Jewish and communist]. We then understood what she meant and from that followed the other. We weren't communists because of our insight or intelligence; rather, we came to communism through our being Jewish. She was always afraid that if we children identified too strongly with Judaism, this could lead again to anti-Semitism. And I think she has changed her mind only in the last few years. But earlier the situation was quite different. I really think that she was right, that it is our major duty, after the last catastrophe that happened here, to be very sensitive to nationalism. SR *presents her mother as implying that Jews inspire anti-Semitism and that if they will only be invisible, then no one will bother them. After the war many Jews did indeed react against their Judaism in order to 'protect' themselves from future prejudice or pogroms.* SR *herself shifts from ethnic identity (i.e., being Jewish) to national identity (i.e., being German) and seems to equate the two.*

And Jewish nationalism is just as offensive as German or Russian nationalism. *This view of nationalism was often behind* GDR *Jews' criticism of Israeli politics.*

My daughter sees it differently. She is sixteen and is very interested in what is going on in the Jewish Community, even though she is not religious [*gläubig*].

J   She is a member of the Jewish Community?

SR   She just applied but hasn't yet been accepted. I don't have anything against it, although I myself couldn't do it. I think that it is a religious Community and that since I am not religious, I shouldn't belong. But of course I also know that we have a different history than all of the others outside the Jewish Community. We carry our family's history along with us. *Although she does not identify with Jews religiously,* SR *links herself to Jews through tradition, history, and common experiences.*

The histories of our families always have to do with persecution or with exile, and it is the same with our circle of friends. My parents' friends are, naturally, other people who were in exile. All the children of these people know each other because our parents all had the same fundamental histories and experiences [*Ausgangsbasis*]. For example, when I told my mother about the man who would become my second husband, she asked, since he was fifteen years older and was born in 1930, what he did during the fascist period. I don't think that my husband was in the army, because he was simply too young, having been born in 1930. Those who were born in 1929 had a very different fate. One year made a big difference back then. But I think that my mother would have never understood if I had married someone who had been in the Nazi army, even if it had been only for a short time and in a completely innocent way.

J   Did she feel like a German? Was she integrated?

SR   No. You know, I think this is our biggest problem. I also don't feel German; I don't feel Jewish; I only feel that I am a GDR citizen. And this is the problem: that in relationship to everything that came before, to history, neither to one nor to the other do we feel that we belong. When we meet people who say, My great-grandfather had this house, and then my grandfather, and then this happened and then that, then you notice that you have a different history.

This weekend I was in the Federal Republic, and for the first time I stood in the street where my mother was driven away, in Frankfurt am Main. My mother had never managed to go there. She was afraid of the memories. I came back to East Berlin yesterday and she was happy, when I told her that in the one and a half hours free time I had in Frankfurt I went to her street. But she herself is very afraid of the memories. I don't know if she will ever overcome [*überwinden*] them. *Although* SR *uses the term* überwinden *rather than* bewältigen, *the term favored by West Germans to describe the process of coming to terms with the past, her remark about her mother shows how the terrible events of the Nazi period cast an indelible shadow on the present. While the notion of memory—in Hebrew,* zakhor—*has always figured prominently in the Jewish spiritual and religious tradition, the Holocaust has unfortunately added an entirely new dimension to the responsibility of remembering.*[1]

J   Is she afraid of the people in the West, as former fascists?

SR   No, she is afraid of the memories of this terrible time. Naturally, one can imagine that the houses out of which the Jews were thrown in 1939 were quickly given to the Nazis. And that was their property then. It is imaginable that children of Nazis could now be living there and that they would open the door. It is not necessarily the case, but it could be. *This idea of finding Nazis or children of Nazis in one's former home illustrates how the home, identified with security, protection, and memories of intimate relations, becomes the locus of fear and anxiety for the refugee who was forced to abandon this trusted space.*

J   Could you perhaps begin with your childhood, with your integration as a GDR citizen? Your memories?

SR   I had a very good childhood. I can say nothing else about that. My parents felt unified with a great ideal, with a great dream. My grandmother joined us later, after we had an apartment here in Germany. My grandmother loved my father and mother, and although she never became a communist, she shared in this great dream. I was the only one in my class who didn't have to go to religion class, and I was for a long time the only one who wore a Pioneer kerchief [the kerchief of the Young Pioneers, the communist youth group]. We were the only ones in the street who had African students in our home, because we didn't have anything against blacks and my grandmother and mother could speak English and the students could speak English. *It is interesting that* SR *characterizes a 'benefit' of emigration to an English-speaking country as the bridge to students of a different racial background.*

They felt comfortable in our home. We children felt like heroes because we could reproach all the others and say that we were against racial separation.

I remember the very primitive interpretations [that came up] when fascism would be discussed. No teacher could explain who the Jews were, and it is very difficult to explain. Mother also couldn't explain it to me, since she didn't want me to think that I was something special. Mother clearly wanted me to be assimilated. s R *uses the term* assimiliert *rather than* integriert, *implying by this usage that she would become just like everyone else by giving up that which made her different, namely, her Jewishness. The distinction between these terms is played out today in the debate around foreigners living in Germany.*

I can give an example of my daughter, when she was ten or eleven, saying to my mother, 'Grandma, please tell me, What am I really? Am I a German [*Germanin*] or a Slav?' *By using the term* Germanin, *an ethnoracial term, rather than* Deutsche, *her daughter is asking about her relationship to Germany based on blood ties.*

She thought that the Jews were Slavs. My mother was horrified and asked, 'Who is asking you such things?' Andrea answered, 'I am asking myself these questions.' My mother turned pale and said, 'But no one can see that by the way you look.'

'She has such a pretty nose and such light hair.' 'No one can tell by looking at you.' Do you understand? This all sounds so funny, but it is very deep, this [sense of] persecution [that she had]. She was born in 1924. In 1933 she was eight or nine years old and she saw her father, whom everyone respected, having stones thrown at him. This lies very deep; it is a trauma, something that she has never forgotten. Lately we have talked with her a great deal about these things, and she has worked through some things [*einiges gelöst*]. But, for example, she did not want my daughter to have a Jewish name. I wanted to name her Miriam. She definitely did not want that. She said, 'Do you want everyone to know immediately that she is a Jewish child?' I think one can understand this in our parents' generation after seeing what they experienced. I still don't feel like a German. Since I studied Russian, most of my friends, and my best friends, are in the Soviet Union. And many of them are Jews, although I don't think that I sought them out. It just happened that way.

You ask why my parents were somewhere else, why the history of my parents was so different. Perhaps I worked that out with my Soviet friends. I had many friends there who never wanted to come to Germany. They had had terrible experiences under fascism. Although we never talk with our Soviet friends about Jewish problems, they are there, and I simply was not on the [German] side because of my birth. When I stand with Soviets at Buchen-wald, I feel no difference [between us]. The first time [I went to Buchenwald] it was very bad. I had good friends during my stu-dent years and we went to [the camp] because they wanted to go, and suddenly as we stood in front of the gate there was such a feeling of alienation. SR *distances herself from Nazism and being German through her Jewish ties to the Soviet Union.*

They didn't know [because of my history] whether [I would feel that I would belong to them]. And when I said that my grand-father had been there, then everything changed. One carries on the guilt. *Because her grandfather had been at Buchenwald and suffered at the hands of the 'Germans,' SR is 'freed' from any guilty associations of being German, even GDR German.*

And even though I think that my generation of Germans is not directly guilty for what happened, still one has to confront this situation. It is all probably easier for me. I notice that even with my countrymen. When you are at international conferences, for example, in Moscow, and you are introduced as a German, I have the impression something stands between us. There was a Cana-dian there, and he was Jewish, and then there was an American there, and he was Jewish, and they ask you, 'What did your par-ents do [during the war]?' You answer and then you need not say anything more. That is a basis [for understanding], and then it's clear. Then it goes much better. Maybe that was only a coinci-dence. I don't know. *For SR being Jewish creates allegiances that transcend national identifications in a vein similar to socialism's pro-gram to eliminate nationalistic rivalries in favor of universal soli-darity.*

J How did it begin—your relationship to the Soviet Union?

SR For us children the Soviet Union was the land of our dreams. We thought that everything there was wonderful and we believed all the fairy tales. And I also had this fairy-tale consciousness. Then I got to know wonderful people in absolutely un-wonderful cir-cumstances. Have you been in the Soviet Union?

J No.

SR The people there are so wonderful. That was the most essential part of it for me. Naturally, my understanding of the country came through knowing these people, without seeing it [any more] as a fairy-tale country. But it is my spiritual homeland.

J   And your relationship to England?

SR   No, none at all. I could speak English. As a child I couldn't speak German. Then my parents were afraid that I would stand out here. It was also an artificial situation. So they stopped speaking English with me. The English that I now know is what I learned in school. I can speak Russian very well and don't trust myself to speak English. I studied in Moscow and was friends with an American couple. The mother of my friend had had the same fate as my parents. We are still friends, and the mother comes every year. And my girlfriend comes to visit. And although she only comes every seven years, when we see each other it is just as if we parted yesterday from our dormitory. I think it is this way also because our parents had the same kind of past or at least a similar past.

J   Can you read English?

SR   Poorly. You know, I can in theory go to the British embassy and have them give me a British passport. Since I was born in England, I am an English citizen. I don't need to do this because I don't have any relationship to England. *SR's discussion shows how the issue of nationality and citizenship which in the former West Germany was connected through race and ethnicity was largely transformed in the* GDR *to an ideologically based notion where* GDR *citizenship precluded ethno-national identifications with a people. She was clearly enculturated first as a* GDR *citizen, to a much lesser extent as a German and very little as a Jew.*

   I am grateful to England because they saved the lives of my parents, but otherwise I don't have a relationship to this country. I would be ashamed to go to the embassy and ask for a passport in my terrible English. *For* SR, *as for other exiles, speaking—or in this case not speaking—the language represents one of the major links to belonging to a national group. In the case of* SR's *relationship to the Soviet Union, however, this national group links her to a spiritual home but not a nation. This may be because she speaks Russian and feels connected to that particular group within the Soviet Union.*

J   You didn't come to the GDR with an English passport?

SR   No, with an English birth certificate.

J   And your parents—did they have English passports?

SR In England they had them, but they certainly had to give them up.

J Was that a subject of discussion for your parents in England? I mean, did they always think that they would return to Germany?

SR Yes, they wanted to come back and to build here a paradise on earth. That's the way it was then. They were young: mother was twenty-five . . . no, twenty-three: my father was twenty-five. They had incredible dreams and ideals.

J When did you begin to think critically about the GDR or about specific political situations here?

SR You know, I always was a critical thinker, but earlier on I thought, My Party is also thinking critically and the others are conservative. I think critically together with the leadership of my Party. Probably as a student I understood that these things were not the same and that I didn't have the same opinion as my Party leadership.

J That was in the sixties, when you were a student?

SR Yes

J Was that connected to any particular event?

SR No, it wasn't. I think it was a continuous process of looking around. I can't specify it. So if you want to hear that it began in 1968, you won't. *SR is referring to the important events in the East bloc, like the occupation of Czechoslovakia by the Soviets with soldiers of five Warsaw Pact states, including the* GDR, *on 20–21 August 1968, not the events surrounding the Shah of Iran's visit to West Berlin. The East had its own set of events that sparked opposition.*

It started before that. I think that I have a lot to thank my Soviet friends for, because I learned from them to see things differently. [These are] people who look at things very broadly. Russian intellectuals always think by comparing and have always done their thinking by making comparisons between the United States and the Soviet Union, whereas we always made the comparisons between the GDR and the FRG. And the prism is much greater when you think of U.S.-Soviet relations.

J In any case, we would like to ask about 1968 and your attitude toward those events.

SR That is difficult. Two days after the [Soviets] marched into Czechoslovakia, I was on my way to study in the Soviet Union. I didn't have Western radio or Western television. On my way to the

Soviet Union, in Warsaw I saw a railroad station full of Hungarians who didn't know how they were going to get home, who couldn't get to Hungary from Czechoslovakia and were traveling to Hungary via Warsaw and the Soviet Union.

I noticed that two days after their march into Czechoslovakia the Soviets suddenly were afraid of us. It had previously been the case in the Soviet Union that when a foreigner came to study there, your living quarters were two small single rooms in a small apartment with a Soviet citizen. In that year they put two foreigners together. [I lived there with] Kate Katzenstein. *This is Kate Leiterer, whose story appears in chapter 9.*

That had never been the case before and is no longer the case. They had a floor for foreigners because they had always been of the opinion that the Czechs had been their most loyal friends. And that had been the case until '68. Then they thought, If the Czechs betray us, what should one expect from the Germans? That was our problem, that as foreigners, as socialists, we were suddenly isolated in this country. That was much more of a problem for us than what had just happened in Czechoslovakia. We arrived right after it happened and wanted to have contact with the Russians. That was more difficult than anything else in that one year.

J Was it an issue that German soldiers were being used?

SR I know that I did not argue with Russians who said, 'When your soldiers came and yelled '*Achtung! Achtung!*' it was like the Nazis.' I said, 'It is just the word in the German language for that.' It hurt me that . . . that something from me should hurt others. *The word* Achtung *calls up memories of the Nazis and German militarism.*

But I couldn't explain it right. I could only begin to think about what had happened after I came back and got information through friends or acquaintances.

J In the seventies many people left for the FRG, people with whom you would have grown up. How did that change your relationship to this country, to this state?

SR None of my closest friends left. I have told you that our circle of friends was different. We were children of idealists and we stayed idealists for a long time. None of my friends left. SR*'s generation of young Jews whose parents returned to the* GDR *was united by a sense of solidarity with their parents' experiences and hope in the* GDR.

J   In 1976?

In November 1976, Wolf Biermann, a well-known political singer and critic of the GDR, *had his citizenship revoked while he was performing in West Germany. And professor Robert Havemann, the spokesman for an oppositional democratic communism, was placed under house arrest.*

SR   Those were not my friends. I think the first whose leaving affected me, although he wasn't a friend but from the circle of emigrants, was, naturally, Thomas Brasch. *Thomas Brasch is a well-known dramatist and director. His brother Peter was also interviewed for this project and appears in the video documentation.*

I didn't know him personally, but our parents knew each other. I couldn't condemn him, because I thought too much of him and because I knew that there was a basis there that was the same as mine. But no one from my closest circle of friends left. Only much later. In 1980 good friends of mine left. SR *'s life is marked by the political events that inspired friends to leave the* GDR *or at least seriously reflect on their reasons for staying.*

What was important for me was the irritation with my own country. I never saw the option—and that is still the case today— to go somewhere else. I can only tell you this: our country can only exist as socialist. If that is not the case, then there will be a unified Germany. And I think that up until now the international situation is such that [the United States] is not interested in having a united Germany. And if there is a united Germany, then I'll pack my bags. I don't want that. I am afraid of that. In any case, I am afraid now because I think that GDR citizens act very snobbishly toward citizens of other socialist countries and I think it is the same with the people from the Federal Republic. I just experienced this yesterday in the train. When I think that this can turn into a wave of German nationalism, then I will pack my bags.

J   So that would be the main reason for you to leave, fear of unity, not politics.

SR   No, you have to understand that the fear of unity is [merely] my subjective problem. My biggest problem is that I would like it to be different here.

J   How would you want it?

SR   I don't see the problem as an economic one; rather, I see that things must go in the direction of *glasnost*. You can probably only stabilize a modern society in this situation through democratization and the development of personality. I am sorry about the fact that in the fifties we had very good preconditions for society that were not promoted. There were many things here in the fifties that were really good. I think of cases where the G D R even created a better basis than the Federal Republic. And that this has stagnated—that is my worry. I think that when there is a war here in Europe, then we will all be gone. Maybe not you, but we won't be here. I am not only sad that people are leaving: I also think that this really intensifies the social tensions within the Federal Republic. *At the time of this interview, thousands of* G D R *citizens were streaming out of the country through Hungary and Czechoslovakia.*

It really bothered me terribly this weekend while I was there to see the hate that surfaces against foreigners because the people there are afraid of losing their jobs. Then the ground is laid for the Republicans. *She is referring to the right-wing party that wants to keep foreigners out. They are thought to be responsible for much of the trouble toward foreigners, asylum seekers, and Jews in West Germany.*

This is terrible that our people are obligated to think not only about our country but also about the resonance of their arrival in the Federal Republic, that it incites all of Europe. This is my problem.

J   Do you regard the Federal Republic as the inheritor of fascism?

SR   I think in the early years, of course. But I would say that because they had an organized and very qualified working class and a certain Social Democracy, essential correctives were undertaken. I understand how difficult it was for our people in the Party leadership to assume the guilt of the German people, when they sat together in concentration camps with the victims, with the Jews. I understand that as a subjective, complicated problem for these people who were interned for twelve years. But the people [*das Volk*] are the same, and these people [*das Volk*] are just as guilty as those on the other side. Just because on this side war criminals were really convicted—and I think they were condemned very severely and justly—one cannot say that the entire population [*Volk*] of the G D R are the inheritors of this victim status. It was not like that, and that is the problem.

SR refers here to a central issue that she obviously sees as a 'problem' in the GDR. Although she does not invoke the term antifascist, as citizens who were more programmatic in their thinking might, the term became a tag for the issue that SR refers to here. In short, it meant that the GDR saw the Federal Republic as the sole inheritor of Nazism, which relieved the GDR and all of its citizens of any guilt or responsibility for the crimes of the Third Reich.

J   What possibilities do you see from a contemporary perspective to deal with the past?

SR   I am in a good position. With me it is different. I don't know how people will manage with this. I think we have to have more information and facts. Once our people were able to travel and get to know other peoples, there should naturally be a more conscious internationalist politics, not just in form, as it always was in the GDR, but rather one that really touched everyday life. I really think that a few more foreigners in the GDR would do the people good.

J   Let's come back to the Soviet Union. How would you evaluate the developments, this entire transformation that is taking place in the Soviet Union?

SR   That doesn't have anything to do with the problems of Jews.

J   No, no, but you have a special relationship to the Soviet Union: it is kind of a spiritual home. *At this time none of us anticipated the mass exodus of Soviet Jewry to Germany.*

SR   This is a big problem. I think that the only chance socialism has is what has been set in motion by *perestroika*. I don't think that either the Hungarian or the Polish method—with their selling out of socialism—is possible, and [I don't think] that this method will bring stability to Europe. This is an incredibly multilayered process. Naturally, the Soviet Union is finding itself in a crisis, and no one can say with certainty what is going to come of all this. It is possible that there will still be a dramatic setback. But I am certain that such a thing wouldn't last for so long. A society that is developing democratically can only continue in this way, and nothing else. And this will also happen. What happened in China can't happen again with those people. They now know too much. *She is referring to the events in Tiananmen Square in June 1989, when Chinese protesters and dissidents were attacked by the Chinese army.*

In September 1989, when the stream of citizens leaving the GDR became a flood, Tiananmen Square was invoked as an example of what could happen in the GDR if protest became too strong and the government struck back.

In the four and one-half years [since the changes in the Soviet Union], there has been so much information there that the people will not let themselves be subordinated. They have become much more self-reliant and incredibly political. This is a great hope for me, and if it doesn't work then I will be very sorry.

J   Do you see, therefore, in Western democracies, in the capitalistic order of things, any possibilities for yourself—that you could find a home, someplace you could go to?

SR   Only if I had to. I can talk wonderfully well with colleagues—although I really don't know so many—who are working in the same field. That is no problem at all. It is not difficult at all to find a common language with leftist intellectuals in the Federal Republic. I can't imagine how I would deal with a life that is always influenced by money. I certainly think that I can work hard, but it would really bother me to have to think about money all the time. I don't know, maybe it is different in the United States. Your country is so large that in one place it is like that and in another place different again. But in the Federal Republic there is this pressure of money, that everything can be bought, everything has a price. That is very difficult for me, and I could only [live like that] when my life depended on it, or the life of my family. I wouldn't be able to feel comfortable because I grew up under different conditions. And wealth is not the most important thing for me. It wouldn't make me happy. I think it is very nice to go into bookstores and to be able to buy books in a less complicated way—here it is very complicated. I think, from all that I have heard about the way libraries run, that my life would be much easier. I would also think it was wonderful if I didn't have to wait in line to buy fruit and vegetables, but rather [could] go shopping in the evening without having to wait in line and to save time. But I have the impression that [people in the West] have to constantly think about money, and that is what would really burden me.

J   Do you think that it is possible that socialism could provide the conveniences and offer a society that was less money-oriented?

SR Yes, I think that it can be so. I only think that the way in which we have practiced it up until now has little to do with socialism. Yes, I think that it can be, theoretically.

J Let's take another direction: anti-Semitism. Have you or your husband ever experienced anti-Semitism—during your childhood, while you were a student, or in relation to your daughter?

SR No. Earlier I always said that without question there was no anti-Semitism in the GDR because anti-Semitism had been discredited. First of all, together with fascism it had been destroyed [*ausgerottet*], and second, because there are so few Jews. Now I think that this problem is much more complicated. I am afraid that it will emerge because we live so close to the West and I think that a lot of things come over to us on this side. *She implies here that anti-Semitism is produced in the West and does not emerge independently in the* GDR.

Since there is a great deal of aggressiveness here and things are not always correctly explained, there is that potential here for such tendencies to arise. Actually it is the same for me whether such aggression is directed against Chileans or against Jews. I think it is now more complicated than it was ten years ago, because people are more aggressive and feel they have fewer ways out. This is what one sees, of course, in the Soviet Union. Where there are social problems, there is nationalism. Perhaps the Jews are in a disadvantageous position here because there are so few.

J Have you thought about the situation of Jews in Germany? Would it be sad for you to imagine that there were no Jews in Germany? Is it important that there are Jews in Germany?

SR I think so. At least for the important reason that if there are no more Jews, then Hitler would have reached his goal. I think that the Jews always belonged to German culture, and why shouldn't they continue to do that? Yes, I would say that.

J That would mean concretely that children like your daughter would have to continue to produce Jewish children.

SR If they want to, they should do it. It doesn't matter to me who my daughter marries as long as he is a decent person. Whether it is a Russian, a Chinese, or a Jew is all the same. But if there are children who feel that they have found their home in the Jewish Community, why shouldn't they do that? I think that is one of the mistakes in the development of socialism here. We have been neutralized much too much and there is too little room for individualism. If one wants to [find one's home] there, then they should do it. Only I have to say that the recent fashion here of being Jewish is very repugnant. I find it disgusting when someone wears it on his sleeve in order to make himself interesting. *In the late 1980s many people in the GDR suddenly 'discovered' that they were Jewish, often as a way to find a community, especially one where discussion circulated more freely than in everyday GDR life. To screen out those who were not really Jews and simply to protect themselves, the Jewish Community in the GDR developed strict rules (based on the traditional Jewish Halakah) for membership in the Community.*

J   Do you think that is now the case?

SR I think that there is a little bit of that. One finds this with people who are not Jews and suddenly have discovered the Jews for themselves and want to get rid of some kind of parental guilt through a sentimental relationship to the Jews. That is fashion and it is offensive. It is probably natural that it is the case since for a long time nothing was done. Then there are such extreme [reactions], and one just has to get through this [phase] until one day it is all dealt with as normal and nothing special that there is a Jewish Community with its own activities and that some go and some don't go.

J   What is your reaction to Israel?

SR If there is a country that I would like to visit, then it is Israel. I cannot explain that to you rationally. Earlier on I always thought, after I read Bruno Bettleheim's book *We Are Children of the Future*, that one could study the kibbutzim as communist utopias, and I thought that they had a lot in common with presocialist ideas in the positive and negative results. After I read this book I really had a desire to go there. But I am terribly ashamed of the Israelis who kill Palestinians. Although I can understand emotionally that the Jews say, It is enough, we will no longer allow ourselves to be brought to the slaughter, it is a disgrace. I think that the English laid the ground for the situation when they left. I don't know how one can solve the problem. I have no idea.

J   Does you daughter have a relationship to the Soviet Union?

SR An incredible one, yes. Because we have such incredibly good friends there and I took her with me from a very young age. She speaks [Russian] well, and she understands [the language] very well. She loves the Soviet Union.

J   Does she still believe in socialism? Is it a part of her life?

SR I don't know. She is sixteen, and everyday we have different discussions. Last night she said to me that she doesn't want to hear anything more about politics. Our politicians don't do it right, and those from the West [don't do it right either]. [The situation] with the refugees [leaving the GDR], she can't take any more. But that can be different tomorrow. She is sixteen and this is quite normal. But when we were in Warsaw and saw Israelis, an Israeli youth group at the Jewish center, she talked to them right away. She wanted to talk with them. That interests her.

J   When you travel together, do you go to Jewish synagogues?

SR She goes, and she is the one who makes us go there. I always have that as tenth on my list. If there is time, then I go. Andrea was in Warsaw and wanted to go with us there [to the synagogue] very much. She was recently alone in Hungary, and she told me that she had seen two supermarkets and had enough: her girlfriends went to a third supermarket, and she went to the synagogue.

   SR's daughter's preference for links to her Jewish identity rather than opportunities to buy goods unavailable in the GDR emphasizes her interest in her Jewishness.

J   Whenever you are traveling, or when you are getting to know people here, and it comes out in the discussion that they are Jewish, do you have the feeling that there is something else between you that would not be there if you weren't Jewish?

SR Yes.

J   Could you describe what that is?

SR I can only say that it is not the case that I like everyone equally. Yes, there is something. I cannot describe it, I don't want to describe it.

J   Would you generally prefer Jews to Germans?

SR No, I can't say that. A Jewish person who is greedy and boring would not be any closer to me than a German who is an interesting person to talk to. No, I can't say that.

J   Was it important for you that you married someone who was Jewish?

SR My first husband was not Jewish and neither is my second husband. We never had problems on account of this issue. My second husband has nothing against the activities of my daughter—that she goes to the Jewish Community or such things. He only says, 'Don't force me to be Jewish.' No one would force him to be. But he understands [her need] completely.

J   As a last question, we often ask people how they would describe themselves with regard to all of these different aspects of themselves in one sentence.

SR I said I am a GDR citizen. I can't say it any differently. However, I realize that I have missed something by not having a history before that. I can't describe it any other way.

SR *responded to the transcript of her interview on 23 March 1991:*

Since we spoke last, one and a half years have gone by. But so much has changed here that I have the impression we talked to each other an eternity ago.

I have never kept a diary. Earlier, I didn't do it because I didn't think of myself as so important. Later, in the last years before the change [*Wende*], I wanted to. My daughter, in fact, pressed me to do it and even bought me a special book in the fall of 1988. Then I didn't write anything in it because I was afraid that the house might be searched. And after the change, time moved in such a swift tempo that I simply could not formulate my thoughts quietly. For about a year it was as if we were being pursued [*gehetzt*].

That's the reason reading my statements today from September 1989 agitated me. I really don't know if I am yet able to write down on paper in an orderly fashion all of my considerations and feelings about the problems that were raised. I will try.

My country no longer exists. My dream, to be able to see a democratic socialism built in the GDR, is destroyed. I am certainly convinced that the idea of a fair and human societal order—and this is how I always understood socialism—is not dead. But I will not be able to experience it. That is bitter. Out of the Federal

Republic and the GDR has grown a larger Germany [*grosses Deutschland*], but I have still not yet packed my bags.

In the winter of 1989–90, when I saw for the first time here in our Berlin the words 'Jews, Get out!' written on a construction truck, I was gripped by fright. I couldn't sleep. Then my sister and I took courage and in spite of our terrible English went to the British embassy in order to apply for a passport. The British granted our request with exquisite politeness.

As I stepped out into the street in July 1990 with a British passport in my hand, my first thought was, Now you have betrayed your country. But then right away came the next thought: Your country betrayed you. Certainly more correct is, You allowed your country to betray you.

And in spite of that, I am still here. I don't know where I would go, although I would very much like to go away.

I used to always think that if I couldn't take it anymore in the GDR, then I would go to my friends in Moscow. Now I understand that I have to stay here in order to help my Soviet friends. Many Soviet Jews are now coming here. I never wanted to live in a world that was ruled by money. Now I have to learn to do that. It is hard for me.

Here in Eastern Germany the original accumulation of capital, as Marx called it, is coming to pass now one more time. I can't say that I am surprised at the behavior of capital. We had studied that and that is simply the so-called Wolff's law of capitalism. That is logical for this societal order.

I am only very, very sad that our people [*Volk*] voted in such a way that so little is left over from the forty-year experiment of the GDR. One thing has become clear to me: our people [*Leute*] didn't vote against the GDR because democracy was lacking, rather because of the economic inefficiency of the socialist planned economy. The consumer society of the FRG simply offered an enormous enticement to most people. People thought that with the West German mark and German unity they would have the social securities of socialism plus the consumer blessings of the West. Now they are shocked because there are the consumer blessings without the earlier social securities, because their situation is much worse than before. The unemployment is horrible here.

It is terrible to see how we are degraded daily by the West and how our people also degrade themselves just to find their way in the new situation [*nur um den neuen Verhältnissen gerecht zu werden*].

The atmosphere in the former GDR strikes me as a carnival in a huge hospital. It is absurd and strangely funny [*irrwitzig*] how this overhasty unification was realized here by us.

Now I feel stranger than ever in my former country. My husband has been unemployed since September 1990; he is receiving pre-retirement money. He was director of the Volksbühne [a well-known theater with a long tradition] in Berlin. He left because he didn't want to have to fire his colleagues so that someone from the West could take over his theater. He was also too proud to have to bow down to the new city fathers.

I belong to the very few Slavicists in publishing houses of the GDR who still has work. I am lucky to have that.

In these new and different times here, I like that I can buy flowers everywhere and any time I want, that I don't have to wait any longer in line for fruit and vegetables, and above all that I can fulfill my daughter's dream to go to France. These are the plus points that I personally can rescue from this new time. It is very wonderful that my daughter now has the chance to see the world. She will be able to do something with that. For us, my husband and me, it is too late for that.

In the summer I will send my daughter to America for summer school. She can speak English, Russian, and French well. Then she will be able to decide for herself later where she would like to live. And when I have any money left over, I want to spend it in this way for my daughter.

My daughter is now a member of the Jewish Community, and I have now also decided to join myself. This is now more important for me than before. I also believe that I can better help the Soviet Jews who come here.

In the meantime, my mother did go to Frankfurt and stood in front of her house. During the last few years my mother has been very critical of socialism in the GDR. She grasped very well how far apart reality and her youthful dreams were. In the fall of 1989 she thought it would get better. Now, considering the economic catastrophe here and the growing xenophobia, she only says she will be able to endure it, that it won't get worse than the Nazi pogroms against the Jews.

Our people here had their identity taken away, in addition to that comes the destruction of the social [system]—xenophobia is a consequence of that.

In September of last year my American friend was here. For many years she has had an English friend in West Berlin and me in East Berlin. The meeting with both her Berlin girlfriends was her own personal unification celebration. It was wonderful as always.

I have the impression that the Americans understand us much better than the West Germans. In any case, my friend was very understanding about all of our worries and fears.

In all of these agitated months, I have not lost any of my friends. All of them have remained true to themselves. Considering the dreadful breakdown of solidarities with each other that is taking place here because of social fears, we are sticking even more closely together. I believe one is very lucky to have in such difficult times good friends and a dear family whom one can depend on.

In the Soviet Union there is the setback that I did not rule out as a possibility one and a half years ago. But I am still convinced today that it will not last forever.

I would like to do some things here in our theatrical publishing house so that our connections to my Soviet writers and theater friends do not come to an end. I hope very much that the Germans will still be interested in Russian culture. The future in Europe can only be peaceful when Germans and Russians act together, only then.

'I was raised to be a radical Stalinist, not in
the aggressive sense, but to be a naive believer.'

Born 1944   England
1947–1950   West Berlin
1950–   East Berlin

While completing research for my dissertation in 1988,
I discovered a book of interviews with workers in a
light bulb factory south of Berlin. I also discovered
that the author of the book, Wolfgang Herzberg,
was himself a German Jew whose parents had been in exile in England. We decided to contact him. He agreed to meet with us but
quickly added that he was not agreeing to an interview.

In our first meeting, on 23 August 1989 in his old, sparsely furnished
apartment not far from the Prenzlauer Berg section of East Berlin, he
began by interviewing us. Unsure about whether he wanted to be
interviewed, he said that most Americans came to the GDR, took
notes, and left—there was no reciprocity, no sense of a relationship
beyond the interview. Additionally, he was already writing an autobiography, and he was working on a book of life histories of German
Jews who survived the concentration camps. (This has since been
published under the title Überleben heisst Erinnern [To survive is to
remember] [Berlin: Aufbau, 1990].) Why should he give us his story?
What did we want to do with it? What were our methodological
assumptions? Wasn't it unusual for the two of us to be interviewing
together? We answered his questions as best we could, and to our
surprise, WH agreed to talk. 'Go ahead, turn on your tape,' he said. We
conducted the interview in German.

WH did not suggest any changes to the transcript of the translated
interview, but his mother, who is fluent in English, made minor
factual corrections and additions, most of which we have included
without commentary.

wh　I was born on 24 March 1944 in Leicester, England. My mother
left Berlin in May 1939. She was born in 1921 and grew up on
Schönhauser Allee in [East] Berlin. Her mother was a sales clerk,
her father a small-time salesman. For a long time he was without
work, and for a while he ran around Berlin, unemployed, with a
hawker's tray. He suffered greatly from this. He never really was
able to get out of this treadmill—to recover occupationally. In '33,
after the Nazis took power, he suffered a heart attack, and later he
died from a stroke, in 1938, still relatively young. My mother
received an affidavit from an English uncle [that enabled her to]
emigrate to England. This uncle had no money left for her
mother, who was then left behind. She was sent to Auschwitz and
killed there.

A few letters still exist from the exchange between my mother
and her mother. My mother has written a kind of autobiography,
not yet published, where she mentions these letters, in which her
mother keeps reminding her daughter to write from England. In
an archive in West Berlin we have recently found the papers that
my grandmother had to complete before she left her apartment,
before she went to Auschwitz. Those are also her last 'signs,' so to
speak. The things in her apartment were valued at 365 Reichs-
marks. We also found an exchange of letters with the superinten-
dent of the building, who wrote to Berlin's *Oberfinanzpräsident*
[minister of finance] that my grandmother owed rent for the six
months following her deportation. This rent was then deducted
from what was left after the dissolution of her household! This is
all written down in the papers.

My father, also born in 1921, comes from Hannover, from a
rather well-to-do family of Jewish businessmen. My grandfather
had a kind of leather goods trade and was also head of the Jewish
Community in Hannover and a member of the Zentralverein der
Juden in Deutschland [the major political organization of Jews in
Germany before Hitler came to power]. Following Kristallnacht,
my father also left Germany, right after he took his mother to the
hospital—she had tried to commit suicide. He had been in training in a boarding school in Switzerland and after this in an agricultural school for Jewish boys and girls. Actually, he should have
emigrated to Israel but went instead to England. My grandmother

was provoked to [attempt to] commit suicide after her husband, my grandfather, was taken to a concentration camp, where he was beaten and crippled. In 1943 she was able to sell the family's belongings to buy [her husband's freedom] from the KZ. They owned a rather large villa in Hannover.

My uncle Bernhard, the oldest brother of my father, left Germany quite early, in 1933. He'd had major disagreements with his father, who was a German nationalist and had, when the Nazis came to power, an old German flag—I believe it was black, white, and red—in order to show his nationalistic support for the Nazis. This brother, Bernhard, who was already on the Left, took the flag down and replaced it with the black, red, and gold flag of the Weimar Republic, which led to a split with his father. Bernhard stood there totally penniless and managed to get on a ship in Hamburg as a stowaway. Although he tried to placate his father and to come closer to him, he was completely ignored.

There's one more story about my grandmother that comes to mind—in order once more to show her orientation. Much later, when she was dying, in South Africa in the eighties, a Polish Jew was lying in another bed in the room. She couldn't tolerate that— to die in the same room with a Polish Jew—and she insisted that she be taken out of the room and be allowed to die elsewhere.

I'll tell you quickly the rest of the story of my grandparents. In 1943, then, in some secretive fashion, they left Germany and went to Cuba. Grandfather worked as a boilerman for ten years. They were thus able to stay afloat before moving to New York, where they also lived okay, though nearly in poverty. By then they were well over eighty years old. Then my uncle Bernhard, who had gone from Hamburg to live in South Africa, sent for them and put them into a home for the elderly there. My uncle had built a chemical trade company in Cape Town and then had fought with South African troops in Italy in World War II. There he was wounded and sent back to South Africa. In the mid-eighties, because of the difficult relationships in South Africa, he emigrated again—to London. The South African regime was keeping hold of his assets, and he wasn't able to free the money he had earned there. Presently he lives in a small London apartment with his family and is still working for his old chemical company, with a home computer. The emigration of my uncle has never stopped.

The entire first half of the interview proceeded in this fashion, following various individual trajectories, all beginning in the Nazi period. However, while WH *presents the lives of family members as many-sided, he describes his own life in terms of only work and identity. Moreover, the narrative, marked by such confidence when he speaks of family members, becomes disjunctive and timid when he talks about himself.*

Still worthy of mention: Aunt Nan, my father's sister, has in the meantime taken up residence in America. She was also in South Africa, divorced her husband, went to Israel, where she advised refugees who emigrated from Germany. She was fired, however, because she refused to take part in the system of bribes by which people obtained better treatment in Israel. She told me that she had to leave when she declined to go along with the corruption. Finally, after various way stations, she ended up working for diplomats and came to the United States, where she worked as a secretary for different embassies. After she retired she moved to Spain and lived in Málaga. Now she lives in a home for the elderly run by Quakers near New York.

J   Whom did she marry?

WH   She married against the will of her father and later divorced the man. She later spoke about the relationship as quite neurotic. Her twin sons had severe psychological problems, and since the divorce she has had hardly any contact with them. One lives in Africa, the other in New York. Also a very difficult life history.

Now let me return to England. My mother worked as a nurse and later in a converted arms factory. My father was interned and was sent to a POW camp in Canada. There he came together with German communists. The Communist Party in England had built an infrastructure and took in young emigrants from Germany. That served as a backbone for them. The communists had a lively political life. They lived in a sort of commune, shared apartments. For these young people, because they left their parental homes at the age of seventeen, [the Party] offered psychological support, also a kind of political *Weltanschauung*. Since the Communist Party functioned as ersatz parents, [my parents] strongly identified with the older KPD members, the *Genossen*. They built a seemingly good political school system and focused on antifas-

cism, as well as on Marxism-Leninism. Thus my parents joined
the KPD. They were members of the youth organization, the FDJ,
Free German Youth.

While my father was in a POW camp in Canada, he was also put
together with Nazis. [This] helped create solidarity among the
leftist groups, who demanded of the authorities that they be separated from the Nazis, who at times attacked some of the Jewish
prisoners. After these protests, they were separated from the Nazi
prisoners and later [were allowed to] return to England if they
wanted. My father worked for the War Agricultural Committee in
Leicester and later joined the English army, where he watched
over German prisoners of war. He returned to Germany in the
uniform (and still a member) of the English army. I think that was
a decision of the KPD—that young Jews should join the British
army and take part in the fight against the Nazis. In her editing,
WH's mother replaced Jews with Party members.

J   Did he already have English citizenship?

WH No, neither of my parents picked up English citizenship, but I did
since I was born there.

J   But he was still able to join the army?

WH Yes. Many male German emigrants were in the army, mostly not
as fighting troops but in support positions. He only had to change
his surname to an English one, for his own protection.

My earliest memories of the atmosphere in England, from the
time I was three years old, are of the amazing solidarity of the
emigrants. They lived together, ate together, took care of the children together, and shared political life together. There was constant discussion about the antifascist fight, about what the Allies
should do, about what to do after the war. They were certainly
well-informed, for many of the people were well-educated and
took a Marxist-Leninist perspective. Certainly, some [of the dis-
cussion] took a dogmatic, illusionary form. But my mother later
explained to me that this opened up for her an entirely new world,
new interpretations of the political world, with social connections
explained in an exceptionally plausible, simple way.

[After the war] the Communist Party decided that all [Ger-
man] Party members should return to Germany to build an antifascist Germany—not yet a socialist one. My parents thus re-

turned to Germany. My father was more intensely tied to the Party line than my mother and thus returned without hesitation, whereas my mother had some reservations since her mother was killed at Auschwitz. My mother was also more self-reliant, also psychologically, than my father, who, as the youngest child in his family, was the weakest and raised in an authoritarian way. He also had an emotional connection to the authority of the Party.

My parents returned on a British troop carrier and finally landed in West Berlin–Steglitz, where other returned emigrants had already found an apartment for us. I still remember this: that it had been occupied by former Nazis. Swastikas were burned on the kitchen stools. This was property of the Nazi Party. We lived there from 1947 to 1950. My sister was born there. My mother stayed at home; my father translated a book from English into German. I don't remember the title. WH's *mother supplied it later:* The Socialist Birth of the World, *by Hewlett Johnson, dean of Canterbury.*

Then he went as a journalist to the ADN [the East German news agency].

Meanwhile, the Party decided that more and more Party members should go to the East to help build the GDR. We moved to a very nice, three-room apartment in Berlin-Weißensee. My father worked up until his retirement as assistant to the head of Radio Berlin International. My mother became a prosecuting attorney, first dealing with youth and later with business crime. Both of my parents had only gone to school as far as the tenth grade.

I went to elementary school. Right away it was apparent that as the child of emigrants I was fawned upon. For example, in first grade I received a toy tractor as a gift. I joined the Young Pioneers. At that time I realized that I must have an unusual background, since I was very lovingly taken in and the teachers protected me. I wasn't very good at school, especially in natural science and languages, where one had to work hard, and my parents had little time for me. This was true for many children of emigrants. We didn't get much attention at home because both our parents worked and they were often pretty tense due to their political work in the Party. *Here as elsewhere in the interview,* WH *often refers to 'emigrants,' which his mother changed to 'Party members.' In fact, most emigrants were perhaps Party members, although most Party members were not emigrants. And the lack of time with his parents that* WH *experienced as a child was due more to their intensive involvement in Party activities than to their being emigrants. Yet* WH*'s emphasis on emigrants indicates that the children of emigrant Party members frequently did not join the Party, whereas they remained marked within the* GDR *by their (or their parents') experiences in exile.*

From 1958 to 1962 I went to high school and completed the *Abitur*. I was good in history, German, and music, not so good in languages, mathematics, and the natural sciences. I was especially good in writing essays and in analysis of the political system. My own political development began at this time, in the ninth grade, as I began to question my parents' ideas as well as my own and those taught at school. A friend of the family introduced me to authors like Ringelnatz, Morgenstern, Zweig, Feuchtwanger, Tucholsky, Brecht, and Kafka. He also prodded me to think critically about this German society and about socialism. I also realized that I was at ease with his irony and humor. I found that many things hadn't basically changed, for example, the bureaucracy, the so-called 'German misery.' Today I know that all this helped to create submissiveness, this subject state, that it had helped the Nazis come to power. There was, unfortunately, a certain continuity after 1945 also.

I began to think critically about Germany and about socialism. I spoke openly about this at school, and I was praised for that by some of my teachers. Perhaps I should add that actually I was raised to be very dogmatic. I was full of illusions. My belief in our politics went so far that I refused to believe even the time of day announced by RIAS [the radio station in the American sector, which called itself Radio Free Berlin]. For me, Stalin was an exceptionally important and fantastic personality. When he died in 1953 and someone in my youth group said, 'One criminal less!' I denounced him. I was eight years old at the time! Because of that he had to respond in front of all of us kids. His parents then went to the West—I don't know if it was because of my denunciation. I was raised to be a radical Stalinist, not in the aggressive sense, but as a naive believer. This devoutness came, naturally, from my father but also from my mother. Thus this friend [who had introduced me to literature] was very important to me, for he encouraged me to think critically about everything. My own world-view developed then out of an ongoing critical confrontation with the dogmatic socialism of my father.

At the age of sixteen I went for the first time to the synagogue on Rykestraße, my first conscious meeting with Judaism. They took me for a West Berliner, since they had never seen me before. They asked me to go to the front and lead the singing. The men wanted to do some petty business with some kind of cigarette exchange with me. I said softly, 'No, no, I am also from East Berlin. I don't have anything.' Nonetheless, it was painful for me, since I couldn't go up front and lead the singing. I felt like a stranger there, but at least I went there to see it. Naturally, I read a great deal of Feuchtwanger, I researched some themes having to do with the history of the Jews, and I asked about this at home.

I have never been to a bar mitzvah, since I was not raised religiously. My parents were not members of the Jewish Community. After the war they quit. It was also a decision of the Party, but my parents would have done it on their own. They were atheists and therefore could no longer be members of the [Jewish] Community because of their beliefs.

There were a few moments, when I think back, when I became conscious of being Jewish. In elementary school I had a friend with whom I was in love. Suddenly she wouldn't play with me anymore. The other students said to me, 'She won't play with you anymore because you are a *Judenjunge* [Jewish boy].' I went home and cried.

Then, a high school teacher once asked, 'Which Judas here is counting his money?' because a child somewhere had counted his money on his desk during school time. My mother or my father went to the school immediately and complained about [the use of] this expression. The teacher had to apologize in front of the whole class. He didn't mean to be nasty or anti-Semitic. It just slipped out. Only later did he realize that I'd been hurt.

Another teacher, a history teacher, wanted to make World War I real to us by bringing in personal experiences. He suddenly began to gush about the *Freßpakete* [food packages] he sent to his mother from France during the war. I realized suddenly that something wasn't quite right. Although he wanted to make it clear that the Germans had unjustly invaded overall, suddenly he was enthusiastically talking about his *Freßpakete*. I should add that other teachers treated me very well, even favored me somewhat, especially the teacher of German. Ultimately, I felt taken care of and secure.

The first real rupture in my life was the divorce of my parents. My father had met another woman. He did not want a divorce and offered to stay with my mother but wanted to continue to meet the other woman regularly. My mother filed for divorce. By then I had a brother and sister. As far as I could tell—I was fourteen at the time—the problem was a sexual one. We were quite inhibited in speaking about it. Only later did I begin to understand better that the ideals held by my father somehow would not unfold with socialism. Therefore this was a severe rupture in my life. I took up a kind of father position for my younger siblings, also for my mother. That has not been good for me, I must say.

Because of this [changed position], I became more neurotic, though I was already disposed to that, due also to the exceptionally confusing times in which I was born, the lack of security at home, the consequences of the Nazi period and the war. My mother left Germany when she was seventeen, my father also. They were still nearly children. I have thought a great deal about this whole area of problems, the increase in neurosis due to family background. I have been in intermittent medical treatment in order to deal better with myself. You in America deal more thoroughly with these themes than we do. The result has been difficulty with the correct perception of [my]self: Who am I actually? What kind of work should I do? Still today I am unclear about this.

WH *then talks at length about the different kinds of work he has done, ranging from intellectual to physical. He describes the content of the different disciplines he has studied and the methods he has employed, the theoretical and practical aspects of each, as well as the way in which he secured entrance into particular programs or jobs. The topic his teachers assigned him for his dissertation was 'the history of the Party's idea of culture.'*

I worked on that for three years. I began to ask what culture actually is and whether this concept of 'culture' [of the Party] holds true for reality. I was almost put to sleep reading about this in these political texts. Nothing came of this work. In three years I produced perhaps fifteen pages. Then they wanted to kick me out of the university because I hadn't delivered. But the FDJ said, 'No, he should stay here to the end.' Many others like me had not finished their dissertations. This was supposed to be a 'research study' that would finish in a state's exam. But the results were practically prescribed before the research was done. The advisers for these dissertations didn't have much of an idea about how we were to go about them because they themselves were recent grads. The science of culture was a new discipline with few old professors who were methodologically sophisticated. We were given overly broad themes and then left pretty much on our own.

I also know now that I didn't have enough interest in [such a] science to be able to successfully complete such a demanding project. After my studies I wanted to go somewhere and hide. [In the GDR] each student was assigned a place of employment. I was supposed to work with Urania, an institution that popularizes [cultural] science [for the general public], somewhere in the provinces. I rejected that. Then I went searching for work on my own. I began as the head of the club in a large company, in a light bulb factory. I did 'culture work' for the labor union for three years.

A short retrospective point here about something really important in my development: In the early sixties, during my student days, I met Wolf Biermann, who at that time hadn't yet been banned from performing in public. *Biermann was a singer-poet-dissident whose provocative and critical writings and performances made him an oppositional cult figure in both Germanies. After a concert in West Germany in 1977 he was not allowed to return to the GDR. Many of the most talented GDR writers and artists rallied to demand his return. This resulted in an exodus to West Germany of a large contingent of the GDR's young, critical intelligentsia.*

He was also a Jew. What he said was exceptionally important for me. My own critique of society was leftist–liberal democratic, and through Biermann I developed a leftist critique. At that time he saw socialism from the Left, originating from the ideals of

Marx and Lenin. For me that was a key for my own private development. It advanced my understanding of the determinants of my own position. The point was not to engage in a general critique measured by the standards of bourgeois democracies but to ask how just or unjust this socialist society actually was. Was the Party authoritarian? Why was that so? I looked mostly for the causes of the discrepancy between ideals and reality. These questions are still with me today, though I've steadily refined them. That's why I went to work in a company after my studies: to see how things work. That's why I went to a club for culture owned and supported by the labor union.

There I developed many ideas. For example, I fought against a ban on [certain] activities of the youth club. I developed the concept and got the materials together for activities outside the company, in an old bar with many rooms, with a bowling lane, a small film room, and a disco. I had quite an interesting confrontation with the Party secretary, an extremely dogmatic type who stood at the top of the Party hierarchy. The disagreement concerned which pictures could be hung on the walls of this youth club. I wanted photos of the Beatles, Stevie Wonder, and Lenin— a mix of different interesting personalities. The Party secretary wanted a picture of Erich Honecker! As a result, the Party secretary dismissed the labor union chair and replaced him with a boss from the state. He made life extremely difficult for me. Above all, he wanted to discipline me. Finally I said, That's enough! After three years, I left the light bulb factory without a secure job elsewhere.

J   Is that when you began your protocols?

WH That was later. While in the factory, I became convinced that one would come closer to [understanding] social reality with the help of biographical interviews. Most important was to follow the development, from childhood to the present, of ordinary people in the company.

In any case the old labor union did recognize [with an award] my work as an 'activist' because I proposed some new ideas. But after that confrontation I realized that I couldn't realize those ideas there. So I tried documentary film. I wanted to document the life histories of contemporary people, ordinary people, not those of some of [our] 'esteemed' personalities. For three years I worked freelance with television and with documentary film-makers, as assistant to the director, as researcher for youth and children's programs. Over time I realized that I wasn't assigned any independent work, that I always had to work as an assistant to others. I couldn't work with my own ideas of documenting on film the life histories of ordinary people.

The reason for this was that the mass media [in the GDR] was strongly controlled by ideology. You were to show only people who were positive examples, who would tell how well they performed their work or how they were political in the sense that the Party used the term. It was made extremely difficult for us to allow people to talk about their own everyday experiences—unless they immediately portrayed some positive hero, in which case it was erroneously believed that the viewer would mimic [the hero]. This was an ideological relic of Stalinism, to think that a positive example would motivate good deeds for the state. There were also some documentary films that came closer to reality, and I had some contact [with the producers], but I never was able to do my own, independent work.

After three years, I entered another dissertation program, at the Academy of Science, Division of Culture History/Folk Culture, that is, ethnography. *WH describes how he researched the personality development and manner of life of workers at the light bulb factory. He selected for extensive interviews twenty-five people, half of each sex, skilled and unskilled, from nearly all divisions of the company. The transcribed interviews filled approximately three thousand pages. In addition to problems with the evaluation and analysis of the interview material, WH had political disagreements with other people in the academy due to his continued support for Solidarity in Poland during a period when the East German government officially disapproved of Solidarity's activities and broke off many ties with Poland.*

As I couldn't extend my studies any longer and I had no desire to analyze the material in the way expected, scientifically, I decided to write as a freelance author. In the seventies I wrote songs and poems. My brother is a rock singer and thought my texts were interesting. In the early eighties he began to use these texts in the rock scene. *The song texts sung by WH's brother, André, for the punk rock group Pankow, were an instant sensation in the* GDR. *The name for the band—Pankow is the area of East Berlin where most of the political elite lived up to the eighties—as well as the concepts behind the lyrics, which focused on the political and the everyday, were* WH*'s ideas. He credits the band for changing and renewing the landscape of rock in the* GDR. WH *supported himself with money earned from the lyrics.*

I reworked the materials from the oral history project and published them in my first literary documentary book, *Nichts wird mehr so sein, wie es war* [Nothing will again be as it was]. This was published in the West under the title *Ich bin doch wer* [I really am somebody]. *The public reception for the book was very favorable. The difference in titles is revealing: The East German title indicates a concern for telling progressive history; the West German title fits the book into the antitotalitarian theme by focusing on the assertion of individual identities in a society where collective forms of expression were preferred.* WH *tells us about the only textual change demanded by the state censors.*

A worker had said, 'Then I had a child by a Russian.' In the publishing house they said, 'No, that's going too far. You may not tell the whole world about rape by the Russians.' Completely crazy! I then went to the Russian embassy, to their cultural attaché, and asked, 'Tell me, are you actually against this being said in public today?' He said, 'We don't interfere in the domestic affairs of the GDR.' That meant that he had nothing against [printing it]. For quite some time GDR books had dealt with the fact that this had happened. It was totally idiotic. The passage was then somewhat toned down. A knowledgeable reader would in any case figure out that while in a camp the woman had a child by a Russian.

As I said, the book sold out—not a bestseller, but since we didn't yet have this kind of documentary literature, where one probed biographies in detail, it was something new here.

We asked about WH*'s project on the life histories of German Jewish survivors.*

Naturally, I came [to this idea] because of my own life experiences and the roots I have in German Jewish history through my own family history. I bring a special antenna and sensibility to this theme. I feel a responsibility to make this clearer in public life than it has been. The general interest [in Jews] has grown a great deal.

J   Could you speak about your own Jewish identity?

WH   That's complicated. I tried once to disassemble that into different levels. First, I am German, because in the broadest sense I was raised in German, not in Jewish, culture. Second, I am a GDR German, because I was raised in this part of Germany, in this cultural milieu, in this society, and I've been strongly influenced by it. Third, I have a critical Marxist-Leninist way of thinking. Then, I am a Berlin resident. Perhaps it's not correct to put these in this order. They are all components of my identity, and I am also, of course, a Jew.

What do I understand by 'being a Jew'? First, ethnically I have a nature [*Naturell*] that is different from the German nature. I have a different temperament, which the Nazis called race. I reject that [idea], but I think that 'nature' isn't too bad, because both of my parents were Jews, and naturally I find that I also share a piece of oriental nature. This conception is somewhat heretical, but it is my opinion that I must define myself as Jewish at least ethnically. I am also determined by the special social structure of the Jews. I ended up in an intellectual occupation, in a journalistic-artistic one. My father was a journalist, my mother a prosecuting attorney. Those are traditional Jewish occupations.

I am also marked by the particular residences of the Jews. Berlin, naturally also the English emigration. I'm also marked through the special connectedness of Jewish history, also Jewish religion, though not in the sense of belief. I feel tied to the human values of the Jewish religion. Often I find an unusual wisdom there that is important to me—how the Jews as humans, so to speak, have reckoned with history in their lives.

[Although] I don't take part in traditional Jewish culture [or] rituals, I know how important they are. I am also connected with Jewish writers, scholars, and artists. I feel connected to the Jewish Community here, though I won't be a member as long as they do not open their doors to atheists. You cannot demand, I believe, from atheists that they go to the synagogue. But I do go to the activities of the Community, [because] I am interested in all of the Jewish themes.

I am also, I want to say in closing, naturally in a certain way bound to Israel. It's clear to me that the founding of the state of Israel is an exceptionally important point in Jewish history, a resource for Jewish people, who live dispersed over the entire world. It represents an exceptionally important cultural and historical phenomenon in world history. Naturally, I am also critical of the politics of Israel. I know of the difficulties in Israel in realizing political equality. I think that the history of Israel is strongly influenced by mutual Jewish-Arabic neuroses of persecution and fear. Apart from the basic economic and imperial interests, [this history must contend with] very difficult psychological questions. I would, of course, be pleased if it would come to a peaceful resolution.

J   What does it mean to you that so much of the talent of your generation has left the GDR [for West Germany]?

WH   That has been very painful, and it has deepened my own critical position with regard to this society. Also, it deepened my critical attitude toward Biermann and others like him. It is my opinion that socialism can only be criticized historically. It is not a matter of just proving moral claims, of showing how bad everything here is, but rather, and this fascinates me in my oral history project, to go deeper into the process and ask why this society [is] what it has become.

J   How do you view the present situation of the GDR?

In the week before our interview, the evening news showed thousands of East Germans fleeing the republic, seeking refuge in Eastern European embassies with the hope of resettling in West Germany.

WH   We are at the beginning of a process of articulating a generational consciousness, of the generation born after 1945, the first postwar generation and those that have followed. We are now at the beginning of a process of recognizing and taking over the responsibility for the history of this country. We—that means those who think about the fate of this society and are not leaving it. Those who are leaving have given up investing of themselves here, and, of course, they think they can live better economically in the West. But those who want to remain politically active here—for them I believe that their consciousness is in its initial stages of formulation, both artistically and theoretically.

There is a tremendous uneasiness, a [sense] of powerlessness, above all about how to make it better, this socialism. I am applying myself, trying to help, precisely on this point, to sharpen the consciousness of my generation. *Here* WH *is articulating perhaps the predominant demand of those critical of the* GDR *before the opening of the Wall. That demand—for a 'better socialism'—was all but lost after the Wall opened on 9 November 1989. It was relatively quickly replaced by a demand for unification with the* FRG*. Unity, in turn, meant the end of the* GDR *and of socialism, as well as embracing the constitutional democracy and market economy of West Germany.*

J　Isn't it the case that many of the most capable members of your generation have already left the GDR and are now in the West?

WH　No, there are many [capable] people here, a large artistic, scientific, and political opposition to the official powers. They are both in and outside the Party, and there is a consensus that socialism is reformable. The problem is that we have no concept, at least in the GDR, about how we can change [things]. [Among the ideas are] more openness in the media, more democracy, more autonomy for individuals and for political organizations. But [I don't yet see] a specific German way of reform. The time is probably not yet ripe.

J　Are the reforms in the Soviet Union [under Gorbachev] a solution for the GDR?

WH　Certainly, those reforms must take place in the GDR, but we need a specifically German solution. This depends on the particular history of the GDR and on the particular confrontation of the GDR with the Federal Republic.

I believe that the generation that would be able to try and solve [the problems] has not yet risen to the top of the political hierarchy. It's like this: very old men rule here, and they've all done service, especially in their resistance to the Nazis. That's perhaps not known in America, but the head of our Party [Erich Honecker] was imprisoned for ten years in Brandenburg; our head of foreign policy, Hermann Axen, was in Auschwitz; [Kurt] Hager, our head of ideology, was in exile in England; the head of our state security [Erich Mielke] fought in the Spanish Civil War. They are all old, proven antifascists who, of course, also have reached the limits of their generation's ability, including the intellectual ability to recognize problems and to deal with them.

It's also the case that the reforms in the Soviet Union, Poland, and Hungary haven't been that successful, at least not economically. Actually, things have partly gone backwards, both in social [policy] and in the economy. The GDR cannot afford that. Therefore, [reforms] must perhaps occur more slowly here, perhaps also following the old German tradition, more from above than below. That's specifically German. You can complain about it, but it appears to be simply the German tradition. You cannot get it out of the people. The belief in authority is so strong, and the ability of the individual to act democratically based on his own conscience is, to this point, just not there.

With the opening of the Wall, WH became active, together with a number of longtime friends, in formulating policy for the since-dissolved party Democracy Today. In the period of transition in which the GDR was dissolved, from December 1989 through October 1990, many intellectuals engaged in a wide variety of political activities, including, among others, participation in the Round Table, Party organization, establishing journals or publishing houses, and writing or giving lectures. WH responded to our request for a written postscript to his interview with a three-page, single-spaced letter on 15 June 1991. Following are translated excerpts from that letter:

The interview was devoted to only a very crass summary of my life history. Much too little could come [forth], also due to time constraints, concerning my inner, psychic development to language, especially my relation to parents, siblings, my own family, and my political and occupational development but also concerning Germany. The struggle for autonomy, from a naive affirmation to a differentiated, equivocal, and positive evaluation, was a painful, contradictory process in each relationship.

Concerning the political upheaval in Germany and what has followed [from that], I was, in my own estimation, thoroughly wrong in August 1989:

1. The 'German tradition' of waiting for reforms 'from above' was contradicted in a surprising way by the pressure of the street and the cry 'We are the people,' and later, 'We are one people.' This was an overtly, thank God, peaceful revolution, because

those 'above' couldn't [carry on] any longer and those 'below' didn't want to carry on.

2. My hope, the hope of most political activists in the GDR, [was] for the possibility of a democratic socialism with a human face. [This hope] was, unfortunately, not fulfilled. WH *describes the reasons for this failure and his own research on the subject. He has already published a book-length interview with Erich and Margot Honecker, obtained shortly after they fled their home in the Wandlitz suburb and before they found refuge in the Chilean embassy in Moscow. In the interview, Erich Honecker repeatedly indicated that he was totally unrepentant about his past. Further, he blamed everyone but himself for the failure of the GDR.*

WH *explains this interview as an attempt to account for the inability to reform the GDR by understanding the lives of the elite. He still thinks that socialism was a worthwhile attempt, that it is and will remain part of modern social and political philosophy. Among the reasons for the failure of socialism he lists (1) the lack of culture and education on the part of the socialist political elite; (2) the lack of material and cultural preconditions of socialism in Eastern Europe; (3) the illusionary idea of skipping over whole epochs of world history, as in the Russian October Revolution of 1919, from feudalism to socialism; and (4) the lack of necessary leadership because of the elimination by Stalinism of what remained of the bourgeois classes.*

The unification of Germany is, therefore, for me the correct [result of events]. People here have correctly sensed that socialism was not capable of satisfying their justified material, political, and cultural needs. In actuality, however, a united Germany offers greater developmental possibilities for the people only when the market economy will fairly [respond] to its social responsibility.

[Thus] I feel freer in the new Germany, which must be a social, democratic, and European Germany and must take up its global responsibility. My life has also become more interesting, livelier, more militant, but also more multifaceted. Naturally, I also now and again fear how high the rents will climb, that my books will have problems [competing] on the open German market.

I do not feel my identity as a Jew endangered. However, I would like the state to oppose more strongly with political and legal means the right-wing, radical scene. The most important point is to attempt [to have] a democratic dialogue with these youths. Prejudices, nationalism, and hate against foreigners can only be fought over the long haul, it is my opinion, not through exclusion, but through dialogue and social integration.

WH *and I met again several times in June 1993, once attending together a small colloquium in Jena on* GDR *identity. At this colloquium he argued strongly that there is a separate* GDR *identity and that it could not be seen as continuing from the Nazi period. Since our first meeting, he has been very productive, publishing several books, including a book of poems and song texts, a number of essays, as well as a book of biographical interviews with the founding members of the East German Social Democratic Party. His work continues to straddle the line between social science and art, both genres about which he is ambivalent. For the moment, he has abstained from involvement in Party politics, maintaining that its clannish nature in Germany means that one must work one's way up the ranks as a functionary before speaking one's mind. He views the attacks on foreigners, specifically the burning of homes in which Turks or asylum seekers reside, as encouraged by the ruling coalition, which refuses to understand these attacks as serious expressions of hatred and acting out of the government's own xenophobic policies toward multiculturalism, foreigners, and asylum seekers.*

Carrying on Tradition

'I am not so good in history. I always left that to my father.'

Born 1946   United States
1947–1955   West Germany,
            then West Berlin
1955–1956   Kansas City
1956–1959   West Berlin
1959–1963   West Germany
1963–   West Berlin

M arion Thimm was born in the United States in 1946 and moved with her mother, Lili Flechtheim, to Germany in 1951. Her father, Ossip Flechtheim, a well-known political scientist, was already in Germany, having been invited to work at the Nürnberg trials. Although MT was only an infant when she left the United States, she makes the point that she still identifies with America, although she could not live there. She feels both German and American, with relatives and friends in the United States but with a German husband, a physician, and two children in Berlin.

We contacted MT at the suggestion of her parents, with whom she is very close. MT was interested in talking to us but did not want to be videotaped with her parents.

Although the interviews with MT's parents do not appear here they are present in their daughter's interview and in the project as a whole. Her father liked Germany; her mother did not. Her mother's first comment was that MT 'came as a child to Germany and always complained about changing schools so often.' Her mother mentioned many times that she would have preferred to stay in the United States, but for Ossip Flechtheim the choice, as he put it, was not between America and Germany but between Waterville, Maine, and Berlin. A leftist and an assimilated Jew before he emigrated, he returned to Germany 'to get involved politically in Germany.' He hoped 'that

Germany would become a democratic-socialistic Republic, neither a copy of America nor the Soviet Union.'

We started the discussion in English, but MT *wanted to switch to German so that she could be precise. Her children came in and out during the discussion, and her husband joined us at the end. Our second interview was two weeks later. The first interview was very open-ended, and she organized it around political history. The second was less coherent, and she complained that she could not understand what we were getting at. After the interview ended, we started talking again about differences between America and Germany and her relations with American and German friends. As we were leaving, she asked whether I was Jewish and correctly assumed that John was not. We wondered how she came to those particular conclusions and why it was important to her. Would she trust me or our collaboration more? I should add that she also asked us to include her middle name, Ruth, when we identified her in the book.*

J   Our first question has to do with how your personal life and the history of the Federal Republic coincide.

MT   Very little occurs to me except that if Hitler had not lost the war, there would not now be a capitalistic Germany, and I certainly would not be here. I believe that I am a child who was conceived after the capitulation and with the thought that Hitler's dictatorship was over. I think that it is clear that my parents did it that way because they did not want to have a child before this terrible period had passed. I would also have to add that since my father always had to confront his relationship to Germany, and because of that the central part of his life dealt with Germany and the Federal Republic, my life was also affected by that relationship. *Already, at the beginning of the interview,* MT *sets the tone—about her significant relationship to her parents, especially her father—that will shape her story.*

I think I was in Germany for the first time when I was six months old. Although I don't remember this time here—it was always anecdotal for me—my mother experienced this typical postwar period in Germany. Misery and misfortune, and chaos. I experienced some of this, even unconsciously. However, it is important to tell the other side. I was not a child that was hungry:

rather a child who always was taken care of. I knew that many Germans lacked [basic necessities after the war], but I did not experience it directly.

J   When did you come to Germany?

MT I was born in 1946, September. I believe my mother came to Germany in 1947. My father was already here, as prosecutor at the Nürnberg trials. I think that the fact that there was a a state here and the possibility to work in this state contributed to my father's decision to return. That was in 1951. At that time I was four years old, and I can still remember that I celebrated by fifth birthday on the ship from America to Germany. I attended the American school. I learned German, and we had many German friends, but I was regarded, and saw myself, as an American child. I didn't feel that I was one of the German children. My childhood in America was happier than in Germany.

The term *child of the occupation* I never knew, since one used this term more for the children whose mothers were German and fathers were American. These were mostly the children of soldiers, and this was a term that was already pejorative. We were much too privileged. I felt like an American, and I didn't feel that I was one of the Germans or one of the Berliners. I felt more like a child of American soldiers that were stationed here. MT *identifies more in terms of national affiliation than in terms of class.*

But that prompted the conflict that my parents were not really typical for army personnel, and our privileges were taken away. The first privilege that we lost was that we couldn't go into the PX, and that was difficult, because I couldn't get the things that my schoolmates had. The second privilege was that we weren't provided with a house but had to look for an apartment, and this really initiated our integration. Then I lived in a neighborhood with German children where there were no American children. I still went to the American school in their school bus.

We went back again in 1955 to Kansas City. I was in the third grade and I felt like an American and not like a German. I never felt like a Jewish child, perhaps that's also important to mention. During this time I also went to 'Sunday school' [*she says this in English*], Protestant, and celebrated the holidays. I surely realized very early that my parents were different than the other American parents. They were relatively old parents according to American standards. It became clearer to me later that we really didn't belong. I said this about us later. This is a feeling that I had my whole life. I am a psychologist, and if I look at threads leading through my life, I see this issue that we didn't belong. We didn't belong to the Americans because my father wasn't in the military, spoke English poorly, and was generally just not American. We didn't belong to Germany because we weren't Germans. I spoke English to my mother for many years or when we were in a situation where the people were anti-German. I can remember that when we were traveling in Holland and France we always spoke English. One simply didn't want to be counted as one of them, quite consciously. MT's *digression from our original question about political history typifies her tendency to underplay the political events while emphasizing her personal life and the problem of belonging. She sees this problem as having to do primarily with national identification (German versus American) rather than with religious or ethnic identification (being Jewish).*

Oh, now I have gotten away from the Federal Republic. The history of the Federal Republic naturally followed me insofar as the decision to return here in 1956, to establish a life here again, arose from the fact that there was a certain security that there was a country in which one could live in safety and work. My father renounced his American citizenship at that point. It wasn't on purpose, but there was no other choice, since he had been living in Germany for four years. For my mother this was a great loss. It created a crisis, and I was indirectly affected because I had been born in America and I still today have an American passport. I have dual citizenship. MT's *notion of being American seems to be related more to the legalities of place of birth and possession of a passport than to experience.*

I think my life was really affected by the Khrushchev crisis with Berlin. Then I was in a German school in West Berlin, and everyone was running around in a panic. It was a decisive moment for me that my parents decided, especially my mother, who was very worried, that we couldn't stay here much longer, that we were in danger. So in 1959, when I was thirteen years old, I was sent to a private boarding school in West Germany. This was a compromise, since my mother would have liked to send me to a school in Switzerland, but then I would have been unreachable. Above all, I had to be out of Berlin and ready to emigrate, if necessary, and not to be threatened by possible imprisonments. *The attitude of* MT*'s mother was not uncommon for the generation of German Jews who returned. The persecution and insecurity of life in Germany was still present. The children of* MT*'s generation also grew up with this fear.*

The only thing that was different in West Germany was that coming home was more complicated. My school friends who were in the boarding school could be home in an hour, whereas we had to cross a border and wait seven hours. Things like that. We, Berlin children, were privileged and got off a half-day earlier at vacations because the trip to Berlin was so long and tiring. It was a school with about 120 children, and there were about 20 children from Berlin. MT *experiences the political* Sonderstatus *[special status] of Berlin in her everyday life as a boarding school student in West Germany.*

Yes, to the history of the Federal Republic. It was, as I said, the time of the famous Khrushchev ultimatum and a period of turmoil and uncertainty, also the time . . . yes . . . let me think . . . I am not so good in history. I always left that to my father.

MT *keeps trying to return to our initial question about the relationship of political history to her personal story, but she continues to return to everyday events, especially about her schooling.*

While I was in the boarding school, the Otto Suhr Institute was founded at the Free University of Berlin and my father was offered a professorship. It became clearer that we would stay in Germany permanently. That became clear in these years, 1959 to 1963. In 1956 the first decision was made. In 1959 it became uncertain again what we would do, since for political reasons there was the possibility to immigrate to the United States, but then at the beginning of the sixties it was decided that we would stay in Germany. I also discussed America with my parents. [As I said], we were there for a year in 1955–56. MT *periodizes her life by her sojourns in Germany or America. These moments codified one or the other identity.*

My parents were often there, and then in the summer of 1964 I spent the summer in the United States. We always visited our

friends and our relatives there. We had a home [*zu Hause*] in
America, especially with a cousin of my father's who was married
to one of his friends from school. They had a house, and that was
always a little piece of home [*zu Hause*]. *The phrase* zu Hause,
more than Heimat, *refers to a concrete place.* Heimat *connotes a
specifically German sense of belonging, familiarity, and security,
which might be located in a feeling, a landscape, or even an idea.*

They always told me that if I didn't feel comfortable in Germany, I could come any time. They thought that one would have
to feel uncomfortable here.

Until the end of high school I thought I would go to a university in America, and I still don't know what stopped me. I think it
had to do with the fact that it was not so easy to find the right
university when one was in Germany. It was difficult with a German *Abitur*. My English wasn't so good, and then [money was an
issue]. When I finished high school here, my father was very sick,
and I think it was personally difficult for me to think of going
so far away, since we didn't know what would happen with his
health. I simply missed the chance to [take advantage of these
opportunities]. I still have friends today with whom I correspond
regularly, whom I always visit.

J Were you influenced by the skepticism of your American friends
and relatives about your living in Germany?

MT I couldn't understand them completely. It actually took a long
time before I understood them, and it was only when I was old
enough to understand historically what was behind their reservations that I knew what they were getting at. It would be a lie if I
were to say that I was unhappy here. I think that my four years in a
boarding school in West Germany, with its very open and sophisticated teaching staff, contributed to my feeling comfortable. The
brother-in-law of the school's director was a member of the Scholl
group. MT *refers here to the anti-Nazi resistance fighters surrounding
Hans and Sophie Scholl, who were finally captured and executed by
the Nazis.*

I understood there that I was Jewish, but that wasn't so important to me. That came later. This happened, I think, when I was
in Berlin during my last three years of school. There was a boy in
our class whose parents came from Israel, and he was the first Jew

whom I ever knew aside from my American relatives. The fact that someone was Jewish was always important in my parents' home [*in meinem Elternhaus*], because it meant that one could trust this person, they had a similar fate, or they had been politically active during the war. *Jewish identity here is based on religious or ethnic solidarity, especially for the generation that lived through the war. Refugees had a great deal in common by virtue of the fact that they had escaped Hitler, lived in exile, and returned. Although their experiences both during and after exile may have differed, they still linked them together.*

J Communists and Social Democrats?

MT It was ideal if there were both. However, I felt completely estranged from my classmates whose parents came from Israel and were religious, even a little religious. In fact I was only confronted with religious laws when I was nine years old. We were visiting our relatives, and they were fasting. I didn't understand, but it was explained to me. I still couldn't relate to it. Our friends and relatives in America always belonged to a religious group. They observed all the holidays.

J Were there German Jews there?

MT It was mixed, but there were many German Jews. Refugees and others, nonreligious people. In school I had very little contact with Jews. I never, never called attention to the fact that I was Jewish. I knew that it was like that. I was always the daughter of my father until I got married. There were never any conflicts. I was always respected. The respect was sometimes mixed with a little fear. Of course, I was in a very small and conservative school, and my parents got involved with my classmates. I learned there that one shouldn't subjugate oneself to authority and that one needn't be afraid of school. However, at the same time I learned that one has to move carefully within power structures. The second generation, growing up after the war, is very sensitive and very careful. My children's generation doesn't do this anymore.

J What political events in the Federal Republic stand out in this phase of your growing up?

MT One's own political activities. I was at the university during the period of the Great Coalition [the political coalition of the liberal-leftist SPD (Social Democratic Party) and the CDU/CSU (Chris-

tian Democratic Party and Christian Social Union), the conservative parties], the [student revolts] of 1968, and the considerations
about the future of the Federal Republic—whether it would be a
country in which one could stay. MT *refers to the same events we
discussed with Ernst Cramer. The coalition was severely criticized by
the student movement as eliminating an oppositional voice in Parliament. This was part of a broader critique of the* bürgerlicher Staat
*[bourgeois state] and its repressive tendencies, which were supported
by capitalism and the 'establishment,' and a demand for reform of the
educational system (Lehmann 1983, 156–57).*

It was also the case that my father always intimated that we were
here with our suitcases always packed. If it didn't work here, we
would leave. My mother always indicated that she didn't want to
stay here at all, that she would leave if she could. She would stay
for the sake of the family. I always thought that they would never
go; I didn't believe this. I also didn't have the feeling that we were
waiting here with packed suitcases. Of course, I believed that if it
became threatening here, they meant what they said, but I never
experienced it here as threatening. They would have to be taken at
their word.

J   What would have been considered threatening here?

MT The rise of anti-Semitism. I think that when one looks at the
development in the last year and a half here, one gets the feeling
that if this had taken place earlier, then I would have gone to the
United States to study. *She is referring to the rise of neo-Nazi and
skinhead aggression toward foreigners.*

It was always the case that I made decisions in relationship to
America. So I never gave up my citizenship; I got married in
America to my German husband. We met here, but I purposely
wanted to get married there. I considered a long time whether I
should have my children in America. I couldn't do it because I
would have had to go very early on—since I wouldn't have been
allowed to fly—and my husband also couldn't come because his
work kept him here. So I gave up the idea and was very unhappy
when I learned that my children couldn't get American citizenship. This [would have been] so important, because the United
States still gives me the feeling of security.

J   Did the GDR ever play a large role in your life?

MT No, or just as something threatening, not as a place to look toward or in which to live. I don't like their whole state system.

J   Do you remember the building of the Wall?

MT Yes, I remember it. We were in Switzerland when it happened, and people asked us in the street if it was possible to go back to Berlin. My father said that for the people in the GDR it would be bad, but it wouldn't affect us much, since the situation in West Berlin had gotten better.

J   Do you have friends in the GDR?

MT No friends and no relatives. Some acquaintances. But I never had the feeling that because [we didn't have such close contacts] I missed much. The GDR never interested me very much. It was a country in which one could stay. MT *refers to the same events we means the 'typically German' characteristics, such as order, authority, and obedience. These traits, which are actually Prussian, are often cited in comparing the* GDR *to Nazi Germany.*

Even today, when I am at the border I have anxiety attacks. It would be awful to have to live there; I would never do it of my own free will. I'd rather go back and forth than live there for two or three months. All this authoritarianism! When you arrive, you have to register, then sign this paper; then your passport is taken away, and you don't know why. All of these things. This arbitrariness, this arbitrariness that one is always subjected to . . .

J   But isn't this bureaucracy typically German?

MT Yes, I do experience that as very German. It is also the manner of bureaucracy, how one deals with people. Certainly, in America there is also bureaucracy, but the manner is different. When one arrives in America, the immigration officers are friendly. You are not subjected to this kind of [unfriendly or hostile] tone.

J   Did you have any influence on your relationship to America?

MT No, I had no influence on my education. When I was nine years old my parents decided to give up their American citizenship, and I had nothing to say about that. I did have the feeling that one could keep some of the tradition and culture, even when one lives here. It is actually more important that one travels there and has contact with the country. I tried later to go back and live there, and I wish that it had worked. My husband tried to get positions three times, but the two systems just didn't mesh. He would have had to repeat parts of his education or we wouldn't have made enough money to live. It was always clear that we really wanted to go, but it was so hard to get the basics in order.

J   How do you feel living in the Federal Republic now, more American or more German?

MT   I think I understand these people [the Americans]. I belong to this group of English-speaking therapists. We now have contact with the military hospital, and when we are together it is all very familiar to me. I don't have the feeling that I am a foreigner or don't belong. I couldn't say that.

I think that I have internalized the fears my mother had. I never experienced what she did. I had a very nice childhood compared with hers. We moved around a thousand times—I went to five different schools and could say that I had some multicultural experience—but I never experienced it as threatening: rather as enriching. MT *acknowledges her mother's concern about constantly moving. Whereas for her mother the mobility was part of her escape from Germany through Czechoslovakia and therefore negative and threatening,* MT *links such movement to positive feelings.*

J   Do you feel threatened in Germany?

MT   I do feel threatened when certain developments take place. In July there was a podium discussion at a church conference about the identity of Jews in Germany. It was very poor, undifferentiated, moderated very badly. It was a real shame. I sat with my non-Jewish friends in the auditorium, and we all realized that my fears and uneasiness were no different than theirs. This is an uneasiness that many people have who think and feel differently, who reject racism and xenophobia.

However, I do feel threatened regarding my children. I made sure when selecting a school for my son that it was one that had little or no anti-Semitism. *Like the German Jews of the prewar generation,* MT *seems to accept that some anti-Semitism is inevitable in Germany (see Berghahn 1988 for further discussion).*

I chose the Protestant high school where they have a very active dialogue between Christians and Jews. Although I am not religious and these issues interest me more from the historical and educational side, I find this kind of school better, and I tried by this choice to shield them from anti-Semitic or neo-Nazi incidents. This has become a problem again. I think I always tried [to understand what prejudice was all about] when I explained what racial divisions in the United States meant. I think I can understand this quite well because I also belong to a minority and feel somewhat excluded and threatened. I also thought it was much worse [in the United States] because one saw the skin color immediately. I think that through my parents I was sensitized to [racism] very early on.

We concluded our first interview here. Twelve days later we picked up again.

J   In relation to the questions that we asked you during our earlier interview, we wanted to ask whether you thought that your being a woman affected any of your responses?

MT   I do think there is a difference. I could imagine that anti-Semitic hostility is stronger with men, but this is only pure speculation. For me, personally, it is difficult to judge. But I hear that the issue of identity plays a greater role for them. They are more often asked, 'Are you a Jew, and if so, how are you so?' Another [part of this, I think, has to do with whether] one feels that one belongs to a religious community—[whether] one can represent it. I never did this myself. The men whom I know are all more self-conscious Jews and stand up for their beliefs and their sense of belonging.

J   What about your mother's Jewishness?

MT   From the perspective of religion, this [has nothing to do with her being a woman]. The outside world is not well informed about the role of the woman in Judaism. This issue bothered my parents-in-law when their son wanted to marry a Jewish woman. That was a bit disquieting for them. It was something strange. In the beginning I interpreted this as anti-Semitism, until I heard that in the Third Reich they had Jewish friends whom they helped. *Like most Jews in Germany,* MT *heeds what people did during the war, especially people who are involved very intimately with her or her family.*

I think that they were afraid that something could come from somewhere that had different traditions and norms and also expectations. Afterwards I didn't even think that it was something Jewish, [but that perhaps it was] because I was the daughter of someone who was well known. Personally I have great difficulty identifying now with this whole idea that women are different, treated differently, or oppressed, because I have experienced an entirely different [kind of] socialization that makes me think that women are treated equally. I have trouble identifying with the notion of oppressed women. I think that the men suffered more during their exile; women were better able to accommodate themselves to the work they got, often very menial work.

My role as a woman is influenced by very enlightened parents, who in 1920 basically had the same ideals. I never experienced that women somehow were not treated equally in the Jewish community. There were very important women that I got to know in my childhood. Politically active women. Women in responsible positions. I was simply educated with the understanding that women were equal. In my father's field there were always very active women. I never experienced that women could not have a career. For me it was clear that I would have a profession. That stemmed, however, from the fact that because of their emigration, or really their return, my mother could not practice the profession that she learned in America. The education that she had gotten in America could not be used here. She didn't want to become a part of the social system, because she didn't feel part of it. She was a social worker, and she didn't want to represent that [profession] in the social system.

J   What about the fact that you have a socially oriented profession?

MT   First, my mother also had this profession. The other source of my interest was the boarding school where I was for four years, which was very progressive. The founders, who also established a school in America, were very rooted in psychoanalysis. I noticed that in this school they did not concern themselves very much with the psyche of the children. I found this to be in contradiction to what I knew from home. It was a milieu in which psychological problems and their relations were seen to be very important. I talked with my parents [about the way certain students were treated], and my father and mother told me that if I wanted it to be different, [if I wanted] to help young people, I should become a psychotherapist. I think that my motivation came from these kind of incidents. I decided, however, not to study medicine and to get psychoanalytic training instead, which was often the pattern then, but to study psychology. The theories came over to Germany and were very successful here, and I decided very quickly that I wanted to do that. I could have done that just as well in America.

In my parents' home there were two topics: politics and psychology. When we discussed things, it was always from the perspective of these issues. My father was always the one who was fascinated by the lives of Marx or others. Politics was too dry for me, had too little to do with people. Therefore I decided to do something else. Of course, I think that my profession has to do with identity, although I could have also turned my interests toward politics.

J   What about your political development?

MT   I never was really politically involved. I signed petitions and so on. I once belonged to a student political group. Naturally, at that time we heard what was going on, but I didn't feel compelled to go into the streets. I also thought that the others could do that, that those who didn't go out into the streets from 1933 to 1945 should now go into the streets. They could confront these events and get beaten up; I didn't have to do that. I experienced the events of 1968 very consciously. I discussed these events with others. *By juxtaposing the issue of political activism (or lack of it) against the Nazis in the thirties with student activism in the late sixties, she seems to be implicitly criticizing those who now are on the streets as latecomers to democratic action in Germany.*

J   How are you politically active now? Do you vote?

MT   If I wanted to be politically active, then I would have to be in an organization. Part of our problem has to do with voting. I voted for the first time this year. I have dual citizenship, and since I have the American I cannot vote in Germany. I cannot vote as an American because I don't have a permanent residence in the United States. But I wasn't prepared to give up my American citizenship in order to vote in Germany.

J   Do you feel more German or more American when it comes to political activities such as voting?

MT   We were in the United States in the summer as the election campaign was going on. We discussed it with our friends, and I understand what is going on. But for us, what is happening in the individual states is much too complicated. It is very difficult to judge from here.

J Do you feel particularly second-generation, the child of German Jewish refugees who came back?

MT Yes, I am very aware that I belong to the 'second generation.' I think that we are the generation that still is very alert to dangers.

J What about your friends?

MT These are people whom I know I can depend on. I am distrustful toward those in my generation, a little younger or older, who have old ways of thinking that are still there or might resurface. This kind of adherence to authority, toward the state [*Staatsdenken*], disturbs me. At work, I just had a father who we assume beats his child and his wife. He has the opinion that children should obey him. His behavior was very aggressive, and I immediately thought that he would be a typical Republican [i.e., a member of one of the newer right-wing parties in Germany]. I have to decide whether I should go to the family or not. Right away I thought, If he knew that you were Jewish! But this is the first time I have thought about such things. Really the first time. This is what things have come to in the last two years. Five years ago this would not have crossed my mind. These are the kinds of situations that one is now sensitized to. Sometimes the clients ask me if I am German or if I am Turkish or Spanish. I look different—with dark hair, and I am not so thin. *Her clients' questions emphasize how some Germans regard those whose features diverge from stereotypical characteristics—white, blond, blue-eyed—that might identify someone as being German. Since German citizenship is still based on racial and ethnic grounds, through blood, these old archetypes are still important.*

J How do you respond?

MT I tell them that I am not that.

J You don't say right away that you are Jewish?

MT No, I am a Berliner, I say. I try to figure out why they are interested in that. I try to figure out whether they are distrustful.

J Do you think that they ask that because they think that you are Jewish?

MT No.

J   Because you look different?

MT It is because there are foreigners in Berlin. For a long time there were a lot of Italians, then Spaniards, and now Turks. Now in the last few weeks the Republicans have started with anti-Semitic remarks.

J   Your distrust doesn't seem directed at a political system, but more towards authority [*Obrigkeit*]. Are you most fearful of that?

MT Yes, I would rather live in a dictatorship in America than in one in Germany. I am really shocked [about what is going on here], and I think that certain social classes quite clearly have passed these tendencies on.

J   What about your circle of friends—how do they react to these issues? Are they also Jewish?

MT Very few Jews. They are academics, intellectuals from the upper middle class, teachers, doctors, university people, and these are people that vote SPD or Greens [the liberal and leftist parties in Germany].

J   Does the topic of being Jewish come up?

MT Yes, every once in a while, but in the sense that one asks or says something, not as something special. Rather, for example, someone will tell something about a book and say the author was Jewish. I don't have the feeling that it is unpleasant for someone to be with me or that it is very important to them.

J   Do you think it would have been better if you had stayed in the United States?

MT No, not at all. It would have been impossible for my father. He wouldn't have been able to build a life there. For my mother, in many ways it would have been better. I can't imagine it for myself. I am a very different person. In America it would have been more problematic and more difficult for me, because I don't have these religious ties. As a child I never belonged to that, and only then does one belong to a Jewish community. If one's parents don't feel that they belong, then one doesn't belong at all. One has to belong to a group [in the United States]—this is much stronger than here. Here there are many people who don't belong to any group. There are many atheists and those who don't belong to any religious group. If I had grown up in the United States, it would have been difficult for me, and I don't know to which group I would have belonged. *This comment raises one of the differences between the American and German Jewish communities. Whereas in Germany one belongs to the Community [the* Gemeinde*], in America one joins a specific synagogue, which is identified with one of the branches of Judaism (Orthodox, Conservative, or Reformed).*

You asked me if I feel threatened here. I was thinking about that. I cannot say that I don't feel threatened, but I can say that I don't feel it as much as my parents' generation, because I really have a very close circle of friends. Because of emigration my parents' friends were scattered all over the world; the people they were close to are no longer there. I think that this feeling of security I have in Germany, I have largely from my friends, who are so varied and close, and from my marriage to a non-Jewish German. The people that my parents interacted with were all people who were either political or very influenced by the time in which they were living. They were also people who very much valued ties of friendship. They realized that one can only live in a circle of friends whom one can trust and who really are loyal to you. My parents found this kind of people again, and I have also found this kind of people who know the value of such friendship.

Two weeks ago I visited one of my girlfriends from school. I was with her for four years in boarding school, and although we haven't been together in this close a way since 1963, I still have deep ties to her family and to her friends. That is also a kind of multinational circle of people. The brother of my girlfriend, for example, married a Turkish woman. The other brother married an American, a Catholic American. There is a multicultural and multireligious mix. I think that I managed to compensate for this feeling of being threatened by becoming friends with people who know half the world, rather than those children who lived in my street. MT's *sense of belonging is tied to universal values and likeminded people rather than to a specific place or locale, which would traditionally be identified with a notion of* Heimat.

J   This word friendship that you keep using, is that a particularly German notion?

MT   This kind of friendship isn't very common in America. When I was a little girl, and even now, I found it so shocking that relationships in America were always based on the here and now. In those cases they are very warm and they can be intense, but they disappear if one moves away, if one joins a different club, if one changes colleges. The letters stop. This is different in Germany. MT *'s experience with friendship or close connection is not untypical for Germans of her generation, who see Americans as being warm, friendly, and open but likewise undependable and unloyal or uncommitted to establishing serious and intimate friendships.*

J Have you ever wondered why that is the case?

MT It is based on tradition. I don't know why it is this way in America. I'll never forget, when I was sixteen years old I met a woman who was twenty years old. She didn't know where the father of her child was. She had already lost contact with her parents. Then she lived three months here and then moved somewhere else for two months. Her life was made up of such stories. I just couldn't understand that, such a totally unconnected life. Homelessness [*Heimatlosigkeit*]. And when I think of my son, I am quite proud that in his twelve years he has only had to move once and never has had to change schools. No ruptures up until now. My daughter is six years old and has never had to move.

J You think this is good?

MT Yes, I think it is important. I think about the limitations of this, but I think it is important to have some roots.

On 11 July 1991 we received her answer to our request for a response to the recent events:

I would rather not say anything about the new political events. My feelings about it are like many other people's, namely, that two smaller German states are more appealing than one large Germany. In regards to the details of the reunification and to the revival of right-wing extremism, others have already spoken.

Jeff did, however, meet with her in her home once more, on 16 July 1991. The following is a transcript of her comments on that occasion:

During the past year I first had contact with a group of people who are trying to build up a psychotherapeutic center for victims of torture, and part of this group is especially interested in Jewish victims and their treatment. Because of this interest, two psychiatrists were invited to speak, and they lectured on the symptoms and repercussions that vary among victims, child survivors, and the second generation. Since I belong to this latter group, I recognize how I have been personally affected [*Betroffenheit*]. I have lost some of my feelings of not belonging that I spoke of in my first interview. I started realizing that there are quite a lot of people of my generation who live in Germany. I started working with a patient who is a child survivor and noticed how similar and painful our identity problems are.

Since the reunification and the Gulf War as well, anti-Semitism is rising again, old fears are returning, concerns and insecurity, especially concerning my children. One once again begins to think whether it is the right decision to bring children up in Germany who are half-Jewish. On the other hand, anti-Semitism is everywhere, although it is more obvious here. I still don't think it is more dangerous to live here than in France or England.

During the recent Jewish Cultural Week, Michel Friedmann from Frankfurt, who is a lawyer and member (CDU) of the city council, was invited to speak, and he emphasized that there is no Jewish identification today in Germany aside from the religious one. Cultural identity has gotten lost. He thought one should think of reestablishing this Jewish cultural identity in Germany, and I agree with that.

'I would say, a committed communist of Jewish origin.'

Born 1943   New York
1953–1954   The Netherlands
1954–   East Berlin

K ate P. Leiterer returned to Germany at the age of ten,
fully 'indoctrinated by American propaganda,' as she
says, fearful of her new home 'behind the Iron Curtain.'
A mutual friend introduced us to her, and when we
approached her about our project in the summer of 1989, she agreed to
meet with us a month later. We had two interviews, approximately
two weeks apart, at her apartment, directly overlooking the Chau-
seestraße border crossing on the Wall. Although our earlier discussions
had been in German, KL suggested that we conduct the interviews in
English. Blonde and fair, she has a very quick humor and an exceptionally outgoing manner.

J   I don't really care where you start, perhaps after your parents
    returned.
KL We came back when I was ten years of age. Back from America
    into the GDR. In 1955. I remember America [only] from my child-
    hood. I was born in New York in 1943. My sister was born in '49,
    [and it's] about that time I start remembering things. My parents
    moved [in 1949], for my father's studies, to Topeka, Kansas. We
    were moving a lot in America. On vacations we drove from Tope-
    ka to my grandmother in New York, and back. We visited some
    parks—which park was it?—Yellowstone Park. *Throughout the in-
    terview* KL *looks to us to correct her memory of America, primarily of
    its geography and of American idioms. We have deleted most of these
    questions.*
J   You still remember?

KL   These are the things I remember about America. For me it was a
      nice time. My mother was home most of the time. She worked
      part-time and studied part-time. She is—how do you say in
      America?—a working therapist, yes?

J   Do you mean work therapist or physical therapist?

KL   No, for work. For real work.

J   Oh, an occupational therapist.

KL   Yes, that's it: *Arbeitstherapeut.* I just translated it [literally]. My
      childhood was really nice, even though my parents didn't have lots
      of money. For instance, they bought an old Nash car. We needed
      the car. Nobody was walking. And trains were, at that time, al-
      ready not reliable. So we had to have a car, and they bought an old
      Nash. They painted the car in the evening in the garage. It was the
      only car in the whole town which was purple. But they loved it.
      These are some funny, nice stories.

J   Did you speak German [at home]?

KL   No. I spoke German [only] up to age five, [before] I went to
      kindergarten and school. [At first my parents] didn't want to teach
      me their incorrect English. [Later] they didn't want me to trans-
      late the things which I learned in school into German. Then we
      returned to Germany.

J   Was the transition from one language to another difficult for you?

KL   I don't remember that. I just remember that what I learned in
      school, I could talk about in English at home. But if they talked
      together in German I understood everything. When we were at
      grandmother's place we spoke German. But they talked. I didn't.

      [After leaving] America [in 1953], my father took a job in Hol-
      land. We didn't have any connections in Germany at that time.
      He wanted to find out which of his friends were already in the
      GDR. We were in Holland [for half a year], and he was working in
      a hospital there in a little town near Alkmar. That was a very nice
      half-year because I didn't have to go to school. My mother knew
      that we were going to the GDR, of course, and she preferred to
      teach me German by herself and not to send me for one year to
      school to learn Dutch.

      We had to enter the GDR illegally, you know, [due to] the
      Rosenberg trial. It was in '53. After we got tickets for the ship to
      leave America, we passed the prison where the Rosenbergs were.

My mother broke into tears and just couldn't stop. She was thinking that this could happen to us. [Therefore] we [had to] return
illegally. [Mother] wanted to visit a relative of hers, an old uncle, in
West Berlin first.

J   After leaving Holland?

KL   From Holland we went on a long trip through Germany, down
the Rhein. From Frankfurt we went by plane to West Berlin to
visit her uncle.

J   As American passengers?

KL   Yes. [Mother] played the crazy American woman who needs all
her stuff with her. She took everything along. We had eleven
pieces of oversize luggage. People asked [about it], of course. She
would say she wanted her own linen, she wanted her fur coat with
her, she wouldn't leave it [just] any place, and so on. She had never
played a crazy woman before. [Also], she had never needed anything on all her trips. Even in the concentration camp [in France,
before she fled to the United States] she had nothing. But she
played this role. And we came to West Berlin and there we met
very nice comrades, communists—West Berlin communists—
who helped us get our luggage. They smuggled the luggage here
in an old car with, you know, with three wheels. In Germany at
that time there was no rubber. And they didn't have enough
wheels. So they built cars like a tricycle, with one wheel in front
and two wheels in the back, [that] could transport some kinds of
goods. We went over [to East Berlin] with the S-Bahn and arrived
just at the time of a festival for German youth, Deutschland-
treffen der Jugend. It was every two years. May '54 was the third
one. There were flags all over, red flags and German flags.

   We arrived at Friedrichstraße. This was one day before the
birthday of my father. Their goal was to be in the GDR for the
birthday of my father, the sixteenth of May.

J   When was he born?

KL   In 1915. They wanted to be back here in safety, as they felt, of
course, that here nothing could happen to them. They came
[back] to their own communist country. *Here* KL *affirms the positive memory of how her parents experienced repatriation, whereas her
own experience of the return, as she describes below, was a traumatic
one.*

J   Had they already established contacts with old friends in the GDR by mail from the United States?

KL   No, they had only with one friend who was in Düsseldorf.

We stop the tape recorder and she goes into the kitchen to fetch the tea.

J   Let us go back to this youth festival and your arrival.

KL   My father took me in his arms and said, 'We will never go back to America again.' And what happened to me? We were on the S-Bahn from West Berlin, and my parents told us: 'Don't speak now till we arrive. We don't want you to speak anymore.' They were afraid that somebody in the S-Bahn would notice that we were from America.

KL tells us about an incident in West Germany, on the way to the East, when they were visiting a woman with whom her mother had been imprisoned in a French concentration camp. They noticed that someone was following them and ran through the streets 'faster, faster, faster, to get rid of this person.'

J   Who was it?

KL   Nobody knows. I don't know anything, but they told us afterwards that they were fairly sure that he was somebody who should follow us and find out where we were living.

J   In the United States had you noticed anything?

KL   I didn't notice anything. Of course my parents know more of that.

J   They hadn't shared all this with you?

KL   No, but maybe they will write it down now. They are writing about their lives. You can ask them.

J   Let's go back to your father. You say your father was very happy to be in Germany.

KL   He said to me, 'We will never go back to the United States. I am really happy now. We are where we wanted to get to my whole life and we will never go back to the United States.' I started to cry, terribly. I realized that I'd never be able to return to America to tell my grandmother and my school friends about the wonderful trip in Europe. And as a good psychologist, which my father really is, he was so angry at the moment with me that he just slapped me. This is what we always remember when we talk about our return and how everything started. It started with a slap.

Here my parents had lots of friends, of course, right up to the

Central Committee. Well, I don't know if they want this to be written. We will talk with them. KL *is suddenly cautious about relating incidents involving people in important positions in the* GDR. *We encountered this kind of Cold War caution with most of the people we interviewed through October 1989.*

J Were these old friendships from the prewar period?

KL No, after [my father] came to America, he went into the American army—[fighting] against the fascists. He worked as a kind of interpreter. But I don't want to tell about this. [The Americans passed] a law that foreigners who had fought in the American army should get so many years of stipend. So this person who was already back in the German Democratic Republic told [my father] to study, and when he finished his studies, he should return. My father had been afraid to contact him earlier, for somebody could have found out. Of course they didn't want to risk anything because of us two children.

When we arrived, he just called him [his friend in the Central Committee] and said: 'I am here. Now I am a doctor in psychology, and I am here.' This was '54, the first year after the death of Stalin. You know what Stalinism meant for the German Democratic Republic. It meant that all people who were returning from emigration in Western countries were not to be trusted, were put into prison or sent back. Lots of these types of things. This man told us to go to some place in the Central Committee to get our papers. The person there told us to go back to West Berlin and wait there for our papers. Then my parents said, 'Do you want a second Rosenberg Trial? Then we will go back.' My father said, 'Put me in prison or wherever you want to, but I won't go back with my family.'

But this person who had told him to [return to America] didn't give us our papers for about two months—till all our Western money was spent. We had to live in a hotel and pay everything in Western currency. Two years later this man left the GDR for the West. He was trying to sabotage [the GDR] and [get rid of the] people who were really needed. KL *then offers an alibi for the Party's distrust of her father.*

It is always hard to know what is right and what is wrong. Of course a person who had a good income in America, a good position, [is suspect]. If he comes back to this country, where there is nothing, he has to be some kind of a spy! This man [handling her family's papers] was not so very wrong. KL *is torn between affirming the mishandling of herself and her family by* GDR *authorities and justifying their actions based on reasonable suspicions of her father.*

It took two months of dealing with this person in the Central Committee and with other people [to get a legal residence].

There were also some very nice things happening [to us] nearly every day. On the street or when we went into the underground or when we went by S-Bahn, suddenly my parents turned around and somebody [else] turned around, and they flew into each other's arms. They were old friends, really happy to see each other after the war. We had lots of friends here.

J Do you remember that as a child—meeting a lot of friends through your parents?

KL Yes, finding new friends and hearing all the stories. They talked about their lives till now: what happened and how they got out of complicated situations in emigration. One of them was an officer during the Spanish War. My father had also fought in Spain. And there [in Spain], during one fight, this man got his arm cut off. My father didn't know where that man was. They met here again on the street. Imagine such things! Yes? The whole evening he just told about how he was brought into a fascist Spanish hospital. The arm started to hurt so much that he couldn't stand it. They brought him to a doctor, [who] looked [sharply] at him and asked, 'You were a fighter here? for the Republicans?' 'Yes.' This doctor had on a fascist uniform. He said, 'You will get a shot now from me, and all the pain will stop.' [Our friend] said that at the moment he got the shot he didn't know if he would still be living [afterwards] or if the doctor was killing him. [These stories] impressed us children very much. This was not a film on TV. These were living people, working, living, trying to make [the world better]. We children were always sitting and listening to what my parents were talking about. That's why we remember these things fairly clearly.

For KL *and her sister, the move to the* GDR *meant immediate integration into a circle of formerly exiled emigrants and their chil-*

dren, some Jewish, all leftists or communists, all of whom had successfully negotiated their way through the chaotic and dangerous period of exile. In terms of contributing to their solidarity, their exile
was certainly equal to, if not perhaps more important than, their
utopian dreams of a new German state, especially as the utopia became increasingly devoid of meaning for some.

We arrived in May, and at the end of August my parents got
work in Brandenburg, not far from Berlin, in a psychiatric hospital. It was far enough away and deep enough in the woods, so
that's how they got rid of us, out of Berlin. *She consistently refuses to
specify who 'they' was when it might lead to direct criticism of the
GDR.*

We lived there for four years. My mother thought that I should
[enroll in] school the first of September. I had been in the fifth
grade in America. I skipped school the next year in Holland. [The
authorities] wanted to put me in the fifth grade again. [My]
teacher gave me something to read, the next day she had me do a
dictation. I wrote almost no word [correctly].

J   I thought you could speak like a native.

KL No. I was speaking German without *der, die, das.*

J   You didn't pick that up from your parents in all those years.

KL They didn't speak much German at home. We spoke mostly English together, because all the other experiences of the daytime
were in English too. *A long-distance telephone call from a friend in
Dresden interrupts our interview.* KL *explains that she has many close
friends with whom she speaks regularly.*

I went to school in September. I won't ever forget [how] the
other children [reacted]. I received a five [on a scale of one to five,
five being the lowest] in one lesson. I didn't think that it was bad: I
knew that I was just starting. The little girls jumped around me
and asked, 'Oh, will your mother punish you terribly at home?
Will she beat you? Should we go with you and support you against
your parents?' I didn't know that they got punished at home when
they got a bad grade.

J   Was this a regular public school?

KL Yes. At that time there were still boys' and girls' schools. In '55, the
next year, they integrated boys and girls, but only those who
started that year in the first grade. I remained in a girls' class.

Next-door was the boys' school. We weren't allowed to go over there and play with them.

We had really good teaching [in this school]. At that time I already wanted to study biology. I really loved biology—what was going on with all the animals and plants, to know the names of all the plants. We took exams after the eighth grade. I took my exams in Brandenburg, and then, in '58, my father was appointed as a clinical psychologist to the Academy of Sciences in Berlin, where he worked to his retirement.

J   Did you feel isolated in Brandenburg?

KL   I didn't, but my parents did. [They] felt very isolated living in the middle of the woods. For us children it was really nice. We had a garden around the house, and I loved to work in it.

J   Did your mother work at that time?

KL   Yes. The GDR had no occupational therapy. People in the hospitals just sat around and drove the nurses crazy. The nurses were in the terrible position of having to beat them [to keep order]. My mother had a hard time convincing the doctors [of the need for occupational therapy]. For twenty years she worked with invalids, mental patients, and orthopedic patients who had lost legs or arms. She worked with these people in the beginning without [official] permission. She created the first training courses for occupational therapists in the GDR.

[The authorities] didn't recognize her American diploma. They said, 'We don't have [that] kind of profession here. That's why we can't even give you the salary of a nurse, but only the salary of a nurse's aide.' She worked for four years for three hundred marks a month, the lowest salary on the pay scale.

J   During this period, did you have any contacts with school friends from the United States?

KL   I wrote them. I wrote to my friends, and I got some letters back, until '58, then it slowed down.

KL *then digresses about the things she still has from America: a Hawaiian hula record with ukulele music and a Girl Scout pin, which she proudly showed us, from the summer she spent in upstate New York. We asked her about her contact with other Jews in America during and after the war.*

KL My parents were not so very [involved in American Jewish culture]. The Jewish committees in Germany didn't always play such a positive role for the Jews during fascism, yes? They didn't really try to support all the Jews. They supported some of the very prosperous Jews. [Thus most of the] communist Jews had left the Jewish communities before the war. Wherever we were we always had friends, many close friends, but I don't think they really knew who my parents were most of the time. KL *explains that she and her parents have maintained contact with many American friends. As early as 1962, less than a year after the Wall was built, Jewish friends from America came to visit them in East Berlin, some traveling in campers for six months through different communist countries. The family also maintained steady contact with her paternal grandmother, who stayed behind in the United States. In 1963 she visited them for the first time, and she returned every two years after* KL *had children.*

J   How did your parents deal with West Berlin?

KL We were never allowed to [go] to West Berlin [or] even to take the train, the *Durchläufer* [which went through West Berlin but did not stop there], because they were very much afraid that the CIA could catch us children and force them to return [to the West].

J   And you never, in the fifties, visited the West again?

KL Never. Since the day we arrived here nobody from our family has ever gone [back] to West Berlin.

KL *began our second meeting with a directive: 'So I think you have lots of questions now. You start with questions.' In the first interview we had let her focus on what she chose, and she had talked about things that would never have come up if she had simply been responding to our questions. In our second meeting, she sought more of an exchange.*

J   In 1968 you went to the Soviet Union, where you studied for four years. You met your first husband in—?

KL Yes, but he is German. We met a few weeks before we left for Moscow. We got married there. We didn't know each other well, only for a few weeks. I said, 'If we want to stay together, then we have to get married, and then we will move to the same town.' [So I left Moscow and] completed my doctorate in Kischinjow, the capital of Moldavia. As you have probably heard, there are nationalist demonstrations there now, as there were back then. All these small countries don't really realize what they get from the big one. They only see what they have to give and are very unhappy about it.

J You didn't see in Moldavia a relationship that worked one way? You saw a reciprocal relationship?

KL Yes, but the people there didn't see it that way.

J You lived in Moscow for how long?

KL For one year, then for three years in Moldavia.

J Did you see a large difference in the standard of living in the two places?

KL I even found that the standard of living in this capital city of Moldavia was better than in Moscow. Of course they had real housing shortages, and it was awful to shop. The same as you see here [in the GDR], but even worse there.

J Did you meet other Jews there?

KL Yes. Moldavia and Odessa are places where there were originally many Jews. It is the capital of Jewish scholars and of Jewish culture [in the Soviet Union].

My husband was a mathematician. He went not looking at the surroundings but to [attend] this school of mathematics. Anti-Semitism, of course, is present wherever many Jews live, in the Soviet Union as in the rest of the world.

J Even then? In '68?

KL Yes, but throughout history. It improved after the war. Still, the Moldavians and the Russians said they didn't want to have a Jewish person in their family. They were kind of loyal to the scientists, very proud that they had so many Jewish scholars and musicians, but in everyday life they tried to avoid contact with them.

The Jewish people [themselves banded] together. My husband is not Jewish, and since [the Moldavians] knew we were Germans, we had a normal, good relationship to the people around us in public life. But when I arrived, *She followed her husband there* and told about my parents being antifascists and emigrants and Jews, all doors to the big Jewish families opened to us. They helped us where they could. In the summertime you have to buy all the fresh fruit and preserve it. They gave us everything [already] preserved.

A woman in charge of the keys and the telephone [in our building] helped us with everything. She brought something for us to eat which she had cooked or baked daily, even though she didn't have very much money.

J   Was she Jewish?

KL Yes. I [still] have good contact with her. It took her ten years before she could come to visit us [in the GDR]. I sent her an official invitation [each year], and every time she went to the police, they told her something else had to be done. Something was always missing. The director of the university called on her and asked, 'Why do the Leiterers invite you?' She said, 'Why shouldn't they invite me?' 'Yes, if they would invite me or some doctors, I wouldn't say anything. But you are just a hostel [employee]. What do you want there?' And she said, 'Oh, you know, I want to go to restaurants.' To go to restaurants is the worst thing you can do as a woman. It means to be a whore. She said, 'Everyday I will read the newspaper *Pravda* to them and tell them what we think of the world.' He said, 'No, we can't permit you to go there.' [That was] the director of the university [speaking]. That's how anti-Semitism [works] in the Soviet Union. Here nobody would ever do such a thing. Here, the anti-Semitism is beneath the surface.

KL *explained that although the Soviet quota system tried to limit the number of Jews entering the university so that their proportion there was the same as their proportion in the population of the Soviet Union, Jews were still overrepresented among the intellectuals. Many who could not get into the university applied for permission to go to Israel. Also, if a person has a relative in Israel, he or she becomes less employable, or is given less preference for higher education, because it is assumed that he or she will go there as well.*

J   Were you integrated only into Jewish circles or also Moldavian ones?

KL The Moldavians don't have very close relationships.

J   Were there any mixed marriages?

KL Yes. Mostly, Moldavian women want to have Jewish men, because a Jewish man will never beat them. A Jewish man doesn't beat his wife, at least not in the Soviet Union. I don't know if this is true in the whole world. And a Jewish man is always doing what his wife wants. That is why they are very keen on them. The Moldavian girls are very pretty, and they try to get a Jewish man. Sometimes the Jewish families cannot stop it. Usually they take this man away from his Jewish family. The wives can keep their names in the Soviet Union, and they keep the Moldavian name and give the children Moldavian nationality, because in the Soviet Union 'nationality' is written in the passport.

J   Jewish is one of the nationalities also?

KL   Yes, even though it is not a nationality, because Jews have no territory. There is a Jewish republic on the Chinese border [Birobidschan], but it is not a real republic. It is in the mountains where no Jews had lived. I have heard there is still a Jewish newspaper there.

J   How did these four years in Moldavia change you?

KL   I have become much more content with all the things that happen to you in life, because I have seen it worse than it is here. KL *begins, though she does not say so, to compare her life in the* GDR *with life in Moldavia. She even compares freedom of movement.*

They told us we were not allowed to move out of Kishinev without asking permission. After a while we just didn't care anymore. At the beginning you are really frustrated and don't do things.

J   Was this frustration lessened by your contacts with the Jewish community?

KL   There was no Jewish community. There were just Jewish families who knew of each other. They advised each other when they needed something, and they helped each other more than they usually helped [non-Jews]. But there was no Jewish community, with all the festivals.

J   When you returned to Berlin, did you then begin to establish a new relationship to the Jews here?

KL   No, I never had any relationship here. About four years ago or so, I was thinking, Maybe you could go there sometime. Somebody told me that on Sundays they had interesting lectures at the Jewish Community. At that time they started to ask Jewish young people, people younger than my parents, for instance, to come to them. And they created this group, Wir für Uns [literally, We for Us]. Sometimes I go there. We are a very big group of Jewish children from communist parents. Only some were emigrants. Some just became communists after the war. Some of them are lawyers and have good positions. Some are friends of mine.

KL *then relates an incident in which the leader of the group insisted on an exclusive definition of membership conflating Jewishness with antifascism.*

We have our feelings which may be Jewish, but we are mostly communist. Many of my friends don't come anymore. I go there primarily because of the really interesting, interesting lectures.

J   What about your children? Do they get a Jewish education?

KL Yes, once they were there. But they don't want to [go anymore]. They didn't like it.

J   Do your children identify themselves as Jewish?

KL They know that they are Jewish. As I told you, here there is anti-Semitism beneath the surface. In the third grade in my daughters' school a little boy said, 'I don't want anything to do with Jews, because Jews are bad people.' My daughter said, 'How do you know that Jews are bad people?' He answered, 'I know that. My parents told me.' But it was not clear if he knew [that my daughters] were Jewish, because, if he had known, he wouldn't have said it. Of course they came home very upset and asked, 'Why do people say such things?' Since then I have begun to explain to them what anti-Semitism is and what had happened during fascism. They know that there are people who would hurt them just because they are Jews. But that is all.

J   Did you lose relatives during the war? And do your children know?

KL Yes, we named my son Günter because my mother's brother was Günter, and he was murdered in Theresienstadt.

J   And he knows that?

KL He knows that and he is very proud to have this name.

J   Is he circumcised?

KL No, because my husband is not Jewish. And he didn't want anything of this kind. And why should I say that it is important?

KL *speaks at length about her attitude toward rearing children and identity. She argues that she does not think Jewish identity is more important than all others. Nor is a specific religion particularly important. The most important aspect of her relation to her children is what she calls open discussion and cultural education. This means being willing to discuss all topics at home and exposing children to a wide range of cultural activities.* KL *explains that she wants always to be available for her children when they need her. Although she avoids mention of her divorce, she does emphasize the special demands on a working mother who has neither a nanny nor a partner to share in childcare and domestic duties.*

J   I am just wondering, after hearing you talk about your children, what do you think makes someone Jewish?

KL   You know, I think there is some kind of a Darwinistic selection which has gone on, and the Jews have lived under repressions for three thousand years. Only the really good thinkers [have survived] all this. I think, under this selection, the Jews I know are very logical-thinking people, warm-hearted people.

J   What was your reference point when you first went to the Soviet Union? Having come from the United States initially, did you think at all in terms of the Cold War?

KL   I was very afraid to go behind the Iron Curtain when we returned [to the GDR]. I hadn't seen it. I hadn't seen this curtain. My parents had, of course, never said anything anti-Soviet at home, but they had never talked pro-Soviet either. They had just let us learn what we had to learn in school, because they were afraid if they would have taught us something else, then we would [repeat] it in school, and everything would be worse. Later we talked about all these things at home. For me it was clear, this is the country of my parents. We won't have it so good as we had it in America, and we have to build up this country which is destroyed by war. I felt that I wanted to build up this [country], too.

J   Was it soon after you came back that you started to feel that way?

KL   Yes. When I went to the Soviet Union for study, it was a big award for being a good student. Only the very best students could study in the Soviet Union. It is still that way. Even though the [standard of] living was bad there, but you could make it.

    KL *describes her integration into the* GDR—*in contrast to the initial treatment of her parents—as marked by* Gastfreundschaft *[hospitality].*

The people really wanted to help newcomers. They were very happy that newcomers were coming in. My parents had studied. That was a big [plus] if someone had studied.

J   As a child, you didn't feel any kind of discrimination?

KL No, not at all. The other way round. Everybody was happy to be a friend of mine.

J   When you went to the Soviet Union, did you make any comparisons with the United States?

KL Yes, of course, I made the comparison. But for me it was always clear that the Soviet Union is our part of the world and the [United States is in the] other part of the world.

J   Still, it seems as if you never totally and finally left the United States, but carried with you certain fantasies and points of reference.

KL Yes, my grandmother, my aunt, and [others] were in America and very happy that we were here. My parents wanted to visit my grandmother for her ninetieth birthday four years ago, but my grandmother said, 'Stay where you are.' She had some kind of feeling that it could be bad if my father came [back]. We always had felt a little bit of fear of America, because America, that is . . . *Das sage ich auf Deutsch, ja?* [I'll say this in German, okay?]

J   *Ja.*

KL *Amerika war unser Gegner und konnte uns schaden.* [America was our opponent and could harm us.] *Translating this sentence would have been no problem for* KL. *It is likely that she felt more comfortable representing America as the enemy or opponent in German than in English.*

They could do something against us, us as a family, because my parents were under this threat, the same thing that was used against the Rosenbergs.

J   Your grandmother, who was in the United States, and aunt— when they found out that you were going to the Soviet Union, were they afraid?

KL Not at all. They said, 'That is wonderful that you can go there and study.' They had no Cold War feelings.

J   Did they have any reservations about your return to Germany in 1954?

KL At that time they did. They were a little bit afraid, and my parents were very much afraid. They didn't know anything [about] what was going on here. They didn't know anything about life here.

J Which events in the history of the GDR, if you think back, do you remember most?

KL Lots of things. In April, student days, *Berliner Studententage*, which they just celebrated for the twenty-fourth time. We created these *Berliner Studententage* when I was a student. One week where the students have special cultural performances, special meetings with specific problems, mostly political, scientific student conferences, and so on. I was one of the first students who presented a scientific paper at the students' conference, scientific students' conference, already in my second year of studies. I got a prize from the university, for young scientists with especially [promising] work. These are really nice things, you know, things you started that go on and become tradition, a good German Democratic Republic tradition. It gives you a good feeling to be part of it.

At the time of our interview, KL did not know, of course, that she had attended the last of these 'German Democratic Republic traditions.' Six weeks later the Wall was opened; one year later the GDR was absorbed into the Federal Republic. KL goes on to list other traditions: the Solidaritätsmarsch, *a march to raise money for Third World liberation movements, the May Day demonstration, the Karl Liebknecht–Rosa Luxemburg demonstration on the second Sunday of January. She emphasizes how special the Liebknecht-Luxemburg demonstration is for elderly communists.*

The people you meet on these demonstrations! I was with my children, and they told me, 'Look Mommy, isn't it funny that most of our good friends we meet at the demonstration?'

J Are these good friends mostly Jews?

KL No. They are [just] lots of really good Party members. I would even say that there are very few Jewish people.

KL then digresses about the relation of the state to religion and norms. She says that she equates communism with humanitarianism and therefore does not see it as opposed to religion per se. Nor does she think that work for the Party is a substitute for keeping one's 'personal life' in order. Many Party members, she implies, neglect their duties to their families, as do many people who just devote themselves to their work.

J   Can you tell us about your own [work] experiences?

Tired of our incessant, prying questions, she fires back that after the tape stops she would like to know something about our experiences. I nod agreement but complete the question.

J   About your experiences working, as a woman. In what way do you feel solidarity with other women?

KL   We shout loudly in our socialist countries, 'We have the *Gleichberechtigung der Frau* [equal rights for women].' But the only states which have women leaders are England and Ceylon and India and Pakistan, Malaysia now, Indonesia. I don't know any socialist country which has ever had a woman leader. And I don't know any socialist country which has a woman in the Central Committee and the Party leadership. But the women are working: 90 percent of the teachers are women, 80 percent of the medical doctors are women, in almost all socialist countries, in the Soviet Union as well as here. Kindergartens, preschool nurseries—all women working there. Where real work is done, mostly women are working. Sewing, the big textile factories, lots of factories where assembly line work is done—almost only women. And the men play the leaders.

Suddenly realizing she had only criticized socialism, she begins to portray the positive side.

Only fifty years ago in Germany, the women were thrown out of the lecture hall. Lisa Meitner, the chemist, she had to listen to the lectures behind the seats. She went into a room behind the [classroom] to listen to the lectures. Once she sat down in the very last row and the teacher said, 'Meine Herren, wenn wir wieder unter uns sind, fange ich mit meiner Vorlesung an' [Gentlemen, when we are again among ourselves, I will start the lecture]. She had to leave the room. That's fifty years ago. Now in universities almost half of the teachers are women, and in some places in the humanities, even more.

Again, she reverses gears and ends with a statement of dissatisfaction.

It will take a revolution against men. It is really hard for a woman to be in a [position of] leadership. The men don't hear what she says. I have often experienced this. She can say lots of good things, but by the next meeting the director will have done nothing [along the lines proposed by the woman]. In my little scientific film association the men gather in the evening together at one table, and when a woman comes they start to talk about something uninteresting. When they talk about how to organize something, to manage something, the women are excluded. And they are very aware of it. There is no equal possibility, maybe equal rights, legally, but no equal possibilities.

J   Do you consider yourself a feminist?

KL No.

J   Why not?

This time she levels her critique against women and undermines her own argument against the discrimination she has faced as a female scientist.

Feminists are fighting for something immoral. I don't know if it would be so very good if there were equal possibilities. [In one area] there is no equal possibility: women have to [get pregnant] and have children. They have to stay at home with their young children. That is just what a man can't do. There is a biological barrier. For instance, I am sure if I wouldn't 'waste' so much time for my children, I would surely have already finished my second doctoral thesis. But if I don't complete the second doctoral thesis, I will never be able to be a professor.

KL *offers an example of her activities as a mother as a sort of defense against, or alternative to, feminist concerns.*

We have *Elternaktive*. There is a group of parents—five, six, seven parents in a class—who organize things for the children which are not organized by the school. I was always in these parents groups. I was a leader of these parents. I think that these small basic things down there are much more important than those of a big leader where you are far [removed from] all the things you say. It is [also] true [that] women, even feminists, even these women I was talking about who just forget that they are women and that they would like to have a family, everything just for work—at some point they don't want to be a leader. They realize that men [at the top] will never really take them in as equals.

J   May I ask you something totally different? What's your perspective on Israel?

KL I feel the same way as lots of communist Jews, friends of my parents, and others who have been there. I feel [that] if Jews who had overcome this Holocaust are doing the [same] things now against the Arabs, they are as bad as the fascists who did such things against the Jews.

The telephone rings and KL *switches to Russian. One of her Jewish friends from Moldavia is coming to visit soon. This unexpected conversation perhaps prods* KL *to focus on a different aspect of Israel.*

The Jews [before the war], the Jewish committees, were talking about a homeland for the Jews. That [Israel] is no homeland for the Jews. It is a normal, capitalist society. The Jews who have much money lead a good life, but there are Jews there who have no good life. The worst thing is that they cannot make some kind of peace agreement with the Palestinians.

J One other question, and you can answer this in German if you like, with a more precise formulation: How would you express your identity?

KL *Doch, ich würde sagen, ein überzeugter Kommunist jüdischer Herkunft* [I would say, a committed communist of Jewish origin]. My father was still educated in the Jewish religion. My mother wasn't educated in religion at all, [though she was] Jewish [by descent].

In countries where German and fascism [are understood as meaning the same thing], for instance, in the Soviet Union, in Poland too, I always say, 'I am not a German,' meaning that I am a Jew. But, of course, I don't know any other country where I would like to stay more than here. My parents are German Jews or Jewish Germans. They had to leave their country. They felt they wanted to come back here [regardless of the extreme] circumstances. They wanted to return to this Germany. And so I would like to stay in this country too.

J Would you call this homeland?

KL In the sense of saying homeland is the place where you feel good and you have everything you need and so, I would say yes, it is my homeland.

J *Wie würden Sie das auf Deutsch sagen?* [How would you say that in German?]

KL *Heimatland. Die Heimat.* I am not an internationalist, but I could feel good in other places in the world too if the surroundings, if my family and so on would be there too. But my family is here. I feel strongly that my parents tried to do right, to do everything right for the family, [following] their convictions. Being a communist during fascism you risked your life. My father risked his life returning here, because in the beginning, they told me, [the authorities] wanted to send us back. My father was a psychologist, a clinical psychologist, and helped lots and lots of people in his life. My mother was an occupational therapist and [created the field here]. Both my parents have *Vaterländische Verdienstorden* [awards for honorable service to the fatherland]. They were not recognized in the beginning, but after everything was accomplished. They had to fight against so much resistance.

♣

We saw KL *quite often during the next several years. Before the opening of the Wall she moved into a new apartment near Potsdamer Platz, the old center of Berlin. Of course, the opening of the Wall and the collapse of the* GDR *had quite an impact on* KL. *She responded to our request for a postscript on 10 May 1991, in a four-page, single-spaced letter written in German:*

Much in the GDR has changed since the *Wende* [change], since October 1989 and since reunification, also for me. The period after the *Wende* in the GDR, before reunification, was a time of hope, of hope for the possibility of a democratic renewal of the German socialist state as an alternative to the capitalism of the Federal Republic. These people [the reformers of the period] deserve our respect. Hans Modrow, Wolfgang Ullmann, Jens Reich, Gregor Gysi. Unfortunately, they have been deeply disappointed, very depressed, about the quick unification of Germany, with destructive consequences for a large part of the population of the former GDR. They had warned loudly and publicly about these consequences.

I am still holding firmly to my humanistic ideals, which I have always held to be correct. The high-handedness of the leadership clique is especially depressing and painful to me. They created many advantages for themselves but increasingly put the majority of the people at a disadvantage. [This] included the worst forms of oppression. They shielded themselves from their own people by means of an immense security organization. What, then, [do I make of] my communist ideals, for which I worked, sometimes under poor conditions, half of my life? For which I engaged and which I still champion?

She lists these Marxist-inspired principles and then talks about some of the negative consequences that have followed the introduction of capitalism into the former GDR.

This is all particularly painful for me, since in my circle of friends we had already earlier seen many errors, with increased vehemence and frequency in the last five years. We knew that these developments had nothing to do with our democratic and humanistic ideals, that they even contradicted them. But why didn't most of us do anything? Why not? Often you had the feeling that you knew too little or had no bird's-eye view of the whole. And you hoped that most [of these developments] were only isolated examples and that it was better elsewhere. Moreover, when you stood up to your boss in your own circle, you often received a clear signal: often, the more you stood up to the general examples [of injustice], the more intense were the repressions.

Another important ideal for me is a humanistic, internationalistic society that is tolerant of others and of foreigners. Therefore I am painfully disturbed by the increasingly vehement hatred of foreigners, especially in the former GDR. In particular, the immigration of Soviet Jews in the last few months has fallen on the fruitful soil of hatred for Jews, which fanned these flames anew.

Another ideal for me in a democratic, humanistic society is that we have no interest in a war. KL *describes her long opposition to war and tells us that she and her daughter took part in demonstrations against the Gulf War against Iraq in 1991.*

Much like other people whom I know, I am experiencing a strong, lasting, and daily repeated feeling of insecurity, even in dealing with daily necessities, from shopping to health insurance. Citizens of the former GDR are in a difficult identity crisis. Almost everybody, whether they admit this or not, considered themselves citizens of the GDR, in both its positive and negative aspects, up to the *Wende.* We had a feeling of identity as a citizen of the GDR. What or who are we now, in these new federal states on the territory of the former GDR? Are we a colony of the Western states? Everything is decided through the Western authorities and imposed on us. Each person must endure this alone. The old ruling principle 'divide and conquer' is functioning superbly.

It has become very difficult today to be on the Left. My children have to think about whether they can wear their Palestinian scarves when they go out in the evening. In December 1990 my son was attacked on the subway by a group of ten boys because of his Palestinian scarf. Now he has dyed his hair red to show his persuasion. I fear that because of this he might be attacked by right-wing youths again.

Jewish life has also changed in the united Berlin. The Jewish Communities in the East and the West have come together. The members of the earlier East Berlin executive committee whom I knew no longer belong to the united committee. I feel good in the circle of people in the Jewish *Kulturverein* [an East Berlin group that is outside the united Community]. They have similar problems that I understand well. I am also glad that the [Community] is reaching out to care for the many Jewish emigrants. Recently Jewish artists who had just emigrated from the Soviet Union gave a concert organized [by the Jewish *Kulturverein*]. These public events are well attended, and the artists are warmly welcomed.

How will the world now develop?

KL *ends her postscript with a list of global problems—environmental catastrophe, world hunger, unequal distribution of wealth. She hopes for a better world but fears that this hope will not be realized.*

KL *informed us in a final letter, in early 1993, that unification has resulted in 'real horror stories!' She was fired from her medical research position at the Charité in November, along with 750 of the other 920 scientists employed there. She is fighting in court to retain her job.*

Rediscovery of Jewishness East and West

'I'm a minority as a feminist and as a lesbian, and that means always sitting in between.'

Born 1954 West Berlin (father in exile in the United States)

Born in West Berlin to a Jewish father who had lived in exile in the United States and a German mother who had converted to Judaism, Jessica Jacoby appears fragile and vulnerable. JJ had to cancel the first two meetings we scheduled in the summer of 1989. We finally met on 25 July. Although our previous conversations had been conducted in German, JJ insisted on speaking English during the interview, for reasons that became apparent. She began, 'I brought this picture. That's my dad. That's just how he came back, as part of the military administration, part of the High Commission.'

JJ thus began her story, not with her birth, but with her father's return from exile in the United States. Clean-shaven with closely cropped hair, dressed in American military fatigues, dark sunglasses resting halfway down his nose, he resembled a 1950s Hollywood-style GI Joe. To JJ, however, he was anything but a generic American soldier. More important, he was a Jew in the American military who had returned to a country from which he had considered himself permanently exiled.]

JJ   He was born in Düsseldorf, went to the Gymnasium, and just a year before his graduation was kicked out because he was Jewish. This must have been around '37. He secretly started studying photography but was caught with his camera by a policeman who was decent enough to tell him that this was trouble, not a good place for a Jew boy to be. My dad heard the message, and he tried to leave.

Bohemia had just been annexed by Nazi Germany. First he tried Israel, but my grandparents were not in favor of his going to

Palestine. He had relatives already in the United States, [includ-ing] a cousin of my grandmother who had gone there in '28. There she married a Jewish man, and they had changed their name to Edwards. [Later, when I visited the United States,] I tried to find the Edwardses in New Rochelle but never managed. They submitted an affidavit to [get] my dad out of Germany but could only do that for *him*, not for his sister. I don't know why that was so, but maybe my aunt had not yet decided to leave. A short while later she went to South Africa, where she still lives. [My] dad went to Rotterdam, accompanied by his mom. She saw him off on the boat, and that was the last time she ever saw him. I think he lost the little money he had in a bingo game. Morale aboard the boat was very low. The young women, who had no money, were pros-tituting themselves. Everybody seemed to be miserable. It was a whole boat of younger Jews leaving, mostly from Germany.

After the Reich's Kristallnacht in '39, my aunt also decided to leave. She wanted to go to Britain but managed only a tourist visa to South Africa. She went there and got married within two weeks —otherwise she would have had to leave again. Surprisingly, she is still married to that man, though it was a marriage of conve-nience, not love.

J   Is her husband Jewish?

JJ   Yes, he's from Hamburg. Both Uncle Ernst and Tante Inge never tried to return, to come back here. My cousins, though—Peter and Leslie—did. They're a bit older than I am. Peter came to live with us for half a year. Leslie, who is now married to a non-Jew, with two kids, came for a few weeks. Peter, who is not married and doesn't intend to, lives with a non-Jewish woman. They used to come here about twice a year to buy scarves and things; they are in the wholesale business. This is the only family I've left. That's why I went into these details.

J   You maintain contact with them?

JJ   Yes, I do. With both cousins and my Tante Inge and my Uncle Ernst. They're older now—he's almost ninety. But they're impor-tant because they're the only family I have left, at least the only family that deserves that name.

Dad was unemployed in the United States for quite a while and worked in all sorts of odd jobs, like babysitter, gardening, cemetery work, things like that. Finally, he decided to join the army and then traveled a lot within the U.S. His place of residence changed almost every other year, perhaps every year. I think he started out in Baltimore, lived in New York, did some training in Los Angeles, continued training at Camp David, and then was in New Orleans for about two years. After Pearl Harbor he went to the Philippines. He wasn't ever in combat, but learned to work with microfilm and worked for intelligence. Later he worked with soldiers who had nervous breakdowns or who had simply gone nuts out of shock. He took care of them, did some sort of work therapy, taught them photography.

He was naturalized. I think he acquired it quite early. He applied right away, and I think after he left Baltimore he managed to get citizenship. But he was not able to hand it on to me. He was just short of the required period for naturalized citizens. A child born to a naturalized American citizen and to a woman from the man's country of birth does not [automatically] qualify for American citizenship. He was missing a very short period of time. Then it wouldn't have mattered anymore whom he married.

It was not my father's idea to return to Germany. He had served in East Asia during the war, returned, still in the army, to the United States after '45, and wanted to remain in the service as a journalist and photographer. He was sent back to Germany, [whereas] his idea was to go to France. The argument then was: you know German.

My father never spoke German again. He stopped writing or speaking it in 1942. You can still see [that] in his diary: he started in German, and from a certain date in '42 on, he stopped.

During [the war] his parents were still in Düsseldorf. Until '41, eleventh of November '41, when they were put on a train to Minsk, after which I've lost track of what happened to them. There are two possibilities: Either they were taken to the Minsk ghetto, which had sections for German Jews from different regions, from Austria as well—many of these inhabitants of the Minsk ghetto were actually shot right there; there is a little pillar of commemoration for them, with an inscription in Yiddish and a yellowish picture of a family—or it's possible, though not likely, they were actually taken to Trostyanets, a little village [in Ukraine], where the inhabitants were cleared out and shot. They dug a ditch and shot people. But I assume that there must have been at least a short period when my grandparents were still alive in the Minsk ghetto [before being moved to Trostyanets].

My dad didn't know much about this. He suffered terribly when he heard about their fate. He used the Red Cross and the Jewish Community to search for them. A few things my grandparents had sent still arrived in the United States. He got a final postcard much later, sent just before they were shipped off. Dad didn't know what happened to them, though their last letters are very, very anxious, fearful and full of death. He tried to get them out of Germany via Cuba but did not manage. My relatives in the United States, most of them, turned out to be a bit of a disappointment, because they didn't do much and maybe could have done more. I'm not sure. Along with [my grandparents], the whole family was taken. Five of my grandfather's sisters. I don't know what happened to my grandmother's parents or cousins. Apparently, except for my father and my aunt [in South Africa], nobody got out. I think my dad must have learned about these things only after '45. This has much to do with the poor press coverage of the killing of Jews and mass murders.

Actually, the Yiddish papers did better coverage, but my father never read Yiddish. As a German Jew, he was not used to it, though, and this is an interesting aside, my aunt did read Yiddish, something I learned only after I started studying Yiddish. I showed her a Yiddish book and she started reading the title. I said, 'I'm surprised you read Yiddish.' She said, 'Well, you know, my in-laws spoke it. I know a little bit. But I don't understand why you bother with Yiddish.' She had been married to a Lithuanian Jew in the thirties and lived in Lithuania then. They divorced, and she has never heard of her ex-husband or in-laws since.

Actually, my father and his sister saw each other only many years later, in the fifties. He visited her in South Africa. It was not a good visit: He didn't like her politics, and vice versa. They fought. It was never a very close relationship. She was much older than he, and he was a bit of a mama's boy [and] she was jealous. At an early age she was independent and did things unacceptable to Jewish parents. With their bourgeois attitudes, they had certain ideas about what a good Jewish girl should be like, and my aunt wasn't that way. She started going out with boys when she was real young, and men were always her favorite sport.

J What were the political differences between your father and your aunt?

JJ My father was a liberal. He had no use for racism, while my aunt didn't care as long as it didn't hurt her. Blacks do all the service, the garden, clean her house. They work for you and you don't mix with them socially. Apartheid seems natural to her. [On his visit] my dad drove to one of the homelands and took some photos, which she didn't like. On another occasion he opened the house bar and invited everybody for a drink. They were happily drunk when my aunt came home. She wasn't charmed.

Still, I consider them family despite these differences. They're the only ones left, and I keep that in mind. These differences also existed between my mom and Peter [JJ's cousin]. My mom always had lots of African friends. When Peter met them here, he said, 'Well, they're very different from our blacks. These are educated people . . . ' There's no way, really, of convincing him otherwise. He would save the Jews there . . .

J He connects this issue with the Jews?

JJ Well, he is a Jew, and everyone sticks with their own crowd. He doesn't mix much with the Afrikaners, nor the whites; mostly he is just with his Jewish friends. Leslie is married to a non-Jew, and Peter's lover is also not Jewish, but that's not very typical. Both my aunt and uncle don't like it very much, though they're tolerating it now.

J Did they start being more religious in South Africa than they were in Germany?

JJ Not really. It's not that they go regularly to the synagogue or are a part of the Community. They're not active in that sense. But they've been very supportive of Israel somehow, in a very uncritical, emotional way. Israel and South Africa, as you know, deal with each other.

I feel a bit uneasy about [Peter's ambivalence about being Jewish]. At the same time, Peter does support me. When my mom committed suicide this January, he came. I asked him to say *Kaddish* with me for my mother. That was a problem because he'd never done it. I gave him a little printed sheet. It was in the Latin alphabet, because he doesn't read Hebrew. He was lost at some point, and I continued alone. But at least he agreed to do it.

J   Do you speak English or German with your relatives?

JJ   English. Peter and Leslie spoke German and English at home, but Peter's German is better than Leslie's. Inge and Ernst speak English with a strong German accent. They still make mistakes. They have been writing down what they remember from the past. Peter would like his father to publish it. And it's all written in this incorrect English.

J   Do you speak English with your aunt?

JJ   No, German. Also with Ernst.

J   Let's go back to your father's return.

JJ   He ended up in '52 in Berlin. But during his first weeks or months [in Germany] he had gone to Düsseldorf to try and find out what happened to his parents, to see the house where he had grown up. He wrote an English article on his experiences there, of what was left of Düsseldorf and his impressions. He then worked for a newsletter to be circulated among U.S. personnel [what later became the *Stars and Stripes*]. He initiated a series with photos of German, or Berlin, women who were in some way antifascist and somehow important people. The first one was René Sintenis, a sculptor. The second was my grandmother, my mother's mother, who at that time was a representative in the city parliament, for the Christian Democratic Party. She was actually an actress, not a politician, but she was known for her anti-Nazi stand and had a lot of Jewish friends in the United States. She was divorced and had raised three children alone. She did not speak English, but she knew Italian and French. She had a very mixed background: Viennese by birth, her father a Czech, her mother Hungarian-Italian, and she was Catholic.

My mother was eighteen or nineteen at the time, also an actress, and knew English well because she had a British friend—woman friend. She volunteered as an interpreter, where she met my father, who offered her Phillip Morris [cigarettes], still a rarity. She was very impressed. He asked her out for dinner. That's how they got involved. He was my mother's first lover. They started very quickly, on the first night, and she just moved out of her home, much to the displeasure of my grandmother, of course, who found this a bit rash. They lived together for quite a while before they actually married, until '53. I was born in '54. It wasn't exactly planned. People didn't think much about contraception in those days. My dad actually felt that he shouldn't have any children because the world was so full of misery and so sickening that it wasn't just to put people into this world. My mom wasn't so keen on babies in general. I had a nurse, a governess, from the time I left the American military hospital in Frankfurt, where I was born.

When I was around, my dad was happy that he had a child. My mother was still very young, much like a kid and immature. Then my dad lost his job, not long after I was born. They fired three people because they wanted to restructure. All were Jewish. My dad was deeply offended.

This was his chance to go back [to America], and he tried. Mom and dad went to New York when I was six months old. They tried living there, but it didn't work out. My mom didn't really have a job—she was just a housewife and bored. Dad was running his butt off to find employment, but there wasn't any.

J   He couldn't work for the military?

JJ No, that didn't work out. Everybody said they would print his articles and publish his photos if he wanted to work freelance, which he did. He found this very stressful. He had agents to promote his work, but he usually went to a place, wrote the story, took photos, developed them, and sold the whole package to a magazine. Sometimes he was also given an assignment and went with an advance; otherwise he had to risk investing his own money. He was also interested in the arts. He went to Japan, for instance, and did a project on the making of Chinese dolls, but nobody cared about that at the time.

In the beginning my mom was still with him, helping him with cameras, drying photos, with all sorts of different things. He was accredited with the American military, so he could use trains, helicopters, airplanes, boats, everything, but only alone, not with my mother. She remained a German citizen, [though] she did convert to Judaism when she married my dad. That was her initiative, not his. She chose to be Jewish. Her Hebrew name was Shoshana.

J   Was it a conscious decision for her to remain a German citizen?

JJ   Not really. The problem was that she didn't like New York much. She didn't know anybody, have any friends. She missed her mother. She found the skyline depressing. She liked green, the outdoors, the countryside. She lived on 116th Street, close to Columbia, in a single room with a lady . . . Russian . . . Jewish-Russian . . . an old lady. They were almost eaten by cockroaches. She hated it.

    I stayed with my grandparents, and didn't see my parents for half a year. All these are stories I was told. My parents returned after that and moved to Switzerland. They stayed for a year and lived near the Zurich airport. That [also] didn't work out. My mom was homesick for Berlin. They returned to Berlin, and we lived on the first floor of a big villa in Dahlem, on Reichensteiner Weg, close to the Free University. My first recollections are of that house. Then we moved to Zehlendorf, into a house which my father could rent cheaply because he had reimmigrated. This was part of a housing project called Neue Heimat, affiliated with the Social Democratic Party and the labor unions. It was tied to the *Wiedergutmachung* [restitution] policy, which my dad did not want but my mom pushed him to accept.

J   Could you explain his attitude toward reparations?

JJ   For *Wiedergutmachung* you had to prove everything you had lost. But you don't have the papers anymore. There was a lot of valuable stuff in my grandparents' flat. My grandmother had jewelry. It was all taken, of course, and dad tried to find out what actually happened. The neighbors, still the same neighbors, refused to recognize him anymore, didn't want to let him into [their houses]. He was convinced that they helped themselves to what they liked. He was very bitter about that. He hated the Germans.

J   Of course when he came back to Germany he spoke German?

JJ   No, he didn't. He refused. Even the very first interview with my grandmother he conducted in English, with my mother's help as a translator.

J   He pretended he didn't know it or just said he wouldn't speak it?

JJ   Well, he just didn't talk about it. I think my mom only learned much later that he knew German. On one occasion he must have spoken it: He was visiting the GDR and for some reason or other he didn't want people to know he was American. Then he must have spoken German. That's the only time, apparently. It was his way of cutting off the language. He hated the Germans, was disgusted with them. He never wanted to live here, but somehow things didn't work out.

My mother had the idea of going to Israel. She was enthusiastic about it and lived there for a few months, but without dad. I was two years old at the time. Mom loved Israel. Dad didn't feel so enthusiastic about it.

As dad was traveling more frequently, mom was increasingly bored with housework and with taking care of me. We had a governess, and my grandmother was crazy about me, so mom didn't really have to do much. She had completed only eight or nine years of school and didn't have any training, so she decided to go back to school to become a vet. During those years I saw little of my mom. She was working hard for her *Abitur* and did voluntary work for the veterinary hospital. I think my dad must have been surprised because he had married a kid.

My dad had more time for me when he was around, which wasn't often. Most often he was gone, though he always sent me postcards from far-off places—from the States and Israel. He was a freelance journalist until his death. He used to buy at the PX. It was possible for American citizens, especially veterans, to shop there. For me as a kid, the PX was something I loved. He would come to school to pick me up sometimes and we'd go to the snack bar and have hamburgers. That was something special.

I went to the American military kindergarten when I was five, for about a year. I was not happy there. I didn't know how to play with the other children. They were different. I spoke a mix of German and English, and people there just spoke English. Also, I think we started reading and writing. I think they could also write their own names already, and I couldn't. Then I learned, quickly, to write and read just a little before I went to school, but English. And when I went to school German was required. I was very confused. My dad wanted me to go to Thomas E. Robert's School, which didn't work out because he was no longer in the military. They changed the rules, so I was put in a German school. After two years there, I switched to the Kennedy school, which was bilingual. My dad had wanted me to go there from the beginning, but no space was available at the time.

At the German primary school I experienced plenty of anti-Semitism.

J   What form did the anti-Semitism take?

JJ For instance, one girl visited me at home, and I showed her some jewelry of my mom's shaped something like a star—it was not the Mogen David—and she said, 'That's a Jewish star.' I said, 'No, that's not a Jewish star. I'll show you what a Jewish star looks like.' And she said, 'Oh, you know, it's something very bad.' I said, 'Why? Why is it something bad?' She said, 'I don't know.' Well, this was a seven-year-old girl. I was in the first grade.

And there were other instances. Another boy always came to my house because I had comic books and Mickey Mouse records —that's why children would come to my place. At one point I told him I was Jewish, and he didn't come any more. My mom saw him on the street and asked, 'Why don't you come to play with Jessica anymore?' He said, 'Well, you know, I better not come. My parents say that I might be a disturbance when you celebrate your Jewish holidays.'

I was also in a Christian religion class and the teacher wanted me to bring my baptismal certificate. I didn't have any, and she wanted to know why. Somehow I was scared to tell her I was Jewish, so I said, 'Ich bin Ausländer' [I am a foreigner]. I was seven at the time! She was puzzled and phoned my parents and asked them what the problem was. My father then insisted that I wasn't going to religion instruction any more. Then I went to the Jewish Community for religious instruction. I really liked my teacher, Ora Gutmann. She was Israeli, a strong woman. In the Kennedy school we had religious instruction in school because there were so many Jewish kids there.

J   German Jewish or American Jewish?

JJ Mixed. One girl, Rosita, was an adopted Bolivian child. Her parents had immigrated to Bolivia and adopted her as a baby. I think she also knew Spanish and was brought up Spanish-German. A lot of kids had German mothers. Jewish men had married German women, and the children were raised mostly Jewish.

When I was five, dad had all these photography books, like a

Polish book called *We Shall Never Forget*, translated in Russian, German, English, and French. It contained pictures of concentration camps and mass shootings. I was looking at these pictures and wasn't sure if they were dolls or people or what. Yet there was something very threatening about them. My dad came in and said, 'You know . . . you know what this is?' I said no. He said, 'This is what happened to your grandparents. That's what the Germans did to us.' I got very scared and said, 'What about now? Are they still that dangerous?' He said, 'No, don't worry. They're not allowed to do that anymore.' That was his reasoning: if they could, they would, but they're not allowed anymore. My mom was angry when she heard about this. I never tried to play with children much, even less with German children. Then my dad said, 'Look, you don't need to bother with the old Germans. But the kids are innocent. They won't do anything. You can play with the kids.' I still didn't want to. They would tease me and hit me. My mom would say, 'Why don't you hit back?' I'd say, 'I can't: I don't even know if these children are insured.' That's the kind of kid I was. Germans really were enemies, and you had to be very careful, especially with the old ones. You don't shake hands with them, you avoid them, you don't trust them, you don't sing the national anthem. There was a lot of 'you don't.'

My grandmother lived in a world of art. After she stopped working in politics, she worked as the headmistress of an acting school, the Max Reinhardt Schule. She felt honored that she had a Jewish son-in-law, but she was a Catholic. I wanted to go to church with her, but my dad said no. She respected that very much. There was one problem, and that was Christmas.

My mom said, 'Well, we can't do this to my mother—not to celebrate Christmas with her.' Dad hated Christmas. He always managed to sabotage it. One way of doing that was to become ill. He always ate something that disagreed with him, and he ate too much of it, so everybody had to take care that he felt better. Another time he knocked over the Christmas tree, and it caught fire. He burned himself trying to extinguish the flames and had to be taken to the hospital. He had his own way of not having Christmas.

J   Did you celebrate Passover or other Jewish holidays?

JJ We didn't. I celebrated other holidays with Ora Gutmann in school, not at home. Usually Jewish holidays meant dad would be home, depressed. You could see things sort of approaching, and he would sit there and stare at the ceiling. It was difficult for him to talk to me. Or else he would just not get out of bed in the morning. He had these phases, particularly on Jewish holidays. He was very, very lonely—never made friends. And he drank. My mom was a social person, with many girlfriends from school. Some of them also married American non-Jewish men. Most were not Jewish. My mother always had her kaffee klatch, where she would make cakes and coffee and invite her friends. Dad would always sit there silently, not talking, listening and eating cake. That's what he always did, even as a baby. He would sit very silently with his mother and her lady friends, who were mostly Jewish, and they would feed him cake.

J   Did some Germans try to befriend him?

JJ Yeah, I think so. *She describes his best friend as Harvey, from Alabama, the husband of one of her mother's friends.*

Both Harvey and my dad had alcohol problems. My dad drank secretly and tried to hide it from my mom. There was a lot of fighting, with my dad just not saying anything. He would avoid conflicts or say, 'Yes, you're right,' and then not do anything about it.

My mother trained me to sniff dad and report whether he smelled like booze or not. I was good at that. Sometimes dad said, 'Don't tell mom.' But I had mixed feelings about that. I mean, my mom sometimes used me in that way. Their marriage was going on the rocks. Once she sent me to the cellar where dad was working to ask him whether he still loved us. He was really shocked at that. The marriage became increasingly unhappy. Mom had her own circle of friends and worked hard at her studies. Dad grew quieter and lonelier, with more frequent fits of depression. Later he hung photos of his parents, who were murdered, over his bed. I had nightmares as a kid, and even nowadays they sometimes happen. Always the same thing: somehow the Germans, the Nazis, or the ss returned to kill me. I always dreamt about boots somehow, boots marching in front of cellar windows. I would wake up screaming and had to crawl into bed with my parents.

J   Do you dream in German?

JJ Those who wanted to kill certainly spoke German, but it some-times sounded like barking dogs too.

I never played with other kids or did what other kids did. I had my books, I read, I went to the theater, to concerts, classical music, except for Wagner. That was a no-no. I hate him. Some-how that's ingrained. At home we didn't listen to any German composers. My grandmother loved Bach and she always played his religious things at Easter and Christmas. I'm not sure dad would have liked it—but he wasn't around much then.

JJ describes the events immediately preceding her father's death: Her mother discovered that her father was having an affair with an Israeli woman and demanded that he choose between them. To take revenge, she began an affair with a Tunisian man. While in Tunisia she was thrown by a horse and her back was broken. At the same time, JJ's father, who was on a freelance assignment in Norway, suffered a fatal heart attack. Only ten years old at the time of her father's death, JJ refused to accept the fact of his death for several years, partly because she was only later informed of it.

JJ Then mom went to Oslo to collect my dad's things, but I still didn't really believe it. Another friend of my mother's, Elizabeth, saw my father in the subway, or rather she believed [she saw] his spirit. She described it as very real for her, a very spooky experi-ence. She lost him in the crowd again but ran to my mother right away to dump the story on her, and I was still around. This reinforced the idea that somehow he was still around but didn't want to have contact [with us]. I wasn't sure anymore who was telling stories—Elizabeth, she and her ghost, my mom. I kept dreaming that he would come back one day until five years ago I dreamt—it was connected with psychotherapy—I saw this monu-ment, which really exists, with a Yiddish inscription of Jews who had been shot on it. It looked just like the one in Minsk. It had Hebrew letters, but it was Yiddish, and it was a monument for my grandparents and my dad. At this point I started to cry, scream-ing, hitting my head against that pillar, this black pillar, ripping my clothes and tearing my hair out, really violently. I woke up crying, and after that dream I never dreamt my dad would come back again.

I excuse myself to make coffee. When I return, JJ *begins to tell us about her own relationships and her involvement in activities of the Jewish Community in Berlin.*

JJ I had a lover who was a bit younger than I am. Her father is also a Jewish man from New York but not an immigrant. He joined the Communist Party at a young age and moved to East Germany during the McCarthy era. He married a German woman and had three kids, one of whom was my lover. I liked him the moment I saw him. He is so much like my father—his whole way, his quietness. He's a chemist and taught at the Academy of Science in the GDR.

J He's still in the East?

JJ No, he died. It was terrible. He must have liked me too: he allowed me to call him David, which was more than he allowed any of his children's friends to do. I went over to visit them regularly. Then he died suddenly, a blood clot in the brain. He was buried in Weißensee. There was a picture of him wearing the U.S. [army] uniform, like my dad.

J How did you meet him? Did you have contacts before with people in the GDR?

JJ No, I met my lover here. After she left [the GDR], she was not allowed to reenter. She once asked me whether I would go over and visit her parents. I agreed. I knew her father was Jewish, and one of the reasons why she was accepted by my mother is because she was such a nice Jewish girl. So when I first met her family I didn't know what to expect. I thought, he's going to be a rigid Communist Party guy. But he wasn't. It's not that I agreed with him so much politically, or that my dad would have. My father was liberal, not communist, though he once had problems with the House Un-American Activities Committee. Why, nobody knows. He also made a point of saying, 'I came to the United States as an immigrant and I'm grateful to the United States.' But he wouldn't have joined the Party—not dad. In that way my lover's father was different: he joined the Party as a young man and was convinced that he was building a new society. He was often disappointed, because the GDR wasn't exactly the way he had imagined it. Most of his contacts were with other exiled Americans who had been Party members.

My lover, Cathy, and I tried to visit him in East Berlin via Budapest, but she was taken out of the train by the police. I threw a fit and screamed, 'Stalin lebt!' [Stalin lives!]. We had agreed that I continue on alone. The whole family was waiting for us, even her brother and sister-in-law, and I had to tell them that they took Cathy from the train.

J   When did Cathy move to the West?

JJ April '86. She has American citizenship now and is in the States. Her father died as an American citizen, even though his passport was destroyed by GDR officials. Cathy had a good lawyer in the States.

J   And your relationship?

JJ My relationship? Cathy dropped me.

J   Have you returned to the United States?

JJ I did research there at YIVO [a center for Yiddish studies in New York City] for my dissertation, on Yiddish songs written in ghettos in the Soviet Union and Poland between 1940 and 1945. The YIVO was an important experience for me. Yet people found it strange that I bothered with Yiddish, when I was a German Jew. Once I had been looking for a person there and I heard an employee say to this woman, 'The German is looking for you.' Just enough to give me the creeps. I'm not German, and I insist I am not. People couldn't handle that, and I felt like a zoo animal. When I would say I'm from Germany, they'd respond, 'Oh, really?' meaning, what kind of freak are you? And I was talking with Jews! People [were very concerned to know] whether you want to live in the United States. But how without a green card?

J   How about Israel?

JJ says that this particular sequence of questions is something she hears all the time from Americans. She then talks about her feelings toward Israel.

JJ I was a Zionist as a young girl. When I was sixteen I went to Israel and stayed for two months. I was very unhappy there. I hated it. I thought it disgusting. I had very unpleasant experiences with men, including attempted rape and all sorts of unpleasantries like that. I was very disillusioned. I disagree with some of the basic ideas of Zionism. I don't believe in a state that is only Jewish at the expense of another nation. I don't believe in an exclusively Jewish state. I lived with a Palestinian family there, coincidentally. I had first lived with friends of my mother. Somehow that changed a lot of my attitudes and beliefs. After I returned, I tried to talk about my experiences with people in the Jewish Community, and no one wanted to listen. Quite the contrary: I was really ostracized. Because I lived with a Palestinian family, people would look at me as some kind of a whore.

J What's your relationship to the Jewish Community now?

JJ Whenever I'm there it's depressing. There is no space for us outside of the temple.

J What about the Jüdische Gruppe [an informal group of Berlin Jews who seek an alternative to the official Community]?

JJ I was there for a while, true. There's still some people there I like and appreciate. To tell you the truth, though, one of the reasons why I decided I was going to leave that group was homophobia. I felt uncomfortable as the only gay person. There *was* another gay man—Arnold, from South Africa, also the son of German Jews— with whom I was on friendly terms.

J Does your feminism or being gay relate in some way with your particular history of being a child of an immigrant?

JJ Yeah, I do believe in some ways. For one thing, I was always very much daddy's girl. I had a closer relationship to my dad than to my mom. I identified with him and he happened to be a man. My mother always made the point that I'm much like him. I personally believe it has a lot to do with my identification with the Jewish part. My mom was a convert, so it's not quite the same. After he died, though, there was a lot of anger also, that he was gone.

Somehow, he loved women, so I did too. [But] some of the feminism came from my mother, though she would have never called herself a feminist. She was ambitious and had to struggle hard as a woman, and she understood that she had to struggle because she was a woman. I always heard her say, 'If I were a man, things would be so much easier.'

JJ *tells us that she suspects that her father was ambivalent about marrying her mother, who 'looked very German, very blonde, blue-eyed.' The Israeli woman with whom he was later involved looked 'very much like his mom.'*

J   When you seek a partner, are you interested in a particular appearance that's Jewish?

JJ   I guess so. I've also had lovers who looked different. Cathy was my first Jewish lover. You don't find that many lesbians around, especially not Jewish ones. I'm sure that's what tied us together, really tied me to her, but at the same time it was dangerous because the breaking up almost killed me, and I'm not sure whether that is worth it. Jewish women have more power to really hurt me.

J   With whom do you feel solidarity?

JJ   This is something very formal. *She shows us her German passport.*

Of course I was raised with the language. I studied *Germanistik* [German language and literature]. It is my mother's language—*Muttersprache*, right? At the same time, I've studied mostly literature written by Jews. That was my choice. I did comparative studies of poetry, German poetry by Jews written after the Holocaust, also Yiddish poetry.

I have roots in Berlin because I have always lived here. I have friends here. I belong to the women's movement in many ways, though I also feel I'm not really part of it. I'm a minority woman. I'm Jewish. I always seek solidarity with Jewish women. But there are very few Jewish women here of my age.

This feeling of alienation is something foreign [to Americans] because they feel they're American first. It's not a problem. They don't say, 'I'm *not* American,' like I say, 'I'm *not* German.' I'm a minority here in the women's group because I'm Jewish. I'm a minority as a feminist and as a lesbian, and that means always sitting in between. I'm very aware of that; it's an awareness that never leaves me. After four years in the Jewish group and four years of struggle against their homophobia, I gave up.

I've started a women's group which is mixed, in the sense of Jews and non-Jews, named Der Schabbeskreis, to have an exchange between those Gentiles who are feminist like me, who are willing to face the past and present with Jews in terms of German Jewish relations. We have other non-German members, and male guests as well, for instance, the father of one woman who helped me find a job. He's Jewish and was lonely after his last divorce, so I always invited him for the holidays. There was one gay man with his non-Jewish lover who stayed with us for a while. And a bisexual man from Riga, who might have started his own group now, of children of concentration camp survivors. He wanted to meet more people with a similar background.

I would say that if I meet women elsewhere and they know that I'm Jewish, they can't handle it. Most of them can't handle it. They want to forget that as quickly as possible. You feel immediately marked, as if someone has spilled the beans.

J You said earlier that your family in South Africa is the only family 'that deserves that name.' What do you mean?

JJ My mother has siblings, a sister and a brother, who are still alive. I have no contact with them. My uncle didn't have any contact with my mother. He certainly didn't show up for her funeral. There is no contact [between us], and I don't care and he doesn't care.

Then there's my mother's sister, who never liked the idea, I think, of my mother marrying a Jew. I had very little to do with her for over ten years prior to my mother's death. When my mother took her life in January, her sister did not want to give her a Jewish funeral, which I insisted on. Eventually, my cousin came from South Africa. He supported me. He said, 'Okay, Jessica, I understand you have strong Jewish feelings and I sympathize with you there. We are one family.' That's why I say he is family, while my mother's sister is not. She even wanted some furniture that was in my mom's place. But the main issue was that she wanted a nonreligious—what can you say—at least a non-Jewish, funeral. I said, 'I will have one even if you won't pay for it. It's me, the daughter, who decides.' There was a terrible fight, and in the end she screamed at me, actually attacked me. We had a fight, with fists.

J How did you know she didn't want a Jewish funeral?

JJ My mother always said something which nobody wanted to hear: 'Give my body to medicine.' That was unacceptable to me, unacceptable for everybody. My mom wanted to save money. I insisted on the Jewish funeral because, after all, my mother did convert. I wanted to have a decent Jewish funeral for all that it's worth, while my aunt wanted a funeral in which she herself played the main role. She's an actress also and runs a theater in Kreuzberg. I also found out from a gay friend of my mother's, who was the last one to talk to her, that she killed herself because of money, for not having money. She was afraid to go broke. She had talked about this with her sister, who has lots of money and who suggested she apply for welfare. That was an unacceptable solution. She was in her fifties, a bit bourgeois, and a doctor. She couldn't do that and maintain her self-esteem as a human.

[My aunt] wanted a notice in the paper, a quotation from Kleist, 'Die Wahrheit ist, daß mir im Leben nichts zu helfen war' [The truth is that nothing was there to help me in life]. This is pure cynicism. I said I would never, never put my name under such a headline. She had her students accompany the coffin to the grave singing, 'Zehn Brüder sein wir gewain' [We were ten brothers]. I found this unbelievable. I studied Yiddish songs for years. This song was made into a concentration camp song, and she had these German students, these kids, accompany my mother to her grave with that song. Also with the last line of the song: 'I die every day because I have no more to eat.' It's about going broke, you know. I thought this was unbelievable. When they lowered the coffin, I didn't wait to finish the song. I just threw dirt on [the coffin, as is customary] and ran [from] the cemetery. I wanted everybody to know that I will never, never again, never have anything to do with this woman.

With my cousin Peter it was different. He tried to say *Kaddish* with me. He was with me after the funeral. I have problems with going to South Africa, but that is the only family I still have that behaves like family. I hate apartheid and I hate the political system, but at the same time I have this family feeling too.

J   Do you maintain a balance between family by blood and family who behaves like family?

JJ This blood relationship between me and my mother's siblings—I cut this off and declare it nonexistent. The social idea of relationship has turned into a mockery. The family in South Africa have proven to be family by their behavior.

My mother was quite lonely in the end. She had these friends, and either they died or petered out. That's why she had to fall back on her sister. She was very proud. In earlier years she wouldn't have anything to do with her sister, but in the end she depended on her. Her business went okay a few years, then started going down. My mother was ill a lot, couldn't keep up with the competition. Competition can become so brutal. It's eaten peo-ple, and it ate my mother too. I don't believe in a system that can do that to people, that's there to eat them up. If she wouldn't have had to be a business woman, but just treat animals, she would have been a happy person. At least in her profession she would have still had some sense of self-respect. She was doing something important, something valuable, something useful. [Yet] she thought that whether she lives or dies would not make any difference. The night from the first to the second of January she took the poison she used to put animals to sleep, to put them down. She used it on herself. Her assistant found her dead in the morning. I got that phone call. *She pauses for a moment before beginning again.*

For me this was a very, very difficult year. I mean Jewish year. Cathy left me in October, mom killed herself in January. I had quite a crisis.

JJ *closed her story, which she had begun with a picture of her Jewish father and an account of his return to Germany, with the suicide of her German mother. Jewish return and German death. Paternal dominance and maternal self-evisceration.*

At that point, after three hours of interview, Jeff excused himself, and I continued talking with JJ *off tape for another two and a half hours. She was still in the middle of a discussion about feminism, the gay and lesbian community, and the intellectual atmosphere generally in Berlin. Following this interview, Jeff and I had an argument about the nature of our project and our responsibility to our discussion partners.*[1]

JJ *sent the following postscript in September 1990:*

After the interview was completed in the summer of 1989, ma-jor changes have taken place in this city.

That summer my Jewish friend Lara was still contemplating to leave the GDR and move West. A few months later I went to pick her up from one of the [border] crossings on a bridge over the Spree. It was a cold, dark afternoon, and the icy, slippery pave-ment made walking a pain in the butt. We were beaming with pleasure upon seeing one another. I was happy to be able to take her to my flat for tea, something that had not been possible before.

Only days had passed since this [opening of the Wall] on November 9th had so horrified me. At first I could not believe what I heard on BBC. Then I saw it. The enthused masses scared the wits out of me. I suffered violent attacks of agoraphobia. I had only wanted to buy ingredients for banana bread I intended to bake for my flatmate's birthday, but, alas, no bananas were to be had. Lara later told me that Cuban bananas rotted in East Berlin while its natives carried off the Western variant from Karstadt, Hertie, and smaller fruit shops. Waltraut called it 'The Day of Many Feet.' I played an old Nancy Sinatra song for her: 'These boots are made for walking, that's all they're made to do / One day these boots are gonna walk all over you!'

For days I had no desire to leave my flat. On TV I watched people dancing on top of the Brandenburg Gate, hearts crying tears of joy. I had a tight feeling in my throat. The streets were jam-packed with stinking Trabi cars; public transport was struggling not to break down. I had given up on trying to ride the packed trains and buses. Cabs no longer managed to get you from A to B more quickly or safely than other transportation. So I resorted to walking and avoided going long distances.

Now, of course, things have normalized. The feeling of being invaded has ceased, and with that the adrenalin waves of panic in the face of impending disaster. I know that this is not much of a political assessment, but it might give you an idea of what I initially felt.

I did not want this reunification. Nothing is left to remind Germans that they actually lost the last war. They won the peace with American help—capitalism, the entrepreneurial spirit that goes with it, hi-tech efficiency. Now their victory was complete.

Don't get me wrong: I don't want the Cold War back either. At the end of the day I did not get the T-shirt saying, 'Ich will meine MAUER wieder haben!' [I want my Wall back!]—for the obvious reason that I didn't want to risk being attacked on the street. Mobs usually don't understand jokes. More than safety considerations, I also didn't want to offend all the black and Jewish lesbians, or straight women for that matter, who have lived in the ex-GDR and whom I might never have met if the Wall would have remained. For them, new opportunities have opened up, privileges that are a matter of course for me. Finally, the GDR nostalgia of some people on the Left began to get on my nerves, almost as much as the glee of the conservatives who had always [thought] that socialism was bound to fail. The GDR as a nation-state, a way of life, a form of arrested development—this was nothing I ever supported or condoned. Why should I do so now that it is gone?

My friend Wendy and I spent days photographing countless T-shirts celebrating the fall of the Wall. Most of them announced, '9. November 1989—Ich war dabei!' [I was there!].

One thing remains that is truly alarming: ever since the cork popped out of the bottle, all the nasty attitudes spilled out. It's unadulterated acid of racism, ethnocentrism, and anti-Semitism. There has been more racist violence and neo-Nazism in the last one and one-half years than since liberation. For black people especially, the ex-GDR has become a very unsafe place to be. I find myself thinking with increasing frequency of places I could consider for migration, despite the fact that I, just like everyone else, have adapted to the new situation, more or less, after all.

In a final letter, in March 1994, JJ informed us that now, with the support of a lover, she felt able for the first time to investigate the German side of her family history. Her mother's father had been a Nazi film director. He had filed for divorce when her mother was two years old. JJ thinks that this explains much of her mother's behavior, such as her conversion to Judaism and marriage to a Jewish man. JJ stressed that her own anxiety about being accepted as a Jew by other Jews and by Germans made her hesitant to delve into this part of her history and made it 'virtually impossible to have a German or German Jewish identity.'

'I cannot say who I am, where I belong. I don't fit.'

Born 1954   Kazakhstan, Soviet Union
1957–   East Berlin (parents in exile
           in the Soviet Union)

Kostja, as he is known, is an imposing but gentle figure. He has a long red beard, red hair, and his demeanor matches his size. His eyes betray his youth and vulnerability. KM's parents were both committed communists. His father, a building engineer, came from a Polish Jewish family in Berlin, and his mother was from an upper-class Jewish family in Berlin. KM's mother's parents did not agree with her political views. His paternal grandparents, although not communists themselves, had connections to communist friends in Moscow.

His own parents voluntarily emigrated to the Soviet Union in 1935 from Parisian exile, his father in January, his mother in October. Like many others of his parents' generation, his father was falsely charged during the Stalinist purges and sent to a forced labor camp in 1937; he remained there until 1951. In March 1952 Ilse Münz was permitted to join her husband. After Stalin's death, in 1955, KM's father was officially 'rehabilitated,' called to an office, and told that he was cleared of all charges. KM's mother worked as a nurse in Moscow until 1942, when she was drafted for work in the military. Thomas, KM's older brother, then six years old, was placed in an orphanage. The war ended in August 1945. In 1947, at the end of her husband's ten-year sentence, Ilse Münz was informed that he would have to serve four more years. They returned to East Berlin in 1956. KM was was three years old.[1]

KM studied journalism at the University of Leipzig. He worked for the International Press Office of the GDR, leading and advising foreign film and TV teams who were granted permission to work in the GDR. (He was, in fact, the official adviser for our video documen-

tary.) In addition, he often gave tours to visitors to East Berlin who were interested in the Jewish Community. In 1988 he began working in public relations for the Stiftung—Neue Synagogue Berlin—Centrum Judaicum, an information and research center on German Jewry. Since unification, KM has worked for the largely West-dominated Jewish Community of Greater Berlin.

Our interview took place in the summer of 1989 in our apartment in the center of Berlin. When we warned KM that our apartment, which had been furnished by the government, was bugged, he told us that he lived freely and could only live in the GDR under the condition that he could say what he liked. He talked for three hours.

J   You can begin where you like. Perhaps with the most important facts. When you were born? Do you have memories from the Soviet Union?

KM   OK, I was born in 1954, on 4 May, in Tschurbai-Nura in Kazakhstan—central Kazakhstan, near the Mongolian border. Karaganda is the largest city of the region. I was born in a gulag where my parents were. I remember that the day after Stalin's death my brother got the money that my father had received for his political rehabilitation. We then belonged to the privileged in this region. You can't compare this gulag with a concentration camp or a closed facility. *While these labor camps were not death camps, many people perished from the harsh physical labor and terrible conditions. However, not all prisoners did harsh physical labor. Some worked in factories, and a few did clerical work, cooking, or skilled labor. The camp in which KM was born was a 'work village.' His mother continued her medical duties. People there were former political prisoners who had been released and were free to move about the area.*

This region where we were was the steppes. Today they use it for space flights. The area extended for eighteen hundred kilometers and went on and on. People could 'move freely,' but there was no place to go. There simply was nothing there, and nobody had anything.

J   What happened after you returned to Berlin?

KM   Shortly after our return my father had a serious heart attack, and I was sent to England, where grandparents on both sides lived. When I came back to the GDR, to a children's home, I had problems—I remember that—because I had been in England. When we painted, I colored the busses red like they were in England, not yellow like in the GDR. These yellow busses were the first busses I ever saw. My grandfather would pick me up, and I would ring the bell as long as I wanted. When I did that here in the GDR, my brother had to pay a fine. Those are my memories. *Alienation and the problem of belonging are a recurring theme in the interview. Even his Russian name, which his parents gave him when they thought they might remain in the Soviet Union, came to symbolize the difference he felt between himself and his surroundings.*

J   You talked about being in a home and being separated from your parents.

KM   I was briefly separated [from them] in Moscow after they came to the GDR. They arrived here in December 1956, and they got the apartment that my mother now lives in in the spring of 1957. We were briefly in a hotel, and then I was with them when they moved into the apartment. But the really traumatic period of my childhood was in this home [in the GDR], which was for the children of the ADN [news service] and government officials.

J   Why were you put into a home?

KM   I was only there during the week, because my mother had to work and after work she went to see my father in the hospital. She didn't know what she should do with me. This was a terrible time for me. It had been very different to be a child in the Soviet Union. All of our playing around, trying to get food, to make a better deal, was normal for the Soviet Union. People loved children, and they were much freer. When I came here I was different, I didn't speak the language. I didn't fit in, and this caused me a lot of problems. One of them had to do with what I call my 'Jewish coming out' [*he says this phrase in English*], and this experience is not specific to the GDR, but takes place all over Europe. *KM's use of the expression* coming out, *commonly used to mean openly declaring one's homosexuality, to describe recognizing Jewish identity is a way of showing how contemporary the problem is and how seriously it affects one's entire life.*[2]

Forty years is perhaps two generations, and that is simply not enough time to balance out six million deaths. Because behind every one of these people who died is a person, a relative, a trauma that exists. I was born in 1954, nine years after the end of the war.

KM *talks about how his childhood experiences in the* GDR *were affected by his being born in the second generation after Auschwitz and about the relationship between individuals in his generation. It was very easy to gather a group of people of his age in East Berlin: they were all living in Berlin, even in the same neighborhoods, children of those who had left and returned to build the* GDR.

What do people do when they return after living for twelve years in exile? They first look for others who also survived, and this was the case with my mother. Somehow her communist convictions were stronger than her Jewish consciousness. She sought out the Katzenstein family [Kate Leiterer's parents (see chapter 9)]. Okay, these people were Jews, but also communists. It was only later that one discerned what was different about these people, whether communists or Jews. What did the children of these people know? We simply knew these people because they had returned from emigration and were like us. But the communist or marxist indoctrination at home was more important than the Jewish information.

J   You mean your parents compared these aspects of people?

KM   Yes, of course. You see, the Jewish Community here was not in any condition to do this. In 1953 the Community split. The fact is there were suddenly two Communities, West and East, and then there existed in Germany what had never existed in world Jewry, namely, that there were good Jews and bad Jews. *A Western European Jew,* KM *is forgetting the difference his parents' and grandparents' generations in Germany saw between themselves and the* Ostjuden, *the Eastern European Jews—between themselves as bourgeois, secularized European Jews and the uneducated village farmers or traders of the* shtetl. *Berlin, in fact, had an* Ostjuden *quarter, the Scheunenviertel, located in an area of the former East Berlin.*

This is really the trauma I was talking about. One was suddenly more Jewish than the other. Since world Jewry does not recognize this split, but rather a division between Jews and non-Jews, we had a major problem. So I think that the trauma that exists here in West and East Berlin has to do with the Westerners trying to compete against the few stalwarts remaining here in the East.

J   Were you encouraged to be a *Kader* [a Party member who could travel to the West] in these years, even though your parents were not in the Party?

KM No, you are mistaken: my mother was in the Party, but my father wasn't. *Encouraged* is not the right [word]. My parents were VDN. My mother was a committed communist, whatever that means. My parents both worked in responsible positions, not in the upper echelons, but they certainly belonged to the 'upper class' [*he says this in English*]. I never had any problems with that. We lived much better than others, and for good reasons, partly because of [our VDN status]. I didn't have any problems with that. They shared similar experiences with many people here who returned from exile and wanted to participate in this experiment, to build socialism in a part of Germany. These people, of course, who were antifascist, were all very close.

As a child it was all quite normal for me that I would be a Young Pioneer, then a Thälmann pioneer [the stage following the Young Pioneers, for students in grades 4 through 7. Ernst Thälmann was the leader of the communists in Germany before World War II], and then go into the FDJ [Freie Deutsche Jugend, the general home for the Communist youth organization]. In school my background and those of the children of my parents' friends sometimes caused problems, because we did come from a different background and received certain benefits. I was often the better Young Pioneer because of my family's experiences. When my parents read stories at night, it wasn't about witches and wolves, but the stories of their fights against fascism, the building of socialism, and such things. So these people they told us about weren't mythical heroes, but people we knew and lived with. I knew how to define for the teacher what a communist was because I had heard it from those people who had built the GDR. When we were eleven years old, Nina Hagen, my classmate, and I would walk down the street singing the love duet from Brecht's *Threepenny Opera.* Brecht was not a famous German writer, but the best friend of my father's friend. This illustrates, perhaps, the background in which I grew up.

Often we kids knew more about politics or political propaganda than our teachers, since the Party officials responsible for this sat around our dinner tables. Things were okay until about 1967, when student protests began on campuses throughout Europe. With me and my friends, these same people who were later in the Wir für Uns group, things started changing. Even though I was going to school in these difficult times, no teacher asked me if I was watching Western TV. I imagine that they would have known anyway. We had a TV from 1960 or 1961, and for my parents watching Western TV was part of their political work, whether it was forbidden or not. The Wall went up at this time, and we were questioned about contacts in the West. For me, having contacts in the East would have been unusual, since I grew up here without any extended family.

But the turning point for me was when my brother left the GDR, on 26 July 1961, and went to the West. We were very close, and I was very traumatized by this event, since it was not just a good-bye but a real division. We didn't see him again until 1972, 20 September, after the Four Power agreement. *On 3 September 1971 the Four Power Berlin Treaty was signed. It improved East-West relations by easing transit between West Berlin and West Germany, travel and visitation of West Berliners in the East, and communication between East and West Berlin and, fundamentally, having all powers renounce the use of force. Thomas left shortly before the Wall was built, when it was not too difficult to actually leave East Berlin or East Germany. The psychological trauma of his brother's leaving was very difficult for KM. For his mother, who had dedicated herself to the GDR, her son's move to the West, while officially an act of political betrayal, on the personal level meant that her family was again separated. She even told us, 'Ich hab ihn zehn Jahre nicht gesehen. Mein ganzes Leben besteht nur aus Trennungen' [I didn't see him for ten years. My whole life consists only of separations]. KM's remembering the exact date of his brother's sudden departure reminds one how the personal and the political intersect in the GDR and mark important caesuras in the lives of its citizens.*

You know, the problem for me is that I cannot say who I am, where I belong. I don't fit. I can't communicate with the Germans and often feel more comfortable with people from France, Italy, or Spain, or England and America. In the years between 1971 and 1975 I was like Jack Kerouac. I hitchhiked all over [the Socialist countries] and would meet people from Scandinavia who would say, 'We're going to Turkey, come along.' But we could only go as far as Sosepol in Bulgaria. We stood there and waved; they moved on. From Schönefeld [the East Berlin airport] to Sosepol, those were our boundaries. *KM's description is similar to the ritualized good-byes that regularly took place at the Friedrichstrasse station, which we ourselves experienced in the summer of 1989, when Westerners left East Berlin at midnight to return to West Berlin.*

Strangely enough, I was always attracted to borders, probably so that I wouldn't lose them for my orientation.

J   Did you have a feeling for the Soviet Union, like your parents?

KM   I was there twice. I never felt like I wanted to stay there, simply because I know too much about life there from my parents. But there certainly was a heartfelt emotional relationship [*Seelenverwandschaft*]. My mother was especially Russified. She was a member of the Communist Youth Group in Berlin at a very young age and was attracted to the Soviet Union not only politically and intellectually but also emotionally. My father was very different: he spoke Russian very poorly and always remained the German intellectual.

You know, my mother came from a wealthy background in Berlin. They never tried to hide that. That was not a problem for me. She made a conscious choice of her own free will to do what she did. I cannot think of anything, or imagine anything, that I missed in my life. I have to be arrogant enough to say, although you would probably hear something to the contrary in the United States, that I didn't miss not having tropical fruit. I don't feel bad about that at all. *Many Westerners, Americans as well as Germans, used tropical fruit as the index for happiness based on consumerism. The banana became the symbol, both in the GDR and in Germany after unification, for the material well-being that the GDR lacked and would now achieve.*

My situation, my birth, is unique, because I was the desired child, an example to the world that my parents survived Hitler and Stalin. Of course I am not one of those people who say that Stalin was just as bad as Hitler, but my parents were in the Soviet Union. My father would never have survived Dachau or any other of these camps, because those who were brought to Dachau, Auschwitz, Theresienstadt, and all those others weren't considered human beings. They were supposed to be turned into wigs, lampshades, or mattresses. Where my father was imprisoned, that was not a death camp. I was born there. I represented the great red hope for my parents and their friends. All of us born in these circumstances were considered very special. We were proof that [some of my parents' generation] had survived! This is not atypical for Jews.

J When did you discover that you were Jewish? Or when did it become important to you?

KM It actually happened without me really knowing it. I had the advantage that my parents never tried to hide the fact that we were Jews. This always played a role; it may not always have been the main concern, but it was always present. We didn't have a menorah or a Star of David in the house, but it was present in what was discussed or noticed. For example, if someone on television was, or appeared to be, Jewish, it was mentioned. I knew that we were Jewish, and there was a time when it wasn't so important for me. Once I asked my father if there were Jewish Indians, because I wanted to play Indians.

But then, suddenly a cousin of my father's who survived appeared from Jerusalem, and she lived in West Berlin. She came every week, and if I hadn't known I was Jewish from my parents, I certainly would have known it from her. And through this cousin, Jossel and Abraham came in the summer of 1966 from Tel Aviv and Haifa. I just remembered this, in fact, and now I see it as a really important memory. These two were very important for me because I was accepted [by them]. They needed me to show them around; and they came every day from West Berlin through Checkpoint Charlie and had to return at twelve o'clock. They were my brother's age, around seventeen or eighteen. I kept up contact with Jossel, and then came the Six Day War and he was dead. In school I learned that this war was imperialistic and aggressive. And at home in the news I saw Nasser saying, 'Throw the Jews into the sea.' If my parents, and especially my father, hadn't been there, I would have gotten myself into a lot of trouble.

It was always important that I was Jewish, although it was not my main concern. I didn't like Bob Dylan only because he was Jewish, although I certainly was aware of that. It is just that I was forced through the special political situation of the GDR, and the way that propaganda and politics were often confused, to find my own point of view and argumentation. There emerged questions about Judaism that weren't answered for me. That was in the period between 1970 and 1973, before the Yom Kippur War. Questions emerged for me about Judaism, not about Israel. We were kept informed about the imperialistic policies of Israel and the events going on in the Middle East.

It was then that I also looked for Jewish writing, Eastern European [Yiddish] stories by [I. L.] Peretz or Sholom Ale[i]chem. I was really naive. I went to the State Library and said, 'I want to read something Jewish.' The librarian looked at me in amazement, and I realized that you just can't ask like that. I went home and asked my father. He responded, 'Why are you so interested in that? There are more important things in the world.'

KM *talks about his involvement with others of his generation in establishing a club to talk about significant world events and political issues that were not discussed among some of his friends who didn't have the kind of parents that he did, those who had more contact with other countries. This was around 1967 or 1968, and up until 1969 they were left alone by the government. They had discussions and planned projects that never would have occurred to the politicians, he says, because they were too old. Socialism could be attractive! They organized concerts such as the Festival of the Political Song or collections to show solidarity with Vietnam.*

I was involved and had friends all over the place, and then around 1975—I don't know why it happened then—I felt like something was missing. I discovered that it was my Jewishness. And I went to Peter Kirchner, the head of the Jewish Community [in East Berlin], and asked what I had to do to become a member of the Jewish Community. Wait a minute . . . it wasn't 1975, but rather 1974? I went to Kirchner, and it was a few weeks or a month later when I figured out where the synagogue was in Berlin. Of course at the time I looked a little weird, with a kind of Angela Davis hairdo and a long beard. On my coat I had all kinds of patches with different political sayings on them. I suspected that he [Kirchner] didn't take me very seriously, and I did feel somewhat rejected, but the most important information I got was where the library was, and I sat down and began to read. I often went to the synagogue but realized that I didn't understand anything.

J   You mean the language?

KM Of course the language, but also the *siddur* [Hebrew prayer book].
I read it all the way through in German. I didn't like it, but no one
told me it was all prayers and psalms. I read it and thought, So
that is what the Jews believe in. I went back to Kirchner, and he
defined the Community as the home of those who have survived.

J   Was that the way he put it?

KM No, but it captures the sense of what he meant. He said, 'We are a
religious community, and for us religion is most important.' I
argued with him but couldn't at that point do so well, but still
making the point that I was still a Jew in spite of the fact that I
didn't agree with him. I had just become a member of the Party,
but it didn't matter. And then I began to get more involved with
this stuff. I started a theater of songs with some friends, and I had
the idea to do a [radio] program of Yiddish songs. They didn't
want to, but they were afraid to say anything against it, since the
Jews are all dead and you can't say anything against the Jews.

Then I got interested in the history of the Scheunenviertel. In
1978 I left the radio and was kicked out of the Party for disciplinary reasons. My last radio program was called 'History is Red:
Stories from Antifascists.' We did portraits and interviews with
antifascists.

J   Not about antifascist Jews?

KM When we came up with the idea, it was supposed to be about
antifascists, but the amazing thing was—and my colleague noticed this—that only Jews came to mind. At that time I couldn't
recognize Jews by name. It wasn't that I was some sort of Jewish
philo-Semite; I even got upset with my mother when she would
pick someone out and say they looked Jewish and they were one of
us. So I asked my mother who we could talk to for these interviews. And this was the way I got into all of this and found my way
to the synagogue. And even with the children of these Jewish
antifascists it was very interesting since we all knew each other
from childhood, [when we] played together since our parents all
were acquainted. Our paths always crossed, [but I never thought
of them as being Jewish]. Irene Runge was one of these people.
We talked a couple of times, and then she came up with this idea
to organize a group in the Community. When we considered who

to invite—they should all be Jewish, we thought—we didn't have to do anything more than open our address books and invite the people we already knew. That was in 1985.

That is where Irene's group Wir für Uns comes in. We got together people who we had always met before to discuss issues and problems, but this time we were meeting in a different context. We hadn't told each other we would all be meeting together, but we had all individually hoped to see each other there. I knew —and I discussed this with Kirchner—that I was not going to be a religious Jew but that people like me [actual Jews] were still important for the Community. I had to learn more before [I could be religious], and even then this Community had to accept other kinds of Jews if it were not going to be the end [*Endlösung*] of this East Berlin Community. KM *uses the same term the Nazis used to describe how Germany would be after all the Jews had been exterminated.*

This was at the end of 1985, the beginning of 1986. I knew that it would take time for the Community to accept this. I did tell him [Kirchner] that I was prepared to be circumcised, since it couldn't be done in Kazakhstan.

Soon after that there was a discussion in the Community about what I call the 'Jewish coming out' about Jewish identity. A friend of mine reproached the Community that they were too orthodox and too doctrinaire, that for him it was [also] important to uphold Jewish culture and tradition. I answered him by saying that if I was interested in changing the political culture of the GDR, then I wouldn't go to the Jewish Community. [If I was going to change this culture], then I would try again to be accepted into the Party, since in the GDR one divides one's work, and to change the political relations through the Jewish Community takes too long. It will not happen that the Jewish Community will replace the SED [Sozialistische Einheitspartei Deutschland, *the* Communist Party of the GDR].

So I was patient and willing to wait to become a member of the Community. On 11 November 1987 I was admitted. *Again,* KM's *remembering the exact date emphasizes that instances when he feels a sense of identity and belonging are specifically marked by moments when his personal, religious, and even political life intersect.*

J Did you feel any different—more Jewish—after the circumcision and your admittance to the Community? Or have deeper feelings of belonging?

KM No. In Germany I had to learn that everything has an ordered relation to everything else. One of the first things I learned in Germany, and [the thing that] was most difficult for me was to accept that there are people who believe that everything that is not expressly permitted is forbidden. I am different and I grew up differently. I never asked for permission; rather I first did what I wanted, and if I had problems I knew that it was probably forbidden. The Germans are overly bureaucratic and tend toward being perfectionists. They think they can do everything better than everyone else. So I have not done anything more now than arranged my life according to German ways of doing things, German points of view, and German attitudes.

I am now a member of the Community. The Germans have fewer problems dealing with me as a Jew [now that I am officially a member of the Community]. For me it was a very important step to accept this. However, this acceptance happened more in my head. As I said, I can be on my own and be alone. I don't need a party, or club, but still it was important for me to join the Community and to have solidarity. If I get a call that someone is needed for a *minyan* [the ten men needed for a Jewish religious service], then I go. If I am downtown on a Friday—I have a yarmulke [skullcap] and *siddur* in the car—then I plan my day so I can go to the synagogue at six o'clock. People depend on me. That is more important to me than the life of the Jewish Community. The Community, in any case, is made up of mostly old people, and the future of the Community rests with those who will live. The Community needs these people since a community only exists through people. Now we're talking about getting a rabbi. *The American Jewish Committee did indeed bring a rabbi from Champaign, Illinois. He was born in Poland and was a survivor of the camps. Unfortunately for the Community, he left after disagreements with the members about how the Community should be run and how he should behave living in the* GDR.

As a Jew living in the GDR, I need a teacher who can teach me what the criteria are for selecting a rabbi more than [I need] a rabbi. Democracy and a community—a Jewish Community is no more than an example of democracy. Democracy only works with knowledgeable and educated people, whether it is a parliamentary or a socialistically centralized democracy. With uneducated idiots one can't have a democracy; one might as well have a dictatorship. KM *seems to be implying that his fellow* GDR *citizens are unprepared for democratic practice. Education and critical thinking in order to make the right choices seem to be his goal.*

J Do you see yourself as German?

KM That is my big problem. I think German, that is, in the German language. I articulate my thoughts in this language. I live in Germany. I live with Germans, and not so badly. But in terms of what you would call the German mentality, I don't feel German. I don't feel like a foreigner and I don't feel foreign [*fremd*]. But when it comes to certain things, I don't think like a German and am not German. Those are the problems that I have, and if someone asks me, 'Who are you?' then I can only follow my instincts and say, 'I am a cow in a barn for horses.' My parents are German, everyone in my family is German, but [I don't feel German].

J We are about to run out of tape, and we have one more question: You discussed having solidarity with the Jewish Community, and just now you talked about not feeling German. How did you feel toward the other children who had come back with their parents from emigration?

KM We knew that we belonged to the same group [*zusammengehören*], and we didn't differentiate among refugees' children, Jewish children, or children of resistance fighters. Our parents may have done that, but we were all the same. All of us who were children of parents who were in the VDN found each other because our parents had similar experiences, had found each other after the war, and were now friends. We found the same friends in their children. And when I was in the orphanage, I knew that if there was a problem I should look for these kids. Our parents had told us all that if you lose your way, don't necessarily look for someone wearing their Party pin; look for the blue triangle of the VDN. This connection was extra. To be a comrade [*Genosse*] is good, especially if you have no one else, but if you find someone who has the blue triangle alone or wears it and the Party pin, then stick to them. KM*'s experience as a child reflects the significance of solidarity established among those who considered themselves antifascists and had been in exile.*

With our final question, we came back to the issue of place of exile, which has been central to our concerns in all the interviews. Now we were asking it of the second generation.

J　Was there a difference between the children who came back from the Soviet Union and those who were in the West?

KM　I always envied those who were in England and America, for example, Thomas Brasch. When I played, I often imagined things about America. Around the corner from where my mother lives, beyond the Greifswalderstrasse, is the Storkowerstrasse. Aside from a five-hundred-meter area that was built up, everything else was bombed out. There is a big field there, and that is where the first new buildings were built in our neighborhood. The trees that are now very large were still quite small then. And if you stared a long time at the place where the new houses were being built, you knew that beyond that was America. Once with my friend Georg, we packed our backpacks, all of the things that were important—a few matchbox cars, a newspaper, and a few other things—and we wanted to travel with our scooter to America.

After the Wall came down and Germany was unified, one of the first things KM *did was to start planning a trip to America. In 1992* KM *and his wife spent eight weeks traveling all over America visiting relatives, from San Francisco to New Orleans and from New York to Florida.*

KM *dictated his postscript in person on 7 July 1991. He was still working at the Stiftung—Neue Synagogue Berlin—Centrum Judaicum, dealing with the repercussions of the unification of the West and East Berlin Jewish Communities as well as the everyday activities of meeting visitors from Germany and abroad, giving talks or tours of the Weissensee cemetery, and doing educational outreach.*

The GDR was never the center of the world for me. This was the reason that many people didn't get along with me.

I divide into two parts what is now called the 'changes in the political relationships of the GDR' or 'the turn': first, the period from June 1989 to 9 November, and second, the period from the opening of the Wall to the elections on 18 March 1990. In the period until the ninth of November I experienced the GDR as completely untypical, because for the first time in the twenty-eight years after the building of the Wall the so-called masses reacted directly to political situations. What happened was the most normal thing in the world. People experienced a situation as unbearable, saw that they were not able to change the conditions, and thus they left—by the thousands. And the GDR government likewise reacted in the most normal fashion, like any other complacent government: they ignored the reactions of the citizens, and when it was no longer possible to ignore this exodus they denounced this emigration and criminalized them. That the citizens' movement [*Bürgerbewegung*] and oppositional groups be heard was only logical. Thus what happened in October was a natural reaction, like had been going on for decades, for example, in Latin America. People demanded a humane politics.

So the period between September 1989 and March 1990 was very exciting and productive for me. I got involved because I saw a chance to be able to create a state and politics without parties. To put into practice citizens' interests rather than group interests. Aside from that, this period was very productive. Even if I, thank God, could keep a satirical distance from all that happened. For example, during the Modrow phase a government commission was formed to create a new media law, and the citizens' committee was not allowed to be represented, although we wanted to be there. The minister of justice, Heusinger, declared, 'Democracy does not mean that everyone can say something, or am I wrong?' Since he was wrong, we did participate and created a highly respected and uniformly accepted media law. Our law, accepted unanimously, was voted on again the same day and became law [*Makulatur*]. The positive effect was that our law was used as a model for new ones in three of the provinces of West Germany.

With the opening of the Wall GDR, citizens already got half of what they had wanted. Ninety percent of the demonstrators in September and October 1989 wanted to go over to the West once and then come back, as they would from one neighborhood to the next. The citizens' groups didn't recognize that the people wanted to do this. It was clear to us that the groups wanted to force political change and gain some power in the GDR. That was natural. With this they became increasingly capable politically, they made the best out of it. Suddenly GDR citizens and the world experienced how democracy moves from above to below.

Even today I still don't understand, although I was there, why those who demanded new local elections in the GDR first permitted the election of a new parliament [*Volkskammer*]. Probably they also wanted to be a member of the Parliament at one time. But with these events the German people showed, just as in 1848, 1918, 1923, and also in 1989, that they had nothing to say. This was for me, my wife, and my friends a very bitter time. When it became apparent in Bonn what was happening in the GDR, they took over the leadership and determined the course of events. This period was so awful because what now determines what goes on in everyday life in the former GDR, I already noticed in November 1989. The growth of social envy and arrogance create conditions like those of a civil war. And based on this background, particular kinds of chauvinistic behavior are growing.

Since November 1989 I have noticed that the search for a country in which I can live becomes more and more important. My questions, which at the moment are still rhetorical, are becoming increasingly concrete. In the old GDR I was often asked why I didn't leave. I always answered that if I left the GDR, then I would have to leave Germany. The Federal Republic was never an alternative. And the conditions in the GDR were never so unbearable that I had to leave Germany as my parents did in 1939. That is an example of the special problem of the children of emigrants. Because we grew up with the large problem of the politically persecuted, I could not leave the GDR as my friends advised me after my firing from the radio. This political problem was relativized for me by my memories of the stories of my parents about their emigration.

One of the strangest and worst memories about the 'turn' remains the ninth of November and the problem of my fellow citizens' dealing with their own past. On the ninth of November I was filming in Leipzig. I heard 'The Wall is down!' As I stood in what at that time was the most expensive hotel in the GDR, exclusively for foreigners, a CBS 'live report' was played [for us] by another CBS reporter in the bar. On the thirteenth of November, when I was on the Kurfürstendamm [the main shopping boulevard in West Berlin] for the first time, I saw people coming toward me wearing T-shirts that said, '9 November, I was there!' Maybe I am stupid, but when I hear *9 November* I think of the burning synagogues and destroyed Jewish shops and those things that in Germany only Jews are interested in.

The worst aspect is that now, for the third time, after only fifty years, again millions of people 'didn't know about anything' and important politicians ask again about guilt rather than about responsibility. My wife's nineteen-year-old son said, 'I don't understand why they all seem not to have known about the suppressions, for example, but I know what I know.' Guilt is a legal category and therefore relevant only in a legal sense. But in the community of people [*Zusammenleben*] all that is important is the willingness to take responsibility for your own history. And because this kind of taking responsibility has little chance in the future, I think I will not be able to stay here.

KM *is still in Germany and continues to work for the Stiftung, where he seems to have become an important asset. He seems to enjoy his work there, especially meeting American academics, journalists, or anyone else who comes from the United States to learn about the Jewish Community. His trip to the United States has enlivened and enriched him, and he wants to go back, maybe for a longer time. Recently, he was encouraging his wife's daughter to apply for study in the United States.*

PART 7. FROM SURVIVING TO BELONGING

Stories of the Returned   *Jeffrey M. Peck*

Based on interviews conducted in the collapsing Cold War order of East and West Berlin, this ethnographic project on German Jewish identity has been highly charged, both politically and personally. *Reflexivity* and *deconstruction* are the terms used in part 1 to refer to our interventions in the construction of German Jewish identity and in our own self-critical, interdisciplinary dialogue about this collaboration. The intense pitch of our work over four years was stimulated by our repeated crossing of boundaries. These boundaries were not only obvious political and ideological ones—East and West, communist and liberal democratic—but also transatlantic (United States and Germany), disciplinary (anthropology and literary study), national/ethnic/cultural (German and Jew), gendered (male and female), and generational (parents and children). This movement created an intensity and depth that characterizes the dynamic exchange and multiple layers of experience (both the interviewees' and our own) that have enlivened this entire project.

These narratives re-present experience on both sides of the Iron Curtain, one of the most rigid, albeit intangible, borders in the history of Europe. Ironically, this dividing line was later literally fortified in Germany as the Wall. These boundaries shaped the experiences of those in the United States and those in the Soviet Union, and then those in the West and those in the East. These experiences simultaneously occurred against the backdrop of persecution in the 1930s, the war and the Holocaust in the 1940s, and return in the 1950s and afterwards. The book and video documentary based on our interviews can never achieve the depth, texture, or nuance of firsthand experience. What we offer is a different (text)ure, composed of layer upon layer, story within story, and enhanced, we hope, by knowledge, sensitivity, and experience.

As an American Jew who has studied and lived in Germany for many years, it was unavoidable for me to be implicated in the questions that this book has raised. Why did Jews return to live in Germany, and who are these people who live what can only be called 'hyphenated identities'? My theoretical training, which had taught me to question identity in fixed, or stable, terms, was put to the test when we were confronted with the category German Jewish in 'real' life histories. Were the identities of the people we interviewed as conditional and susceptible to historical transformations as I had thought? Was our participation—as American academics, one Jewish—in the process of reconstructing these life histories as significant as contemporary ethnographers were making the subjectivity of the ethnographer out to be?[1]

My being Jewish in Germany and in German Studies has been an issue throughout my career. However, only with this project did I convert a longtime preoccupation into a scholarly enterprise.[2] The frequent questions about why Germany was the object of either my personal or my professional interest came not only from American Jews. They also came from non-Jewish German friends, who asked why I in fact 'sojourned' in the country toward which they felt such ambivalence. Like American Jews, they also wondered why German Jews would return to live in the land of their murderers. This past weighed heavily on them, at least on this postwar generation, the children and grandchildren of those Germans who lived through World War II. I became increasingly fascinated by that past, by the way it continued to reach into my life and drew me closer to Jews in Germany today. I was equally fascinated by the Germans' experiences with these living Jews (many of whom were Americans), as well as by their feelings about the conspicuous absence of a Jewish tradition in Germany, which was a lost part of their own history.

As I look back now on these interviews, my commentary, and the way I have represented these people in the essay that follows, I realize that my emplotment of their stories was affected by emotional responses tinged with a certain pathos. I was clearly moved by these people and their stories. I could have taken an exclusively academic and therefore, supposedly, more dispassionate approach. I might have pursued, for example, the Jews as a symbol of modernity threatening the more idealistic, romantic, and ultimately regressive irrational urge propagated by the Nazis. This was already prepared for by defeat in World War I by the Western standard-bearers of modernity, which led to a humiliating resolution for Germany in the Versailles Treaty. The German Jews, hyphenated as a very specific subgroup, actually never fit, although Napoleon, a French invader, granted them civil rights in German lands and began the process of assimilation, which was never as symbiotic as one was led to believe. Although I do not want to imply that decisions about what and how we study are not subjective, I indeed admitted more of my person than I had imagined. In fact, I was lionizing our interviewees because they were Jews who not only had struggled for something they believed in but also had an even more ambivalent relationship to the Germans than I had. I had always acknowledged my *Gebrochenheit*, my 'broken' relationship, toward the Germans. Still I had only studied them, been involved with them, and sojourned for lengthy periods in their country. Our subjects had survived to come back and lived among the Germans, proof that Hitler's Final Solution had failed. The potential for high drama was clearly there. Was their return the ultimate revenge or only a pathetic (in the literal sense of the word) reminder of loss, disorientation, and profound sadness? I vacillated between these explanations, neither of which satisfactorily answers the question why Jews live in Germany today.

Perhaps their presence in Germany today is my major motivation for writing this book. If anthropologists are prone to unearthing and revealing secrets, I was fascinated by discoveries as well, in this case the contradictions in being what John Borneman calls a 'third,' this other identity of the German Jew. I too had to see myself as a kind of 'third,' as a German friend pointed out to me in the summer of 1989, when I was running back and forth across the border between East and West Berlin. I too was trying to find a home, a place to belong. I too kept returning to Germany. I admitted that I did indeed identify with these people who returned. And writing about and within their lives through these narratives continued to remind me of the position I occupy when I study, talk, or write about these German Jews or the Germans in general. In other words, this project has been a unique occasion for experiencing the complexities of identity construction, for me as well as for our subjects.

♣ ALIVE AND WELL AND LIVING IN GERMANY?

Yes, 'die Juden leben,' as the German Jewish author Rafael Seligmann announces in an essay in the German newsmagazine *Der
Spiegel* (1992). He cites an event that has come to symbolize (East)
German insensitivity and ignorance of Jewish life, a Rostock politician's question to Ignatz Bubis, the leader of the Central Council of Jews in Germany: 'Is Israel your homeland [*Heimat*]?' Seligmann tells us that this event marks a turning point for German
recognition of Jews in Germany. Not only are their deaths memo-
rialized in symbols of the Holocaust but their lives are touched by
the question, 'Do the Germans accept the Jews as part of themselves [*ihresgleichen*]? And: Do these Jews living in Germany understand themselves as Germans?' (75).

Seligmann's questions remind us of the central issue of German
Jewish identity, which prewar Jews so grossly misjudged. Assuming that they were as German as the Germans, if not sometimes
more so, they did not expect exclusion and persecution and then
death and destruction.[3] But Seligmann confronts us rather brutally with the point that some Jews did indeed survive. He wants
the Germans to acknowledge these living Jews in their midst and
not to think that by immortalizing those who have died they have
adequately dealt with the living. While 6 million died, some managed to make it through the camps, others went underground,
and the majority went into exile. At least 278,000 German Jews
went into 'the emigration,' as it is referred to in Germany (Benz
1991a, 37 n. 46). From that group a small number came back to
Germany—to the Western zone, which became the Federal Republic, and to the Soviet Occupied Zone, which became the
German Democratic Republic. These people, specifically those
who were in the Allied countries, were the subject of our research
for this book and the video documentary, which focuses exclusively on East Berlin.

♣ TALKING, LISTENING, WRITING

Because of the vast amount of literature on the Holocaust, it is
important to situate these chronicles and the chronicling process
in that tradition. I mean the variety of narrative forms that have

been used for talking and writing about the Holocaust and the representation of the testimonies of people who survived the camps or escaped by leaving Germany and going into exile. In recent years books such as James Young's *Writing and Rewriting the Holocaust: Narrative and the Consequences of Interpretation,* Berel Lang's edited volume *Writing and the Holocaust,* and Lawrence Langer's *Holocaust Testimonies: The Ruins of Memory* have drawn attention to the relationship between the experiences of Holocaust victims and the interpretive consequences of the testimonies they give or the stories they write. In Young's words, 'What is remembered of the Holocaust depends on how it is remembered, and how events are remembered depends in turn on the texts now giving them form' (1988, 1). Acknowledging criticism of 'overly critical readings,' he recognizes 'the fear that too much attention to critical method or to the literary construction of texts threatens to supplant not only the literature but the horrible events at the heart of our inquiry' (3). While I agree with this statement, it is clear, especially in ethnography, that the representations of these events and the discourses (written or oral) that mediate them are not merely stylistic vessels into which the 'information' or 'facts' are poured. Imagination and the vicissitudes of memory implicated in what is called, for a lack of a better term, 'the poetic' are not impediments to 'getting at the truth' nor a sugar-coated version of an awful reality. They are a constitutive part of the testimonies recounted by the victims. For Langer, 'it took . . . some time to realize that all of them [those giving Holocaust testimonies] were telling a version of the truth as they grasped it, that several currents flow at differing depths in Holocaust testimonies, and that our understanding of the event depends very much on the source and destination of the current we pursue' (1991, xi).

Both Young and Langer concentrate on the testimonies of Holocaust victims who were in the camps, and both deal with comparisons of written narrative and video documentary forms. Young concentrates more heavily on the first, and Langer on the second. In this project we moved between these forms but focused on the narrative forms, the stories, those people told and the process of re-presenting them in written and video form. This made the process of transcription, translation, editing, and commentary as important a part of the chronicling as the 'information' the interviewees gave to us. In short, the interview became a process that did not begin and end when the tape recorder or video camera was turned on and then off. Our interviewees' identities were being reformed and reestablished as we asked them questions, found appropriate forms for their words, and put this volume and the documentary film together.

For someone trained as a literary critic and theorist of German literature, ethnographic fieldwork has provided a firsthand education in interdisciplinary practices and methods. My own reflections on subjectivity, for example, are certainly the ruminations of a literary critic, not an anthropologist. But collaboration of this sort has meant venturing into unknown intellectual and cultural territories that were traditionally reserved for anthropologists, whose traditional object was the so-called primitive. Now (urban) Europe is a legitimate site for fieldwork. But more importantly, working in a different discipline has taught me that the skills and insights of textual interpretation can be brought to bear on real, living peoples, whose experiences can also be textualized.[4] I mean here interpreting life stories through their textual forms, always acknowledging how this rendering shapes the lives of those whose stories are re-presented and affects the way they are understood. Therefore, scholars in foreign languages and literatures who also study 'culture' share more with anthropologists than they might think. These fields have more in common today since many practitioners in both fields have recognized that they are united by notions of text and context, culture and the practices of narration and representation, and poststructuralist theorizing.[5] The interview, based on ethnographical techniques of participant observation and replete with possibilities for philological interpretation, became a proving ground for representing personal experiences and historical events that are part of the Holocaust.

Particularly in Holocaust testimonies, what Langer calls the 'principle of discontinuity' foregrounds the desire of the ethnographer-critic to create coherence and make some sense of the disparate images, memories, and statements the interviewee offers. Contemporary interpretive ethnography, however, reminds us that 'coherence—and it always creeps into ethnographic texts—is generally forced upon the gathered data and witnessed events ex post facto. All happens as if—the die of fieldwork having been cast—the odd bits and pieces, the undigestable morsels, the weird fragments, and everything else, all fall in place at once. And yet, at the moment when one is confronted with a specific ritual or hears a specific story, one is unlikely and often unable to grasp what is going on' (Dumont 1992, 3).

In Holocaust testimonies problems of discontinuity and incoherence endemic to anthropological analysis are magnified by the unique situation of those recounting their horrific stories, which are themselves products of the most existential forms of displacement. In short, ethnographic analysis of the Holocaust— the sort of experiences, both ours and our subjects', that we have struggled to present here—reminds us of the double bind of doing this particular kind of documentation. Persecution, exile, and genocide, all part of the catastrophe of the Holocaust, undermine any semblance of coherence, unity, or totality of vision.

In fact this particular kind of 'Jewish ethnography' plays a special role for Jonathan Boyarin, one of the few anthropologists who defines himself as a practitioner of this field, who comments, 'It may be more rewarding in the long run to explore the lessons for ethnography in the Jewish interpretive model of multiple and diffuse authority, of dialogue with and through a narrative, textual source whose potential meanings are never exhausted, and hence never fixed. Narrative—about Jews especially perhaps, but also narrative in general as a human faculty—keeps alive the 'Jewish question' after genocide, but in order to stay alive, it must remain a question' (1992, 75).

Indeed, this volume is based more on complex questions than on simple answers, the supposedly definitive answers that often are assumed to be found by more quantitative, social scientific methodology. Our goal was not a representative or statistical study of two generations of German Jews: rather, we were interested in the range of responses peculiar to the historical experience of living as a German Jew of a specific generation in divided Berlin. Our focus is on the process of heterogeneous identity construction in different political contexts, on what it means to be

German or Jewish, communist or liberal democrat. How do the
life constructions converge or diverge from each other in the
different social and ideological systems? In short, we were absorbed by stories, not data. We welcomed the individualization in
each life history, and we were particularly interested in the interaction between the many contexts—political, social, cultural, religious, gender, class—that produced the subjects' experiences and
the individuals' own efforts to shape their lives by decisions they
made consciously or unconsciously. In other words, the relationship between individual agency and social structure was always
considered (see Personal Narratives Group 1989). In the words of
the Personal Narratives Group, such life histories 'provide evidence of historical activity—the working out within a specific life
situation of deliberate courses of action that in turn have the
potential to undermine or perpetuate the conditions and relationships in which the life evolved' (6).

Taking into account the historical dimensions that produced
such stories makes us acutely aware that the interviews in this
volume are not Holocaust testimonies in the strict sense of the
term. These people lived out the Holocaust in the United States
or the Soviet Union, England or France. However, as Wolfgang
Benz points out in his interviews with the people he calls 'die
kleinen Leute' [the little man or woman],

*Man wird dem Exil nicht gerecht, wenn man es nicht auch als Ver-
folgung begreift, die über die damals verfolgte Generation hinaus-
reicht. Die innerfamiliären Konflikte mit den Kindern und Enkeln
der Exilierten, die Aggressionen und Berührungsängste, die auf der
ganzen Skala vom lebenslangen Schweigen der Opfer bis zur Anklage
der Nachgeborenen artikuliert werden, sind untrennbar mit der Tat-
sache verbunden, dass die Emigration lebensrettend war. Am Syn-
drom der Überlebenschuld leiden beileibe nicht nur die geretteten
Opfer der Konzentrations und Vernichtungslager.*

*[One does not do justice to exile if one does not also understand it as
persecution that affected generations after this one. The internecine
conflicts with the refugees' children and grandchildren, the aggressions
and anxieties about intimacy, that were articulated in the lifelong
silence of the victims and the accusations of their offspring can not be*

separated from the fact that the emigration had saved them. Those who survived the camps are not the only ones who live with this syndrome of feeling guilty for having survived.] (1991a, 11)[6]

Clearly, those we interviewed did not suffer as much as their fellow Jews who did not get out in time, nor perhaps even as much as those Benz describes, who remained in exile. However, our sojourners experienced other kinds of prejudice, other forms of indignities and persecution, not the least of which was the hostility of Jews who did not want them to go back to Germany, especially to 'Communist Germany.' Therefore their status as refugees and temporary inhabitants—sojourners—in the countries that were the victors in the moral battle of the World War II makes them unique. They entered these countries as survivors, not always with the warmest welcome.[7] And they returned to Germany for professional, familial, and, especially in the case of those returning to East Berlin, political and ideological reasons. Even for those who came back to the 'new' East Germany, 'das bessere Deutschland,' as Cordt Schnibben (1991) called it, feared what they might find. As the interviewees readily told us, living in the United States during the McCarthy era or in the Soviet Union during the Stalinist purges remade their lives in ways they never imagined. Already forced by Hitler's Nürnberg Laws to acknowledge a Jewishness many of them had ignored or forgone, after 1935 and then after Kristallnacht in 1938, the stage was set for repeated interventions by history and politics, especially in the 1940s and 1950s. The victory of the Allies (1945), the division of Germany into four occupied zones (1946), the founding of the state of Israel (1948), the founding of the Federal Republic of Germany and the German Democratic Republic (1949), the hearings by the House on Un-American Activities Committee (1954), the Workers' Rebellion in the GDR (1953), *Wiedergutmachung* in West Germany (begun in the 1950s), the building of the Wall (1961), the visit of the Shah of Iran to West Berlin and the Soviet-inspired Warsaw Pact's march into Czechoslovakia (1968), the fall of the Wall (1989), and finally reunification (1990) are only the most obvious markers of when these people's lives took dramatic turns.

Already a part of their lives, these events led to the return to Germany, the most significant decision of their lives. They returned to a country that had been defeated, divided, and left in ruins by both the Nazis and the Allied bombs. While they may not have been able to choose their place of exile, they could decide which part of Germany to return to. Their decisions situate the stories in this volume, ambivalent experiences of migration and homeland interlaced with horror and avoidance. The people whose stories are told here are not physically marked by torture or malnutrition. They are not burdened with the pain and anguish of Holocaust victims struggling to recollect their thoughts. Our interviewees talk of escape and of life during the Holocaust and afterwards. We are as interested in the experiences since their return as we are in their sojourns in foreign countries. They were spared much of the immediate horror, and yet as Benz points out, their stories are nonetheless colored by hardship and duress. They are a significant piece of the puzzle that constitutes Jewish identity in Germany since the war.

Presenting testimonies of Holocaust victims raises an ethical dimension that underlies any ethnographic project, especially one that deals with lives altered by persecution and atrocity. Literary critics, for the most part, are not confronted with the kind of moral dilemmas engendered by the ethnographic responsibility involved in re-presenting experiences of catastrophe and death. In undertaking our project,we were ethically bound to recognize the vulnerabilities and sensibilities of our interview partners.

When we first entered the GDR, we feared that answering our questions might endanger our interviewees. As we discovered, they were anything but circumspect in their responses. Given the chance to talk, they let flow what seemed to have been bottled up for years or only shared with each other. That we were Americans and that I was Jewish created avenues of discussion that were astonishingly open. For Kate Leiterer, Marion Thimm, and even Hilde Eisler, we were from the country that had given them or their parents refuge. My being Jewish made us trustworthy. And the fact that we both were university scholars [*Wissenschaftler*], which some of them had trouble believing since we did not fit Germans' traditional image of a professor, meant that we were serious about them and our work.

After reunification, we asked them to respond to transcripts of their initial interviews. To my surprise, after being 'freed' from the oppression of the regime, they were often more reluctant to expose themselves as having been too willing to accept the status quo or to be regarded as what came to be known as a *Wendehals* [turncoat], someone who quite suddenly was critical of the GDR. In the process of editing both the book and the video documentary, it became clear that our ethical responsibility was not so much a question of erasing or emending anything they might have said as it was a question of presenting them in a way that respected the different viewpoints on issues that were obviously of existential proportions.

Returning to the country that had persecuted and killed their families was always a very difficult decision. In West Germany returnees confronted the continuing anti-Semitism in the postwar years and the presence of former Nazis in high government positions. In the East they found a regime that made the West the inheritor of the Nazis and encouraged GDR citizens to believe that because their leaders had also been imprisoned and theirs was a new state made up of antifascists, they were free of guilt or responsibility. Accepting the GDR regime's restrictions on travel and free speech or even the regime's neglect of the Jews' place in the Holocaust compromised many of these people's ideals.[8] They knew and yet often didn't want to admit how compromised they had become.

That our acquaintance with this particular group of people inspired particular ethical considerations only complicated the interview process. The most trivial gesture suddenly had to be considered. How should we introduce ourselves? How should we go about setting up interviews? When we visited people in their homes, should we take flowers, cake, nothing at all? If prospective interviewees were disinterested or even hostile, how could we convince them to see us? The chain of often banal events associated with the interviews are as much a part of these life histories as the interviews themselves. While some critics find Claude Lanzmann's film *Shoah* manipulative and artificial, I was impressed precisely with the way he made the interlocutors, whether translators or interviewers, part of the film. Especially in video testimony, as Young put it, 'the interviewers' questions do not merely elicit testimony but quite literally determine the kind, shape, and direction survivors' stories take. Depending on the training and knowledge of the interviewers, their own experiences and memory of the Holocaust, their preoccupations, and their own perceptions of their task, interviewers may be as much a part of the survivors' testimony as the survivors themselves' (Young 1988, 166). The exigencies of video testimony draw our attention to our responsibility as interviewers and as witnesses.

Nowhere does the hermeneutic imperative raise its head so prominently as where the textual product is so conditioned and caught up in a web of interpretive demands. Geoffrey Hartmann, a Yale literary critic who also turned to recording Holocaust video testimony, sums it up as follows: 'These testimonies are texts, not because we wish to study them as literature—that would be another way of profaning them—but because they are unintegrated, exposed, fallible memories that need interpretation' (quoted in Young 1988, 170). Interviews, testimonies, or oral histories, especially those based on the Holocaust or those by our interview partners, lead us to share with our audience all the conditions under which they came to be. Most collections of interviews, such as Peter Sichrovsky's well-known *Wir wissen nicht was morgen wird, wir wissen wohl was gestern war: Junge Juden in Deutschland und Österreich*, published in English as *Strangers in Their Own Land: Young Jews in Germany and Austria Today*, present interviews to the reader with the implication that these are their 'real' voices, unadulterated and pure, without the kind of interventions we call attention to here. This form, while perhaps easier to read, does injustice to the interview as a literary-ethnographic genre of which the process of self-reflection and involvement is a constitutive part.

♣ LONGING TO BELONG
Themes and (Dis)connections in the Refugee Experience

Keine Deutsche Regierung hat die noch Lebenden gebeten, aus ihren Zufluchtsorten zurückzukehren, selbst die juristisch definierbare Schuld wurde allenfalls halbherzig festgestellt, und am Antisemitismus konnten auch die vereinten Kräfte der Allierten nicht viel ändern.

Ein wesentlicher Teil der deutsch-jüdischen Geschichte ist Seelenge-
schichte. Für diese gelten andere Zeiten und Zäsuren.

[No German government requested of those who were still alive that
they return from their places of refuge. Even the guilt that had been
legally defined was only halfheartedly used on the guilty, and thus
even the combined strength of the Allies could do little to counter the
anti-Semitism [still in Germany]. An essential part of German Jewish
history is a history of the soul [or spirit]. For this kind of history there
are other kind of epochs and caesuras.] (Mattenklott 1992, 124–25)[9]

In one of the most perceptive and well-written German books
about Jews in Germany, the literary critic Gert Mattenklott reminds us that Jews and Germans mark the trajectory of their
identities differently. The Jews in Germany, as our interviews
show, have unquestionably been shaped by the turn of historical
events. They have, however, another story to tell, one that, as the
Holocaust brutally revealed, often contradicts what could literally
be called the 'master narrative' of those who forced the lives and
life histories of German Jews to take a different direction than the
one most of them had surely planned before 1933. The *Seelen-*
geschichte [history of the soul, or spirit] to which Mattenklott
refers may be the story of an oppressed and persecuted people, the
wandering Jew, who took centuries to find a home, a desire still
unfulfilled for many Jews even with the establishment of the state
of Israel. But the Jew's story was unalterably recast by the Holocaust, which not only wiped out a generation but also literally cast
a generation to sea in search of a home. This special story may also
be what the German Jewish émigré and filmmaker Peter Lilien-
thal notes in his interview with Mattenklott:

Ambivalenzen, Widersprüche, das lachen über sich selbst . . . [Jüdi-
sche Menschen] sind nicht erlöst. Es gibt für sich noch eine Zukunft.
Sie warten auf den Messias. So lange ist alles in der Schwebe.

[Ambivalences, contradictions, laughing at themselves . . . [Jewish
people] are not redeemed. For them there is still a future. They are
waiting for the Messiah. As long as they are, everything is still up for
grabs.]

To which Mattenklott responds:

Bei meinen Forschungen über jüdische Leben in Deutschland muss ich mich oft fragen: meine ich nicht diese Komplexität und Unentschiedenheit, wenn ich jüdisch sage?

[When I am doing research on Jewish life in Germany I often have to ask myself, Do I mean this complexity and indecisiveness when I say Jewish?] (188)

In an interview, not unlike our own, with a German Jew who emigrated to Uruguay in 1939 and returned to Germany, Mattenklott reminds us of the *Seelengeschichte* of the Jews, which is so prominent in the stories we present here. Ambivalence, contradiction, irony—all markers of unfulfilled desires, frustrated hopes, and the tenacious struggle for connection. While these tendencies may be typical for Jewish history, they are even more pronounced in the stories of these German Jews who left and returned. While they are differentiated by generation or gender, by country of exile or site of return, the parallels that emerge— most obviously among those in the East and those in the West, but even beyond ideological demarcations—are striking. Common threads seem to wind their way through all the stories. Of course, some of this symmetry emerges in response to our questions focusing on the coincidence of political and personal identities and the subjects' relationship to their country of exile and the country of return, as well as to questions about anti-Semitism or xenophobia. Our choice of informants from the limited pool that met our criteria also contributes to particular points of view, orientations, and experiences common to two generations of German Jews who returned.

Home/Heimat

What more potent metaphor among those who have sojourned in foreign places during the Holocaust than the search for home! Some had it easier in the United States. Conditions were brutal in the Soviet Union during World War II. The German term *Heimat*, which is practically untranslatable, evokes even more specific feelings associated not just with a particular place—a city or the street of one's birth—but often with a landscape, the nation, or a feeling.

Our subjects left Germany, their *Heimat*, in the years 1932 to 1939, during the formative years of young adulthood, and they returned middle-aged. While they returned to the country they left, which many of them called home, they returned seasoned by experiences, as different people, to a very different world. Since they were exiles, the question of return was open, especially for those committed to communism and the eventual rebuilding of a new Germany. While many of them, especially Ruth Benario and Kostja Münz's mother, Ilse, were very integrated in the Soviet Union, others, such as Hilde Eisler, felt persecuted in the United States because of their political views. Ernst Cramer and Marion Thimm's parents, Ossip and Lily Flechtheim, felt comfortable in their American exile. But feeling comfortable was not necessarily the same as having a *Heimat*, and the Nazis, with their ethno-racial programs of 'Heim ins Reich.' [Come home to the new Germany!], ideologically transformed an idea of homeland to one that would exclude Jews or anyone not considered to be pure German. Since the war the English term *home* and its German equivalent, *Heimat*, have had less and less in common. Today, in fact, the discussion around *home* and *Heimat* continues as xenophobia spawns attacks on foreigners, asylum seekers, and new refugees to Germany (see Peck 1992). None of our interviewees returned from exile because of a romanticized love of *Heimat*, although they have varying degrees of satisfaction or comfort in Germany.

Among the second generation, the children of those who went into exile, the response to the presence or lack of *Heimat* is particularly forceful and often even poignant. Born during their parents' exile, experiencing childhood in places as dissimilar as Kansas in the United States (Kate Leiterer) and Karaganda in the Soviet Union (Kostja Münz), and returning to the two Berlins, depending on their age at return, almost all of them—Kate, Kostja, Marion, and even Jessica—felt disconnected in their new German homes. Susanne Rödel is the only one who seems fully integrated. For some, like Kostja Münz, Jessica Jacoby, and Marion Thimm, the question of belonging was the dominant motif. They did not feel German, but rather more Russian or American. All of the children's stories and feelings of belonging or alienation, in fact their identities in general, were intimately linked to their parents' stories or lives. Kostja Münz and Marion Thimm admitted that their births were a direct result of the war: they were to be living symbols of victory and hope for the future. The children of refugees, as Benz points out, may well have serious problems stemming from their parents' war experiences. These children bore the burden of carrying on a German Jewish life in Germany in a world from which their parents were disconnected when they returned. The question of citizenship in a country that had taken it away from their parents was never to be taken for granted. German citizenship could never give them security, since it had not proven before to be a shield against anti-Semitism or persecution.

The stories of this younger generation, of course, often begin with their birth. Without being asked, they immediately told us about their parents' exile and their previous lives: their identification with being Jewish, their political affiliations, class, and social status. They spoke little about their emotional relationship to their parents, although they often talked about why they felt uncomfortable in their new homes and how that was influenced by their relationship to their parents. Kostja Münz was placed in an orphanage when his parents came back to the GDR, because they had to work. Marion Thimm was sent off to boarding school in West Germany so she would be safe in case political tensions in Berlin mounted during the Cold War. These children who often suffered from disconnection were the products of a very particular generation. Ruth Benario reminded us how 'crazy' life was for members of her generation, who were 'scattered [*durchgeschüttelt*] to so many places.'

Ruth Benario's assessment seems right. Feeling secure and at home in their German Jewish identity in the twenties and early thirties, these people were murdered, in hiding, or 'scattered' to far corners of the earth, and the Jewish diaspora expanded, ranging from Shanghai to San Francisco, from Havana to Istanbul. New York, Moscow, and London were popular centers, and those who sojourned in the Allied countries did indeed have additional burdens influencing their choice to return. *Heimat* had been lost, and by few, if any, would it ever be regained.

Language

'Die Sprache ist ein unüberwindbares handicap' [language is an insurmountable handicap], Georg Grosz wrote to Walter Mehring on 12 May 1939 (Middell et al. 1983, 22). The mix of English and German might seem to imply that Georg Grosz has integrated America into his identity. However, this complaint appears in a lengthy warning in which Grosz encourages his friend not to leave France for the United States.

Walt, Du gibst viel auf, wenn Du dort fortsegelst—ich habe Dir zu sagen, dass Du hier ganz von vorne beginnen musst. Empfehlungen und freundschaftliche Bindungen von drüben her versagen—und vor allem es fehlt an einem gewissen 'intellektuellen Milljöh'—es gibt in diesen Sinne keine Cafes. . . . Es gibt keinerlei Aussichten hier für Dich.

[Walt, you give up a lot if you leave. I have to tell you that you will have to start all over again here. Recommendations and friendly connections that you have over there won't help. Above all, a certain 'intellectual milieu' is lacking here. In this way there is no appreciation of places like cafes. . . . There is no future for you here.] (22–23)

The letter is part of a discussion between intellectuals, one of whom is lost in the New World. The Old World was in chaos. Emigration disconnected them from their home, and yet what they could take with them most easily—their language—hindered their integration, in this case into America.

Since our interviewees are all intellectuals in the broadest sense of the term, communication was an issue, even in everyday conversation. Language figures prominently in almost all of the interviews, since language, constitutive of thought, is linked to home, childhood, and family. For Jews especially, language ties them to a religious tradition steeped in chanting, praying, and invoking holy words that will call upon God to listen to his people. In the eighteenth- and early-nineteenth-century German tradition, language functioned to unify a specifically German *Kulturnation* [nation of cultivated people] when political action had failed.[10] While our interviewees may have been largely secularized and not consciously aware of these rich histories of language, as Germans and as Jews they were influenced by language's ability to shape identity and create connection. However, even with this background, none of our interviewees expressed themselves in such an extremely stylized and romanticized fashion as the refugee interviewed by Marion Berghahn: 'We were Germans, otherwise all that happened later would not have been so horrifying, so shattering. We spoke the German language, so dear to us, our mother tongue in the truest sense of the word, through which we received all words and values of our lives, and language means almost more than blood. We did not know any fatherland other than Germany and we loved the country as one loves one's fatherland, a love which was to become fateful later on' (1988, 48). While some nationalistic German Jews may have identified with the 'fatherland,' another version of *Heimat*, our interviewees' responses were never so formulaic and regularized. Even Ernst Cramer and Albert Klein, who sentimentally remembered the artifacts of German culture, were much more restrained in their expressions of enthusiasm for things German.

For the first generation, language did serve as a link to what they were now losing and might regain; for the second generation the connection was to a tradition that they might never experience firsthand. For many, like Ossip Flechtheim, who had a high professional profile as a professor of political science, the inability to master the foreign language (and practice one's scholarship) hindered integration into American life. For him it made a return to academic life in Germany all the more appealing. For those in the Soviet Union, language was less of an issue, perhaps, as in the case of Ilse Münz. A youthful member of the Communist Party in Berlin, she was already oriented toward the Soviet Union, went there early on, and became extremely Russified. Albert Klein reminded us that in Berlin between 1920 and 1930 more Russian than German was spoken on the boulevard Kurfürstendamm.

Those in exile often spoke German at home, and the children were usually raised bilingually. Especially for the children, like Kate Leiterer and Marion Thimm, the German language, which had been a hindrance for their parents in the United States, became a link for them to the country in which they were born. With both women we discussed conducting the interview in English, and Kate Leiterer especially enjoyed practicing her English. Some of our video interviews were conducted twice, once in each language, to give the interviewee the best chance of expressing him- or herself. Especially in the GDR, where Russian, not English, was the preferred second language, speaking the language of the 'number one capitalist imperialist enemy' still gave Kate Leiterer enormous pleasure. It attached her to the United States even amidst GDR propaganda. Some experiences lived in the foreign culture can, of course, only be related in that language, and as she proudly pulled out her Girl Scout pin, Kate Leiterer told us in English about her years as an American Girl Scout with her mother as Girl Scout leader. Susanne Rödel spoke English when she came from England but soon lost it in the GDR, especially as her allegiance to the GDR and her interest in the Soviet Union grew. She now speaks Russian fluently but no English. Ruth Benario felt that her daughter, who spoke Russian and had been brought up in the Soviet system, could not have stood 'the shock' of going to West Berlin. For others, like Marion Thimm, speaking English with their parents even after their return connected these family members to a unique experience that they had shared together and reminded them of their continued links to family and friends in the United States.

Language could also set these children off from their schoolmates and friends. Kostja Münz returned as a small child from the Soviet Union speaking Russian and bearing a Russian name. For Kostja Münz, in fact, language represents his feelings of isolation after coming to Germany. He related what he calls 'a terrible experience' on the first day in the apartment his parents received in 1957. His parents were at work, his brother was gone, and he was home with a woman who was to take care of him. He tried to tell her that he wanted to go to the bathroom, and since she didn't understand Russian, he went in his pants. Kostja Münz relates how this single experience of feeling uncomfortable about communicating about something so personal reflected his sense of Germans' general attitude toward children. It was quite unlike what he remembered from the Soviet Union, where 'there is nothing so important or so wonderful as children.' His following years in an orphanage sponsored by the Party only intensified his feelings of not belonging. These were what he calls the most 'traumatic memories' of his childhood.

Gender: Reconfiguring 'Family' and Professions

There are more women than men among our interviewees because, on the one hand, more of the men have died, leaving women to tell their stories and, on the other, we are both very interested in gender and feminist issues. The choice of the categories 'family' and 'profession' and how they are traditionally gendered also reflects the particular situation of our interviewees. Women were caretakers of family and children who simultaneously sought professional fulfillment; the men had the privilege of attaining the latter without the same conflict between family and profession. It made it all the more interesting that conventional expectations of women and men were both maintained and confounded in the dislocation and trauma of emigration and return. These specific experiences add a complicating dimension to conventional gender roles and even to contemporary critiques of such conventions.

With similar concerns, Leo Spitzer discusses the gendered aspects of assimilation and marginality, comparing the experiences of exiled people on three continents. In an 'Afterthought' on gender to a chapter poignantly titled 'I belong nowhere, and everywhere am a stranger,' he notes,

Although their husbands and male relatives generally expected their emancipatory and assimilationist journey to lead to access into the sphere of public and professional activity, the women were socialized toward a different expectation. Having been relegated to a separate, 'domestic,' sphere by the division of labor reflected in bourgeois ideology and the social construction of gender roles, they attempted to attain the material benefits and status of bourgeois life through their link to husbands and male relatives. When they perceived exclusion from the public spheres of the dominant realm, they did so only indirectly: through the experience of their men. And because it was the consciousness of an impeded goal—of a barrier—to acceptance within the public sphere—that stimulated many of the men to explore their predicament and articulate their plight, the absence of female voices becomes more understandable. For the women . . . marginality was thus a predicament-once-removed. From the perspective of the dominant establishment, they were not just the 'Other,' as Simone de Beauvoir has argued, but the 'Other's Other.' (1989, 172–73)

At first glance, the predominance of women in our study, particularly those that seem so independent-minded, would seem to contradict Spitzer's claims about silent women. In fact our work gives 'voice' to more women's lives than it does to men's. Our project would also contradict Spitzer's vision of women's passivity, which posits that they even experience exclusion through men. However, the life histories of women who speak in this book and in the video documentary are intertwined, even in the socialist GDR, with the 'bourgeois ideology' that, according to Spitzer, supposedly condemns them to silence.

But let us first look at the life of Lily Flechtheim, Marion Thimm's mother, whose story conforms most prominently to Spitzer's model, especially after she returned to the more confining context of Germany. (Unfortunately, because of their length, we could not include the Flechtheims' interviews in the book.) Trained as a social worker during her exile in the United States, Lily Flechtheim had to give up her profession and became, one infers from the interviews and our observations, a proper German professor's wife who was, however, very frustrated in having to give up her career. Lily Flechtheim went back and forth between America (Waterville, Maine) and Germany a number of times with her husband, Ossip, who first was called on to work with the legal staff at the Nürnberg trials and then was offered a highly esteemed professorship at the newly established Free University of Berlin. Lily Flechtheim admitted that she left America reluctantly and that this decision caused a great strain on the family and her marriage. Marion Thimm talks about this tension in her interview as well. Ultimately, the family stayed together in Berlin. Ironically, as her husband grew old and became sick and retired from the university, Lily Flechtheim directed his affairs; she became his voice, so to speak. As we interviewed them both, when we directed questions to her husband Lily Flechtheim often interrupted and tried to speak for him. While Lily Flechtheim was probably always very talkative, she may well have been adjusting and compensating for her own frustration and may only have achieved the opportunity to make herself heard after her husband no longer held a privileged position.

But what of the other men we interviewed? All of them were professionals, all quite successful in their chosen fields. Albert Klein was the head of the office for foreign journalists, and Ernst Cramer was the righthand man of Axel Springer, one of the most powerful newspaper magnates in Germany. Among the children of the second generation, Kostja Münz worked in public relations at the Centrum Judaicum Foundation, and Peter Brasch (who appears in the video documentary) was becoming a well-known director. In the case of Ernst Cramer and Ossip Flechtheim, their return was based on opportunities offered to them as exiled Germans. Most of these men born between 1905 and 1915 never acknowledged the privilege and advantage they enjoyed simply by being male. Certain stereotypical assumptions of job and family were simply taken for granted. Men of the second generation, like Kostja Münz and Peter Brasch (both from the GDR) did, however, seem to be more sensitive to gender and sexual difference. They acknowledged the vulnerabilities and burdens of what it meant to be a woman or to be gay or lesbian and recognized how reactions to being 'different' in these ways engendered prejudices based on race or ethnicity. Although experiencing xenophobia does not necessarily inoculate these people against their own prejudices, the second generation seems to be more self-critical and sensitive to such problems.

Although the lives of all of our interviewees are in between, the women seem to have occupied a more precarious place in the upheaval of exile and return. At first glance, it may seem that Lily Flechtheim is the only example among our interviewees of what Spitzer describes as women passively caught up in the process of movement, assimilation, and marginality. But more interesting, I think, are the ways that other women were actively moving between, on the one hand, their bourgeois roles as mother, wife, caretaker, nurturer and, on the other, having a professional career or being divorced, unmarried, or lesbian.

Hilde Eisler upon her return to the GDR did indeed fulfill her dream of becoming a journalist when she was named editor of the prestigious GDR cultural journal *Das Magazin*. Yet she admitted to us that she actually liked living in the United States but, married to the well-known communist labor organizer Gerhart Eisler, who was arrested, released, and then escaped, would not give the American government 'the satisfaction they would get if the widow of Gerhart Eisler stayed behind.' Whether it reflects the loyalty of women of her generation to their husbands or her ideological commitments (which were not unlike her husband's), Hilde Eisler's explanation of her choice was conditioned as much by traditional gender roles as by the political events of her time.

Under the more trying physical circumstances and hardships of life in the Soviet Union, Ruth Benario and Ilse Münz had to carve out new forms of survival in difficult and often tragic circumstances. Ruth Benario followed a man to the Soviet Union, then another to China; however, she prided herself on the fact that she never married the men she lived with. She tells us with some humor how she married one of her 'husbands' only after he was already dead. And her last 'husband' wanted to return from the Soviet Union to West Berlin, but she unequivocally refused and told him to go if he wanted. She was definitely staying in the GDR! Ilse Münz waited fifteen years for her husband while he was in a Stalinist gulag. Having become very Russianized, Ilse Münz wanted to stay in the Soviet Union and return to Moscow. Having suffered so many years in the gulag, her husband prevailed, and the family returned to the GDR. During her twenty years in the Soviet Union, she raised her two children largely alone. A nurse during the war, she worked in the GDR as a journalist and an active fighter against fascism.

It is fascinating how these women negotiate competing claims and make sense out of mixed patterns—conscious rebellion and acceptance of traditional behaviors. One cannot but be impressed by their independence, stamina, and self-reliance as they moved back and forth between the shifting demands made on them. I do not want to trivialize their struggles with contradictory experiences by making them heroes or conventionalize their unconventional lives by scripting them as what some might see as typical modernist narratives of suffering women. However, I am reminded how gender, in this case female gender, is socially and historically constructed out of a nexus of material, ideological, and cultural factors. The contradictions we see in these women are perhaps to be expected given the competing claims made on their lives as women, as Jews, and as communists whose 'unconventionality,' as I have called it, is still mixed with the more traditional conventions of the societies around them. Ruth Benario's pride in never having 'real husbands' and Ilse Münz's acceptance of long separation from her husband can be understood as responses to the dominant culture's middle-class values.

The women of the younger generation, except for Jessica Jacoby, have less dramatic histories and have led less uprooted lives, partly because they returned as children and grew up in their respective Germanies. Susanne Rödel, successful in her career in a prestigious publishing house, claimed that she would not leave the GDR because her husband would not go. Marion Thimm, a licensed psychologist who married her German husband in the United States, would have liked to have her children in the United States (to protect them from the event of future political upheaval in Germany) yet ultimately did not move back to the United States because it would have been too difficult for her husband to become a licensed physician there. During our interviews Kate Leiterer was divorced and living alone with her children. Since unification she has lived with a partner who is also from the former GDR. Jessica Jacoby struggles against both anti-Semitism and homophobia in her respective feminist and leftist circles. Jessica is the most marginalized, trying to find ways of connecting and building a family of sorts outside the bounds of conventional values.

The life histories of these women constructed as narratives say more about our own methodological orientation than about the women's acknowledged self-awareness of how their lives are entangled in gender issues. Indeed, feminists would agree that gender and narrative form are closely linked in autobiographical writings such as personal narratives (Maynes 1989, 103). We originally wanted gender to be a focus of discussion, so we were unnerved by the fact that among our interviewees only Marion Thimm and Kate Leiterer considered gender an issue worth discussing. This may have been because they saw other claims being made on their identities as more pressing at particular historical moments. But this position would deny the foregrounding of gender. Their position does not, however, prevent us from problematizing gender. I am keenly aware that, in the words of the Personal Narratives Group, 'since feminist theory is grounded in women's lives and aims to analyze the role and meaning of gender in those lives and in society, women's personal narratives are essential primary documents for feminist research' (1989, 4). This does not, however, mean that we ascribe feminist consciousness to our interviewees; rather, it means that we acknowledge our own theoretical interests in constructing these narratives and draw attention to certain important aspects of gender, unreflected as they might be, in these people's lives. While the women often defied or circumvented gender stereotypes, they were still caught up in conventions that shaped responses, behaviors, and actions that could be interpreted as grounded in more traditional 'bourgeois' standards.

As persecuted and displaced people, our interviewees felt very keenly the need to belong and to feel solidarity with other human beings, especially after they returned to their former home. While for those from the East the political collective formed their ideological foundation, for all of the returnees family is the central structure of their stories. Ilse Münz and Eva Brück, both of whom appear in the video documentary, leave their families for their commitment to an ideology. The former travels to Paris and Zurich as a communist organizer, and the latter leaves what she calls 'her comfortable life in England' for the GDR. Yet Eva Brück, whose ideals had dissolved by the early 1950s as she became disillusioned with the GDR, 'runs to the synagogue' in her despair. Ilse Münz, a committed Communist Party member even after the state began to dissolve around her and unification became a reality, also admits that she has become a member of the Jewish Community. The failure of a political group identity has obviously left a wound that these women feel the Jewish Community can help heal. Their ethnic, religious, cultural, and political priorities have to be dramatically resequenced.

Both Ilse Münz and Eva Brück have moved back and forth in their lives between various affiliations. They left their families to pursue ideological agendas, yet neither disconnected herself completely from these familial ties. The Jewish Community may indeed represent for them the possibility of creating a new group bond that is capable of sustaining them when other collectivities have failed or died away, yet Ilse still remains a committed communist. In a project focused so intently on the constitution of multiple identities, it is important to recognize the many shifting affiliations that compete for dominance, especially after reunification, which has, if only superficially, erased the differences between East and West.

As sojourners, these people, women and men alike, relate the incidences of their lives as part of families divided, dispersed, and dislocated, literally in between two worlds. They feel this in-betweenness most acutely in terms of the bonds broken by departure, by persecution, and by death. In Hilde Eisler's words, 'They are all dead, all. From my mother's side, from my father's side, no one is still living. They all lost their lives.' Such themes echo throughout our interviews. Yet, finding one's friends again on the streets of Berlin after so many years was a special joy. In fact, with families destroyed by exile and death, friends became even more important, carrying on a tradition and identity. One could find something familiar in these reattachments, and they could help one begin to reestablish a life in a country that had changed dramatically. This reconstitution of 'family,' collectivities in the broadest sense, becomes a metaphor for the potential to rebuild new forms of affiliations and bonds in a Germany transformed once again, where for these GDR Jews the political 'family' disappeared. The questions that remain are, of course, What will be the basis of any new German collectivity? How are race and ethnicity imbricated in the constellation of identity that centrally acknowledges gender?[11] and, the most direct, Who belongs to the new Germany?

❦ FOUR YEARS AFTER REUNIFICATION

Reunification becomes the overwhelming metaphor for the mirage that closure has taken place. The war and the postwar situation were for many Germans and Americans now concluded because Germany was reunited. Even we could not avoid changing our research plan and this book. History had overtaken us. We were forced to continually shift our position, to accelerate and brake to accommodate the new political and personal situations of our subjects and our relationship to them. As I interviewed many of them again for the video documentary during the year 1990–91, the year of reunification, I was struck by the way that the war and the Nazi period, which had obviously figured so prominently in their interviews, had receded. The ninth of November, the date of Kristallnacht, was now to be remembered as the day the Wall fell and subsequently attached to the end of the GDR and the unification of Germany eleven months later.

Those in the East were mostly preoccupied with what it meant for them to live in a new country. For Ilse Münz, Ruth Benario, Hilde Eisler, Eva Brück, Susanne Rödel, Kostja Münz, and Peter Brasch, the world they or their parents had consciously chosen to return to was now gone. This was without a doubt the overriding concern at the time, especially in the euphoria of reunification and the naive dreams of many, including the politicians, who believed that this transformation would proceed with little discomfort or maladjustment.

Four years later much is different. No one would deny the problems faced by those in the East even as they enjoy new freedoms. The Westerners have also recognized that their Federal Republic and the lives that they led are also definitively altered. The rise in xenophobia and anti-Semitism, the attacks on asylum seekers, and the murders of Turks in Mölln and Solingen are reminders of the events that forced these Jews to sojourn in other countries during the war. I do not mean to equate these two historical periods.[12] Nevertheless, since these tragedies in the reunited Germany, many of our interviewees have questioned whether they should remain in the country. Particularly those in the former East Germany find themselves citizens of the country that they purposely chose not to return to. They were being dislocated for a third time. The GDR Jews are like refugees again, this time in a country that is supposed to be their own. The proverbial packed bags of the Jews who lived in Germany after the war were pulled out of storage, dusted off, and made ready to accompany these frightened and insecure people on a potential new journey.

The movement of refugees into Germany (now called asylum seekers) rather than out of Germany as during the war is a stunning reversal that still seems to be marking Germany as a country without much tolerance for difference.

What is to come remains to be seen. The Jews we interviewed admit that they have less to worry about than the other minorities, especially those who are racially marked. The Rostock politician's asking Ignatz Bubis if Israel is his homeland reflects not just ignorance but also the gap left in a Germany without Jews. This space is unfortunately being filled with hostility and aggression toward all 'foreigners,' of which the Jews, even the few German Jews, still remain a part. The identity of Jews in Germany is in the process of changing, their lives now more intertwined with the lives of others who are marked as 'different' or 'foreign' by the Germans. 'Die Minderheit Juden [*zählen*] jetzt wieder zu den Fremden im Land' [the Jewish minority are now being counted once again among those in this country considered foreign]. This is a point made by sociologist Alphons Silbermann, another Jew who returned to Germany, who recently published a study of anti-Semitism in West Germany. He is cited in an article entitled, appropriately, 'Die Juden sollen sich nicht verstecken' [The Jews should not hide] (Dachs 1992, 2). Like Seligmann, Silbermann is trying to educate Jews and Germans to this new situation created by the first attacks on asylum seekers in Rostock. What followed was a rededication to the problem of xenophobia of all kinds in Germany. Identity has become a central issue for the Germans, whose self-image is being transformed, first by reunification and then by the recognition that they are indeed a 'country of immigration,' made up of many peoples who are not ethnically German.[13]

That the Jews contributed to German culture is indisputable, but a contribution of this magnitude is unlikely to be repeated. Too many people perished in the Holocaust, and too many live out their lives elsewhere. However, there is a newly evolving German Jewish identity that is being reconfigured by the hard questions 'Jews living in Germany' (a term that describes them more appropriately than *German Jew*) are asking about themselves and their relationship to the Germans, especially after reunification.

The influx of Soviet Jews, for example, has added a new and complicating component to the mix of Jews in Germany.[14] Some of our interviewees who were in the Soviet Union feel especially committed to helping these people. The fate of the new German Jewish Community is linked to these other 'foreigners' who are populating the new Germany. Let us hope that the Germans as a group will be willing to practice tolerance, since neither the hopes of financial restitution in the West nor the ideals of antifascism in the East succeeded in wiping out the pernicious tendencies that contributed to the dislocation and disconnection of the people whose stories are told here. More drastic, concrete measures will have to be taken to ensure the safety and integration (not assimilation) of 'foreign' peoples in Germany, including the Jews. The issue of 'foreignness' in Germany manifested in the debate around asylum and immigration is clearly about tolerance and integration. How difference will be handled politically and personally will without a doubt be *the* question for the Germans to answer in the coming years.

Part 1. *Identifying German Jews*

1   The word *community* is capitalized when used in the institutional sense.

2   The number of people emigrating from the GDR to West Berlin declined from 103,507 in 1961 to 6,179 in 1962 and 2,468 in 1986 (Borneman 1992, 62).

3   The Hallstein Doctrine, formulated in 1955, was part of the attempt to isolate the GDR. It established the principle that the Federal Republic was the sole, sovereign representative of all of Germany and that, therefore, if any state granted political recognition to or established diplomatic relations with the GDR, the Federal Republic would immediately break off diplomatic relations with that state and react with sanctions.

4   For a different but parallel perspective on the relation of materiality to 'the construction of subjective agents of history,' see Leslie Adelson's rich theoretical discussion (1993, 1–35). Focusing on the body as object, she writes that 'bodies constitute a nonontological, material ground for action at specific moments in time. Such ground is, moreover, subject to diachronic shifts as well as synchronic instability' (14, 15).

5   Schmitt's (1976) insight into the shifting nature of the political and his criticism of liberalism's dangerous tendency to depoliticize and negate what is essentially political are extremely important. One must, however, disagree with Schmitt with regard to where the authority to decide on the exception should reside. Although he is critical of the reduction of politics to state doctrine and thereby questions the sovereignty of the state, he also argues that the state (which represents a homogeneous majority) should be the ultimate arbiter of disputes. However, by *state* he does not mean the liberal idea of state as opposed to society, which he criticizes for simply reversing the Hegelian idea of state as 'a realm of morality and objective reason' (77). Instead, he defines the state as founded in a historically determined and contested 'political.' It follows from this empirically valid claim that states constitute one of many instances of authority in a competition over defini-

tions. For me, then, the state has no a priori grounds to justify its claim to ultimate moral authority; this authority must be continually earned and reclaimed (see Borneman 1992, 1–36, 74–118).

6 Between 1990 and December 1993 approximately five hundred thousand Jews left the former Soviet Union, about fifteen thousand of these going to Germany (*Der Tagesspiegel* 1993, 5).

7 The jus sanguinis principle of the citizenship law of the Federal Republic of Germany can be traced back to a 1913 amendment to the 1870 *Reichs- und Staatsangehörigkeitsgesetzes*. The 1870 law basically limited citizenship to those with at least one German parent, but not all German people were citizens of the Reich. Though 'German' was already, in 1870, a category broader than that of the citizen, it emerged as a central legal concept only with the 1913 revision, which defined a German as a person with citizenship either in one of the federal states or in the Reich. National Socialist racializations of this citizenship law were nullified when the 1913 statute was put back into effect with the passing of the Basic Law in 1949 (Grawert 1973).

8 For an interesting exchange on being a German or a Jew, as well as on 'assimilation,' see Jaspers and Arendt 1992, 19. For a summary of the debate about this question as posed in 1848, see Wördehoff 1993, 74. On the effects of 'symbiosis' today, see Benz 1991c; and Diner 1986.

9 Much excellent scholarship exists about the various meanings attributed to 'the Jew' in late-nineteenth and early-twentieth-century Germany, a review of which goes beyond the purposes of this book. The critical historiography, specifically on the creation of Jewish stereotypes and race, includes Mosse 1985a; and Gilman 1985. Both writers have explored the importance of a Jewish stereotype and the use of race in the creation of Otherness for German culture of this period.

10 I undoubtedly give Marx a one-sided, favorable reading here. For a more critical view, see Gilman's careful reading of this essay (1986), along with Marx's later rewriting in *The Holy Family*. Gilman argues that Marx's hatred for what he called the 'Sabbath Jew' and the 'finance Jew,' along with his virulent attacks on Lasalle, were the result of 'his antithetical self-image: thus his confusion and the vehemence of his own rhetoric when confronted by the contradictory aspects of that 'Jew' which he sees within himself' (208).

11 Boyarin also addresses the relative exclusion from anthropology of

Jews as objects, as subject matter, even though, or perhaps precisely because, many anthropologists, Boyarin included, are themselves Jewish. In a review of Boyarin's book, Virginia Dominquez elaborates this point, drawing a parallel between the ghettoization of Jews (and Jewish studies) and the closeting of gays (and, I would now add, queer studies). Dominquez argues that, on the one hand, closets and ghettoes 'produce . . . room in which self-acknowledgment, assertiveness, and experimentation can take place safely,' but, on the other hand, many differences are tolerated on the condition that they do not actively assert themselves (1993, 622).

12 For example, a major exhibition, 'Jewish Lifeworlds,' opened in January 1992 in Martin Gropius Bau in Berlin. At issue for some of our East Berlin Jewish friends was that only the learned, textualist, and religious traditions were represented and that the Jewish 'antifascist resistance' was ignored. One of our interview partners even sent us a clipping of a critique of the exhibit. They understood the exhibit as part of an effort to delegitimate communist and political contributions of Jewish culture.

13 Opinions indicated in surveys often are unreliable indicators of what people actually do, since they usually reflect back the opinions of the questioner. Usually, moreover, the more meaningful or penetrating the questions in such surveys, the less people are able to understand their own responses and thoughts. In this case, the questioner was the American Jewish Committee, which, though perhaps naive in approach, presumably had no interest in skewing the responses to show West Germans to be more anti-Semitic than East Germans.

14 The two earliest, and perhaps most renowned, examples of European ethnographies are Zborowski and Herzog's *Life Is with People* (1952), which constructed the East European *shtetl* and its generic Jew as an ethnographic possibility (a minority culture in a ghetto), and Laurence Wylie's *Village in the Vancluse* (1957) a study of a French peasant village. In the introduction to Zborowski and Herzog's book, Margaret Mead explains that this study was part of Ruth Benedict's postwar project (aborted due to her untimely death) to do ethnographies of European nations. The initial goal of this particular study was to document the national variations in Jewish selfhood within Europe, not to construct a generic *shtetl* Jew. For an illuminating discussion of

why Jewish collective identity has been difficult to conceptualize eth-
nographically, see Boyarin 1992, 52–76, 77–93. German Jews are doubly difficult to fit into this older ethnographic paradigm, for not only
are they urban instead of rural but they are a minority that distin-
guished itself as quintessentially Modern instead of primitive, intent
on transcending the tribal, or *völkisch*, assumptions of group identity.

15 For an example of the work of someone who has made an academic
career arguing from a position of ethnic essentialism, see Horowitz
1985. Widely recognized as one the foremost 'experts' on ethnic conflict, Donald L. Horowitz makes the crucial error of assuming that
ethnic conflict develops out of already existing ethnic differences
(throughout the world); he fails to understand that ethnic differences
are generated out of and are an expression of other kinds of already
existing conflict. He ignores the way ethnicity is constructed and produced. Ethnicity is a historically changing and politically sensitive
mode of representing political and economic power. Of course, it may
be, and often is, reified and treated as if it were primordial, and in this
respect, acts as a cause of violent conflict.

16 This argument parallels that of Eve Sedgwick with regard to the definition and study of homosexuality in the twentieth century. Sedgwick
sees the act of 'minoritizing' as one in which homosexuals are regarded
as a 'small, distinct, relatively fixed' minority, in contrast to a 'univer-
salizing view,' according to which one sees homosexuality as 'an issue
of continuing, determinative importance in the lives of people across
the spectrum of sexualities' (1990, 1; see also 82–86).

4. From the U. S. to East and West Berlin: Ernst Cramer

1 Dutschke's death, in December 1979, is often attributed to this 1968
attack. We thank Leslie Adelson for this information.

6. From England to East Berlin: Susanne Rödel

1 Critical studies such as Young 1988 and Langer 1991 necessarily devote
considerable attention to the issue of memory in Holocaust writing.
The struggle to remember and retell their 'stories' becomes as important as the experiences the survivors are recounting. Perhaps most

important for understanding the role of memory for Jews is Yerushalmi 1982.

10. Rediscovery of Jewishness: Jessica Jacoby

1   The disagreement proved to be enlightening for the demands of the ethnographic project. I had chastised Jeff, he felt unfairly, for leaving the interview before it was over. I had insisted that our discussions were more similar to fieldwork than to journalistic interviews and that thus we had to hold ourselves to a different standard of behavior with regard to our partners. While they were offering us many different things—friendship, intimate stories, painful memories, and opportunities for career advancement—we were offering them only one thing: that we would listen to them. We made no other promises regarding publishing their life histories nor promises of monetary compensation or any other form of remuneration. Thus, I argued, if they had the urge or even compulsion to narrate beyond the point where we could fit it to our own uses, it was our duty to listen at least to the point where they no longer wanted us to listen. Jeff insisted that our responsibility did not extend to listening beyond 'the interview,' which, he said, was over once the taping ended. My problem with this perspective was that it assumed the journalistic rather than the ethnographic meaning of *interview*, that it viewed the interview as a monologue we listen to instead of a dialogue to which we must respond, even if only by our presence.

To resolve our dispute, we agreed not to make appointments that might conflict with lengthier 'interviews' by forcing us to close prematurely the interview. Unless, that is, we stated ahead of time, before the beginning of our discussion, that we would have to leave at a certain time. By the end of the project Jeff himself emphasized how his notion of the ethnographic interview had changed.

11. Rediscovery of Jewishness: Konstantin Münz

1   We thank Julie Allen for allowing us to use material from a paper on the interviews with KM and his mother.
2   For a very interesting and provocative discussion of the parallels between Jewish identity and homosexuality that are implicit in using the expression *coming out* for both, see Virginia Dominquez (1989).

Part 7. From Surviving to Belonging

1 In her study *Continental Britons: German-Jewish Refugees from Nazi Germany* Marion Berghahn also addresses her personal involvement— 'complicated emotions on both sides'—as a non-Jewish German in a sociological analysis based in large part on interviews. She, however, seems to be either apologetic or defensive about her personal connection. 'I would like to stress that it was not guilt feelings and an attempt at *Vergangenheitsbewältigung* [dealing with the past], as a number of individuals interested in my research have argued, rather it was a purely scholarly interest which originally motivated me to undertake this study' (1988, 4).

2 As American scholars increasingly pay attention to disciplinary histories, they recognize their own involvement in the standards, expectations, and roles of its practitioners. In redefining traditional work in German literary studies [*Germanistik*], Sander Gilman has made an important contribution regarding his own Jewish identity (see Gilman 1989a).

3 I have simplified here the very complicated relationship between Germans and German Jews before the war that John Borneman discusses in greater detail. Also there are many studies on German Jewry, such as Berghahn 1988, which discusses this relationship in depth, as well as Mosse 1985a; Richarz 1989; and Rabinbach and Zipes 1986.

4 See James Clifford's discussion, based on Edward Said's *Orientalism*, in the introduction to Clifford and Marcus 1986.

5 See Daniel and Peck 1995, in which strong arguments are made for the link between anthropology and literary studies.

6 Benz's title, *Das Exil der kleinen Leute*, plays on the multiple connotations of the word *klein* in German. While it means 'the little man,' it also literally means 'average,' 'small,' or 'unimportant.' His point is that for many of the writers, artists, politicians, and other prominent people who went into exile, the emigration was often less traumatic than it was for these average people.

7 Even though German Jews were fleeing persecution when they went into exile, they were often treated with disdain and hostility in the receiving country, which still saw them as 'aliens' and even the 'enemy.'

8 For a more detailed discussion of the GDR and the Holocaust see Peck 1995.

9   Albert Klein's interview would seem to dispute the point that no German government asked those in exile to return, since he emphasized to us how the East German government, unlike the West German government, did in fact encourage some prominent people to return.

10 From the late eighteenth century in Germany, especially during German romanticism, thinkers like Johann Gottfried Herder and Wilhelm von Humboldt up to Jacob Grimm have promoted a theory of language intimately bound to national identity. For further analysis see Peck n.d.

11 For a detailed and important discussion of the neglect of race and ethnicity in gender debates in Germany, see Adelson 1993, esp. chapter 2, 'Anne Duden's *Übergang*: Racism and Feminist Aesthetics: A Provocation'; and Lennox 1993.

12 For a more detailed discussion of this issue in the context of recent attacks on foreigners see Fijalkowski 1993; and Peck 1993.

13 Foreigners make up approximately 7 percent of the population and are visible throughout Germany, yet Germany has never acknowledged itself as an official 'country of immigration.' During the Cold War, West Germany had one of the most liberal asylum laws in Europe but no laws regarding immigration. Concern with abuses of the asylum law led to its removal on 1 July 1993. One of the justifications offered for restricting the right to asylum was that the curtailment of asylum seekers entering Germany would lessen attacks on foreigners. Presently, Germany still lacks an explicit immigration law, so officially there are no immigrants in Germany.

14 For recent contributions to this emphasis on Jews living in Germany today, see Seligmann 1992; and Silbermann and Sallen 1992. For a more recent study from a largely North American viewpoint, see Gilman and Remmler 1994, which emphasizes questions about the possibilities of a Jewish culture in Germany today. The essays deal with topics such as 'Jewish Life in Germany,' 'Politics, Religion, and Immigration,' and 'Literature and Sexuality' and focus on issues such as visibility, absence, and representation.

Adelson, Leslie. 1993. *Making Bodies, Making History*. Lincoln: U of Nebraska P.

Beigel, Greta. 1953. *Recent Events in Eastern Germany*, 1–18. New York: Institute of Jewish Affairs.

Benz, Wolfgang. 1991a. *Das Exil der kleinen Leute: Alltagserfahrungen deutscher Juden in der Emigration*. München: Verlag C. H. Beck.

——. 1991b. 'Die Legende von der deutsch-jüdischen Symbiose.' *Merkur* 45:168–74.

——. 1991c. 'Der schwierige Status der jüdischen Minderheit in Deutschland nach 1945.' In *Zwischen Antisemitismus und Philosemitismus: Juden in der Bundesrepublik*, edited by W. Benz, 9–23. Berlin: Metropol Verlag.

Berghahn, Marion. 1988. *Continental Britons: German-Jewish Refugees from Nazi Germany*. Oxford: Berg.

Bodemann, Y. Michal. 1983. 'Opfer zu Komplizen gemacht? Der jüdisch-deutsche Bruch und die verlorene Identität Anmerkungen zu einer Rückkehr in die Bundesrepublik.' *Die Zeit*, 30 December, 28.

——. 1994. 'A Reemergence of German Jewry?' In *Reemerging Jewish Culture in Germany: Life and Literature since 1989*, edited by Sander Gilman and Karen Remmler, 46–61. New York: New York U P.

Borneman, John. 1992. *Belonging in the Two Berlins: Kin, State, Nation*. Cambridge: Cambridge U P.

——. 1993. 'Uniting the German Nation.' *American Ethnologist* 20 (2): 288–311.

——. 1995. 'Education after the Cold War: Remembrance, Repetition, and Rightwing Violence.' In *Cultural Authority in Contemporary Germany: Intellectual Responsibility between State Security Surveillance and Media Society*, edited by Michael Geyer and Robert von Hallberg. Chicago: U of Chicago P.

Boyarin, Jonathan. 1992. *Storm from Paradise: The Politics of Jewish Memory*. Minneapolis: U of Minnesota P.

Brague, Réne. 1993. *Europa: Eine Exzentrische Identität*. Frankfurt am Main: Campus Verlag.

Brubaker, Rogers. 1992. *Citizenship and Nationhood in France and Germany*. Cambridge: Cambridge U P.

Caruth, Cathy. 1991. 'Introduction.' *American Imago: Studies in Psychoanalysis and Culture* 48 (1): 1–13.

Clifford, James. 1988. *The Predicament of Culture: Twentieth Century Ethnography, Literature, and Art.* Cambridge: Cambridge U P.

Clifford, James, and George Marcus, eds. 1986. *Writing Culture: The Poetics and Politics of Ethnography.* Berkeley: U of California P.

Dachs, Gisela. 1992. 'Die Juden sollen sich nicht verstecken.' *Die Zeit,* 20 November, 2.

Daniel, E. Valentine, and Jeffrey M. Peck. 1995. *Culture and Contexture: Explorations in Anthropology and Literary Studies.* Berkeley: U of California P.

Derrida, Jacques. 1981. *Dissemination.* Translated by Barbara Johnson. Chicago: U of Chicago P.

Diner, Dan. 1986. 'Negative Symbiose: Deutsche und Juden nach Auschwitz.' *Babylon* 1:9–20.

Dominquez, Virginia. 1993. 'Questioning Jews.' *American Ethnologist* 20 (3): 618–24.

Dumont, Jean Paul. 1992. *Visayan Vignettes: Ethnographic Traces of a Philippine Island.* Chicago: U of Chicago P.

Dwyer, Kevin. 1982. *Moroccan Dialogues: Anthropology in Question.* Baltimore: Johns Hopkins U P.

Fabian, Johannes. 1983. *Time and the Other: How Anthropology Makes Its Object.* New York: Columbia U P.

Fijalkowski, Jürgen. 1993. *Aggressive Nationalism, Immigration Pressure and Asylum Policy Disputes in Contemporary Germany.* Occasional Paper 9. Washington D C: German Historical Institute.

Fischer, Erica, and Petra Lux. 1990. *Ohne Uns ist kein Staat zu machen: D D R-Frauen nach der Wende.* Köln: Kiepenheuer & Witsch.

Foucault, Michel. [1975] 1979. *Discipline and Punish: The Birth of the Prison.* Reprint. New York: Random House, Vintage.

Garber, Marjorie. 1992. *Vested Interests: Cross-Dressing and Cultural Anxiety.* New York: Routledge.

Gay, Peter. 1978. *Freud, Jews, and Other Germans: Masters and Victims in Modernist Culture.* New York: Oxford U P.

Gay, Ruth. 1992. 'What I Learned about German Jews.' *American Scholar* 54:467–84.

Giesen, Bernhard. 1993. *Die Intellektuellen und die Nation: Eine deutsche Achsenzeit.* Frankfurt am Main: Suhrkamp.

Gilman, Sander L.. 1982. *On Blackness without Blacks: Essays on the Image of the Black in Germany.* Boston: G. K. Hall.

——. 1985. *Difference and Pathology.* Ithaca: Cornell U P.

——. 1986. *Jewish Self-Hatred: Anti-Semitism and the Hidden Language of the Jews.* Baltimore: Johns Hopkins U P.

——. 1989a. 'How and Why I Study the German.' *German Quarterly* 62 (2): 192–204.

——. 1989b. *Sexuality: An Illustrated History.* New York: John Wiley & Sons.

——. 1991. *The Jew's Body.* New York: Routledge.

Gilman, Sander L., and Karen Remmler, eds. 1994. *Reemerging Jewish Culture in Germany: Life and Literature since 1989.* New York: New York U P.

Grawert, Rolf. 1973. *Staat und Staatsangehörigkeit.* Berlin: Duncken & Humbolt.

Hammer, Manfried, and Julius Schoeps, eds. 1988. *Juden in Berlin, 1671–1945: Ein Lesebuch.* Berlin: Nicolai.

Hannerz, Ulf. 1992. *Cultural Complexity: Studies in the Social Organization of Meaning.* New York: Columbia U P.

Herzberg, Wolfgang. 1990. *Überleben heisst Erinnern: Lebensgeschichten deutscher Juden.* Berlin: Aufbau.

Hobsbawm, E. J. 1990. *Nations and Nationalism since 1780: Programme, Myth, Reality.* Cambridge: Cambridge U P.

Horowitz, Donald L. 1985. *Ethnic Groups in Conflict.* Berkeley: U of California P.

Jacobmeyer, Wolfgang. 1983. 'Jüdische Überlebende als "Displaced Persons."' *Geschichte und Gesellschaft* 9:421–52.

Jaspers, Karl, and Hannah Arendt. 1992. 'The Idea of the 'Chosen People': An Exchange.' *New York Times,* 19 September, 19.

Keesing, Roger H. 1993. 'Theories of Culture Revisited.' In *Assessing Cultural Anthropology,* edited by Robert Borofsky, 301–19. New York: McGraw-Hill.

Kirchner, Peter. 1991. 'Die jüdische Minderheit in der Bundesrepublik.' In *Zwischen Antisemitismus und Philosemitismus: Juden in der Bundesrepublik,* edited by Wolfgang Benz, 29–38. Berlin: Metropol Verlag.

Klüger, Ruth. 1993. *Weiter Leben: Eine Jugend.* Göttingen: Wallstein Verlag.

Lang, Berel, ed. 1988. *Writing and the Holocaust.* New York: Holmes & Meier.

Langer, Lawrence. 1991. *Holocaust Testimonies: The Ruins of Memory.* New Haven: Yale U P.

Lehmann, Hans Georg. 1983. *Chronik der Bundesrepublik Deutschland 1945/49 bis 1983.* München: C. H. Beck.

Lennox, Sara. 1993. 'Divided Feminism: Gender, Race, and German National Identity.' Paper presented at the annual meeting of the German Studies Association, Washington D C, October.

Lévi-Strauss, Claude. 1966. *The Savage Mind.* Chicago: U of Chicago P.

Luize, Wilhelm, and Richard Höpfner. 1965. *Berlin ABC.* Berlin: Presse-und Informationsamtes des Landes Berlin.

Marcus, George, and Michael Fischer. 1986. *Anthropology as Cultural Critique.* Chicago: U of Chicago P.

Martin, Biddy, and Chandra Mohanty. 1986. 'Feminist Politics: What's Home Got to Do with It?' In *Feminist Studies/Critical Studies*, edited by Teresa de Lauretis, 191–212. Bloomington: Indiana U P.

Mattenklott, Gert. 1992. *Über Juden in Deutschland.* Frankfurt am Main: Jüdischer Verlag.

Maynes, Mary Jo. 1989. 'Gender and Narrative Form in French and German Working-Class Autobiographies.' In *Interpreting Women's Lives. Feminist Theory and Personal Narratives*, edited by Personal Narratives Group, 103–17. Bloomington: Indiana U P.

Mendelsohn, Moses. 1993. 'On the Question, What Is Enlightenment?' Translated by Hans-Herbert Kögler. *Public Culture* 6 (1): 213–17.

Middell, Eike, Alfred Dreifuss, Volker Frank, Wolfgang Gersch, Thea Kirfel-Lenk, and Jürgen Schebera. 1983. *Exil in den U S A : Kunst und Literatur im antifaschistischen Exil, 1935–1945.* Vol. 3. Leipzig: Philip Reclam.

Moore, Sally Falk. 1994. 'The Ethnography of the Present and the Analysis of the Process.' In *Assessing Cultural Anthropology*, edited by Robert Borofsky, 362–75. New York: McGraw-Hill.

Mosse, George. 1985a. *German Jews beyond Judaism.* Bloomington: Indiana U P.

——. 1985b. *Nationalism and Sexuality: Middle-Class Morality and Sexual Norms in Modern Europe.* Madison: U of Wisconsin P.

Ostow, Robin. 1989. *Jews in Contemporary East Germany: The Children of Moses in the Land of Marx.* New York: St. Martin's P.

Peck, Abraham J. 1988. 'Zero Hour and the Development of Jewish Life in Germany after 1945.' In *A Parish People? Jewish Life in Germany after 1945: A Symposium*, 3–11. Cincinnati: American Jewish Archives.

Peck, Jeffrey M. 1992. 'Rac(e)ing the Nation: Is There a German Home?' *New Formations* 17 (summer 1992): 75–84.

——. 1993. 'Comment' on *Aggressive Nationalism, Immigration Pressure, and Asylum Policy Disputes in Contemporary Germany*, by Jürgen Fijalkowski. Occasional Paper 9. Washington DC: German Historical Institute.

——. 1995. 'East Germany.' In *The World Reacts to the Holocaust*, edited by David Wyman. Baltimore: Johns Hopkins U P.

——. n.d. '"In the Beginning Was the Word': Germany and the Origins of German Studies.' In *Medievalism and the Modernist Temper: On the Discipline of Medieval Studies*, edited by R. Howard Bloch and Stephen Nichols. Baltimore: Johns Hopkins U P, forthcoming.

Personal Narratives Group, ed. 1989. *Interpreting Women's Lives: Feminist Theory and Personal Narratives.* Bloomington: Indiana U P.

Rabinbach, Anson, and Jack Zipes, eds. 1986. *Germans and Jews since the Holocaust: The Changing Situation in West Germany.* New York: Holmes & Meier.

Richarz, Monika. 1988. 'Juden in der Bundesrepublik Deutschland und in der Deutschen Demokratischen Republik seit 1945.' In *Jüdisches Leben in Deutschland seit 1945*, edited by Micha Brumlik, Doron Kiesel, Cilly Kugelmann, and Julius Schoeps, 13–30. Frankfurt am Main: Athenäum.

——, ed. 1989. *Bürger auf Wiederruf: Lebenszeugnisse deutscher Juden, 1780–1945.* München: C. H. Beck.

Schmitt, Carl. 1976. *The Concept of the Political.* Translated by George Schwab. New Brunswick NJ: Rutgers U P.

Schnibben, Cordt. 1991. 'Das bessere Deutschland.' *Der Spiegel* 15: 154–67, 16:146–64.

Scholem, Gershom. 1976. *On Jews and Judaism in Crisis.* Edited by Werner Dannhauser. New York: Schocken Books.

Sedgwick, Eve Kosofsky. 1990. *Epistemology of the Closet.* Berkeley: U of California P.

Seligmann, Rafael. 1992. 'Die Juden leben.' *Der Spiegel* 47:75, 78.

Sichrovsky, Peter. 1985. *Wir wissen nicht was morgen wird, wir wissen wohl was gestern war: Junge Juden in Deutschland und Österreich.* Köln: Kiepenheuer & Witsch.

———. 1987. *Strangers in Their Own Land: Young Jews in Germany and Austria Today.* Translated by Jean Steinberg. New York: Penguin Books.

Siegel, James. 1986. *Solo in the New Order: Language and Hierarchy in an Indonesian City.* Princeton: Princeton U P.

Sievers, Leo. 1983. *Juden in Deutschland: Die Geschichte einer 2000 jährigen Tragödie.* Hamburg: Wilhelm Goldmann Verlag.

Silbermann, Alphons, and Herbert Sallen. 1992. *Juden in Westdeutschland: Selbstbild und Fremdbild.* Köln: Verlag Wissenschaft & Politik.

Spitzer, Leo. 1989. *Lives in Between: Assimilation and Marginality in Austria, Brazil, West Africa, 1780–1945.* Cambridge: Cambridge U P.

Spivak, Gayatri Chakravorty. 1988. *In Other Worlds: Essays in Cultural Politics.* New York: Routledge.

Stern, Frank. 1991. 'Philosemitismus statt Antisemitismus: Entstehung und Funktion einer neuen Ideologie in West Deutschland.' In *Zwischen Antisemitismus und Philosemitismus: Juden in der Bundesrepublik*, edited by W. Benz, 47–62. Berlin: Metropol Verlag.

Der Tagesspiegel. 1993. 'Unsicherheit und Sorge nach dem Sieg der Rechten in Moskau.' 15 December, 5.

Unger, Roberto. 1983. *The Critical Legal Studies Movement.* Cambridge: Cambridge U P.

Wördehoff, Bernhard. 1993. 'Sind deutsche Juden Deutsche?' *Die Zeit*, 28 May, 74.

Wylie, Laurence. 1957. *Village in the Vancluse.* Cambridge: Harvard U P.

Yahil, Chaim. 1971. 'Berlin: Contemporary Period.' *Encyclopedia Judaica*, vol. 4. New York: Macmillan.

Yerushalmi, Yosef Haim. 1982. *Zakhor: Jewish History and Jewish Memory.* Seattle: U of Washington P.

Young, James. 1988. *Writing and Rewriting the Holocaust: Narrative and the Consequences of Interpretation.* Bloomington: Indiana U P.

Zborowski, Mark, and Elizabeth Herzog. 1952. *Life Is with People.* New York: International Universities P.

In the *Texts and Contexts* series